ARE WE CIVILIZED?

ARE WE CIVILIZED?

Human Culture in Perspective

BY ROBERT H. LOWIE

AUTHOR OF
The Origin of the State

HARCOURT, BRACE AND COMPANY

NEW YORK

PRINTED IN THE UNITED STATES OF AMERICA
BY QUINN & BODEN COMPANY, INC., RAHWAY, N. J.

To the memory of

ERNST MACH (1838-1916)

PROFESSOR OF THE HISTORY AND THEORY OF THE INDUCTIVE SCIENCES AT THE UNIVERSITY OF VIENNA

PREFACE

In this book on human civilization I have tried to be both accurate and popular. Except for the geologist's "Pleistocene," for which no substitute exists, I think technical terms are wholly lacking.

While engaged on this work I have sought, above all, the judgment of lay friends—too many to be all cited by name. For valuable comments and for considering major parts of the volume I am especially indebted to my sister Miss Risa Lowie, and my friends the Misses Suzanne and Radiana Pasmore, Mrs. Mary Ellen Scott Washburn, Mrs. A. Isaacs, Miss Marietta Voorhees, Mr. Donald Clark, Professor Frederick E. Breithut, and Professor J. S. Schapiro. To Mrs. Gladys Franzen I owe a lifelong debt of gratitude for referring me to the writings of Alfred Franklin on French culture-history. By pointing out recondite Spanish sources Professor Erasmo Buceta has been equally helpful.

My anthropological auditors have been Professor and Mrs. A. L. Kroeber, Drs. E. C. Parsons, Erna Gunther, Ruth Benedict, M. Mead, Dr. and Mrs. Jaime de Angulo, and Dr. C. D. Forde. I hereby thank them all for their patience and their valuable suggestions.

I have to thank *The American Mercury* for permission to reprint in the chapters, "Education" and "Hygiene and Medicine," some material originally published in that magazine.

A careful reader will note that my comments on the Nordics are directed only against the votaries of race cults. Since I do not believe in a Nordic race today, I cannot be prejudiced against it. Of the Scandinavian *cultures*, on the other hand, I have always been keenly appreciative. I have never felt happier anywhere than in Sweden and Norway, am an associate of the American Scandinavian Foundation, and have for years been a member of the Scandinavian Club of the University of California. For that very reason I feel that the truest Nordics living should be protected from those "friends" who are cloaking their own sinister designs with a pro-Nordic propaganda while at the same time sneering at Scandinavians for having become a civilized people.[1]

ROBERT H. LOWIE.

Berkeley, Cal., 1929.

[1] See page 30 f.

CONTENTS

ILLUSTRATIONS

ARE WE CIVILIZED?

CHAPTER I

CULTURE

IF YOU saw a man spitting at another, you would infer that he was expressing contempt for the victim. Well, that would hold in France, but you would be all wrong if it happened in East Africa among the Jagga Negroes. There spitting is a kind of blessing in critical situations, and a medicine-man will spit four times on a patient or a newborn babe. In other words, it is not "natural" for human beings to expectorate in order to show loathing. Such symbolism is purely conventional. Raise a Frenchman in Jaggaland, and only as a well-wisher will he spit on a fellow man. Bring up a Jagga in France, and he will not dream of spitting on a baby. His behavior will depend, so far as spitting goes, on the company he keeps.

Most of us harbor the comfortable delusion that *our* way of doing things is the only sensible if not the only possible one. What is more obvious than eating three meals a day or sleeping at night? Well, in Bolivia there are Indians who think otherwise: they sleep for a few hours, get up to eat a snack, lie down for a second rest, rise for another collation, and so forth; and whenever they feel like it they do not scruple to sleep in the daytime. *We* drive on the right-hand side of the road; and what is more logical for right-handed folk? But the custom of England, Sweden, and Austria is precisely the reverse, though left-handedness is no more common there than elsewhere. But surely it is natural to point with the index-finger? It is not. Many American Indians do so by pouting their lips. Again, there is nothing eternally fit about weaning a baby at nine months: among the East Africans and the Navaho of Arizona a boy of four or five will come running to take his mother's breast.

In short, there is only one way of finding out whether any particular idea or custom is natural or only conventional, to wit, experience; and that means not our limited experience in Ottumwa, Iowa, or the United States, or even in Western civilization as a whole, but among all the peoples the world over.

Human beings generally act and think as they do for no other reason than that they have picked up such behavior and thoughts from some social group of theirs, whether family, gang, church, party, or nation. Every newborn unit of this sort is bound to invent some little tricks, badges, songs, and what not of its own. How, otherwise, would one college fraternity stand out from its neighbors? It's the particular Greek letters, and the pin, and the ingeniously unique way of hazing the novice, that give it individuality. Every human being belongs to a number of such social groups, some important, some trivial, from a philosophical point of view. Each group has somehow developed its peculiar style of thought and behavior and thrives on adding to its quips and cranks. Accordingly, every one of us does a vast number of things that are imposed upon him as a member of some group. The way he eats, courts, loves, fights, worships, is not his individual invention, and it is largely independent of his mental make-up. All we have to do is to place him in a new setting, and at once he follows new rules for the game of living in society. An American Negro does not speak Bantu or Sudanese, but English; he does not pray to the spirits of his dead ancestors, but takes communion in the Baptist Church. Indeed, standards change even without a change of residence. What a difference between England under Queen

Bess and under Cromwell! Or, to come nearer home, what a difference between our generation and its immediate predecessor! Thirty years ago American women wore long skirts and called legs "limbs"; it is no secret that they have become less fastidious.

Anything and everything a man thus acquires from his social group is called a part of its "culture." Learning from one's fellows is a peculiarity of mankind's, for even the highest apes have nothing of the sort. Put a banana outside a chimpanzee's cage so that he can not reach it. His craving for the fruit will goad him into tool-making. If bamboo sticks are at hand, he wedges one into another, and, if his pole is long enough, he will sweep in his prize. He has made an invention—raw material for culture. If his neighbors imitated him, if he taught them his trick and they all passed it on to their offspring, chimpanzees would be on the high-road to culture. But they do nothing of the sort. Apes are not the imitators they are cracked up to be, and the inventor cares not a fig whether his brilliant idea becomes part of chimpanzee behavior in the future. That is why apes hover on the outskirts of culture but never quite get there.

Of course there are scores of things chimpanzees hand down to their progeny, but it is by a different mechanism altogether. A chimpanzee is born with projecting canine teeth that are not affected in the least by the horde he associates with; nor can any of us develop such teeth by fleeing the company of our fellows and dwelling among apes. The heredity of men and of apes is not the same. When a male chimpanzee cohabits with a female, the sex cells that unite to form a new chimpanzee in embryo contain some tiny particle that makes for projecting canines. The sex cells of human beings lack this particle, and so human beings have teeth that do *not* jut out.

Men and apes alike get innumerable traits in this way. Our American Negro may be a Baptist and a Republican, but he neither turns white nor loses his kinky hair. He may use anti-kink effectively enough on himself, but his children are born with hair as kinky as his own at birth. So Indians along the Columbia River were not satisfied with the natural shape of their skulls and flattened their babies' foreheads in the cradle. But in order to achieve their end, pressure had to be applied in each individual case. Since man, however, has many traits that are social as well as many that are hereditary, he worries us with questions that we may ignore in studying the chimpanzee, who is without culture. Which of the human traits are inborn in all men as distinguished from other animals, and which are determined by culture? Are some of the inborn traits peculiar to special races, such as the Negro or the North European? Even if group behavior depends on social convention, may there not be some residue that is fixed by heredity? If a West African village were steeped in all the atmosphere of Athens at the time of Pericles, would it produce great philosophers, sculptors, and poets? Or is there a definite limit to Negro effort because the Negro sex cells lack ingredients which the Greeks had and passed on in the act of cohabitation? A chapter will be devoted to this important question.

Certainly the enormous variation of culture in time and space calls for some explanation. Why do Siberian nomads milk cows while their Chinese neighbors do not? Why do early tools from India resemble so amazingly those from far-off Spain? What made Californian life so different in Indian days from what it is now? Why did the Peruvians of 1500 A.D. lack iron tools when the Egyptians had them about 1500 B.C.? Why do the Japanese copy our science and industries but stop short of Christianity? Why does

Aldous Huxley write novels that would have shocked his bold grandfather far more than he himself shocked Victorian England as a champion of Darwin? These are but a few of a thousand intriguing puzzles. Some of them can be solved.

CHAPTER II

VISTAS

How did culture begin? It cannot have started simply from the inspiration of a single genius. Our chimpanzee is something of the sort, but his inventiveness remains culturally barren so long as his companions are unable to grasp a novel idea and make it their own. So a human prodigy might make discoveries that thrilled him to the core; yet unless he had a receptive audience that passed his message down to posterity it would be lost. Hence, for culture to take shape, the star performer must have had from the very start a supporting cast.

Can we set a date for the earliest collaboration of this type? Geology gives us a clew. Some implements are found side by side with the bones of animals that have been extinct in what the geologists call the Recent period, that is, within approximately the last 10,000 years. The tools, then, are also older than that: they, too, belong to the so-called Pleistocene period. In this division of the earth's history climate, flora, and fauna were not what they are today. In the Sahara, for instance, there are districts where no human beings could nowadays support themselves. But in these very spots there are sprinkled hundreds of tools, and also the skeletons of animals that have since moved south or died out altogether. Man and beast must have lived here when North Africa enjoyed an Age of Rainfall. At about the same time the inhabitants of France were hunting reindeer, making lifelike engravings of their game animals, and manufacturing harpoons from their antlers. The climate of Western Europe must have been much colder then than it is, or reindeer could not have thrived there.

Here, then, is proof that man shaped tools and practiced art in the Pleistocene. Not *one* man or a few random craftsmen of talent, but whole schools of workers, for the artifacts and drawings are too numerous to be explained in any other way, and whole series of them cling to the same style. In other words, they are tokens of a cultural tradition.

Western Europe happens to have been more thoroughly explored than other areas; accordingly we know a little more about its prehistoric remains. For example, the reindeer-engravers, judged by their skulls and the rest of their skeletons, were men of our species, *Homo sapiens*. Before them, however, there came a more remote kinsman, related to us somewhat as the ass is to the horse. He belongs to the same genus as ourselves but to a distinct species, *Homo neanderthalensis*. This Neanderthaler—a squat, stooping, flat-skulled man with apelike ledges of bone above the eyes—lived possibly 25,000 to 50,000 years ago. Wherever he and the reindeer-engravers occupied the same site, his artifacts lie in a lower stratum, so that they are undoubtedly older. He, too, had to cope with a frigid climate and sought shelter in caves, where his fireplaces and tools are found. These latter are largely stone scrapers suited for dressing hides such as he may have worn to protect himself against the weather.

By no means all of these implements, however, lie alongside of the skeletons of Neanderthal man. Similar forms occur without human bones in Eastern Europe and China. Sometime the skeletons of their makers may be dug up, and they may turn out to belong to other Pleistocene races. Perhaps several types of man hit upon the same ways of working stone. Or, more probably, one of them made the invention and the rest copied it. Modern archaeologists can produce similar tools. Take a lump of flint and strike off slivers with a stone hammer (Figs. 1, 20). Discard the big core, touch up the little flakes on one face only, and you

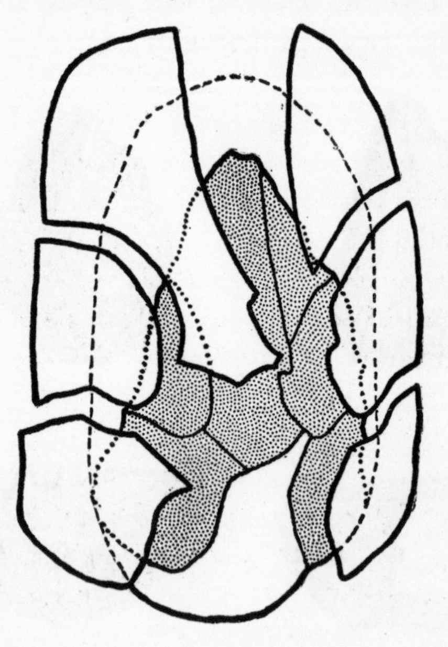

FIG. 1. STONE LUMP OR CORE WITH SLIVERS KNOCKED OFF (*after Neville Jones*)

have an assortment of Pleistocene points and scrapers (Fig. 2). This is not the only possible way of handling the material, but a purely conventional one. The worker could reject the flakes struck off and cling to the lump. That is exactly what the people of Western Europe did before they went in for manufacturing scrapers and points on a large scale. For their main implement they used the core, knocking off flakes on both the upper and the lower face of the flint until a large almond-shaped affair was left. This could serve as a cleaver or hatchet held in the hand, there being no evidence of a handle (Fig. 3).

Human remains have not been found with these fist-hatchets; so we do not know what manner of man first made them. Like the scrapers, they may be the product of several distinct types of humanity, for they crop up in

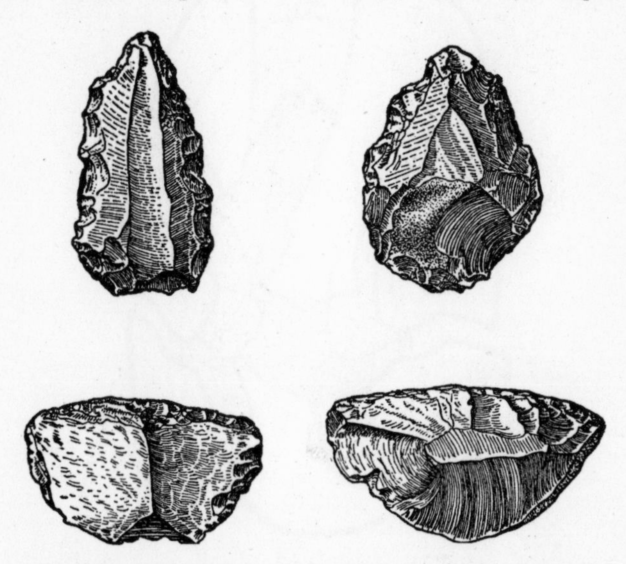

FIG. 2. SPANISH TOOLS MADE FROM THE DETACHED FLAKES (*after Obermaier*)

Africa and India as well as in France and England. Science also leaves us in the lurch in another matter. Fist-hatchets are older than the scraper vogue in Western Europe. But are they older than the scraper school of China and Eastern Europe? Here there are as yet no signs of core tools lying below the sliver tools (Fig. 4). It is therefore entirely possible that men in different areas of the world independently developed two different techniques more or less at the same time. The West Europeans may have later invented the sliver method or taken it over from Eastern neighbors. That would explain why hatchets occur in lower

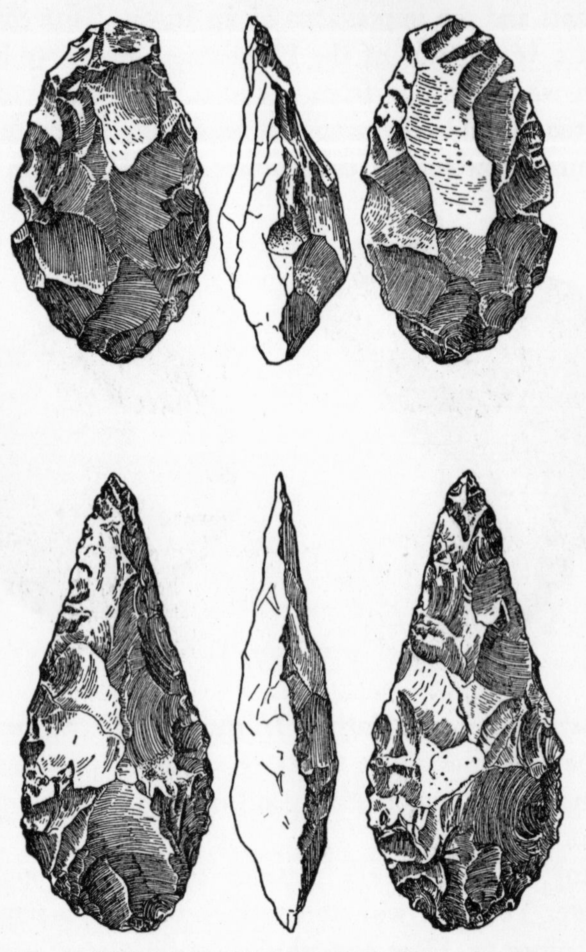

FIG. 3. SPANISH FIST-HATCHETS OF CRUDER AND FINER TYPE (*after Obermaier*)

horizons than scrapers *in the West*. But it would prove nothing as to their relative age in the world as a whole.

Fortunately science makes one positive revelation that is

very helpful in fixing the age of culture. The older hatchets of France do not belong to a glacial period like that of the Western scrapers, for they are found with the bones of elephants and the impressions of fig leaves. Thus they fall within a *hot* division of the Pleistocene. Hence we have to reckon with a change from hot to cold climate, and again from the glacial to the temperate conditions of France today. We must grant further that culture may be older in Africa

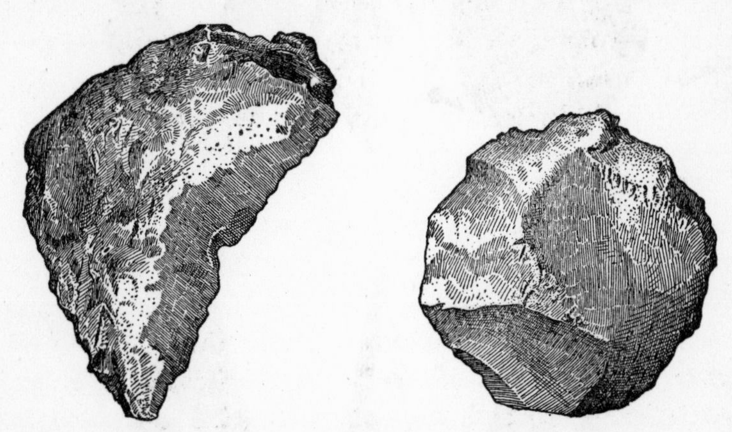

FIG. 4. CHINESE TOOLS (*after Licent and Teilhard*)

and Asia than it is in Europe. If, then, the Recent period of Europe goes back about 10,000 years, the total age of culture may be set conservatively at the good round number of 100,000 years.

Many scholars would consider this a most niggardly estimate. Yet even with this modest figure amazing vistas open before us. How miserably short by comparison is the span of the higher civilizations! In Egypt and Babylonia they date back six or seven thousand years, but what is that compared to the preceding era? The essence of culture cannot be learnt from these mushroom growths; we cannot ignore the more than 90 per cent. of its course before there were written records. Let us then try the long-distance view of the entire range. Iron was first smelted about 4,000 years ago; 2,000 years earlier the most advanced nations of the earth, the Babylonians and Egyptians, began to reduce copper ores. Before that—during more than nine-tenths of its existence—humanity shifted without metal tools. Wherever men have used such at all in later times, they previously had nothing but stone, bone, shell, and wooden implements. And only the more progressive branches of mankind ever lifted themselves out of this incredibly long Stone Age. For many tribes—for the Australians and most American Indians, for instance—that stage was literally interminable.

Within the last twentieth of the history of culture fall writing and stone architecture, wheeled carts, and the plow. Farming with hoe or digger and the breeding of live stock are older, but not much. In 15,000 B.C. and more likely in 10,000 B.C. there was not on the surface of the globe one grain of cultivated corn, one head of man-bred cattle, one metal tool, one pottery vessel. For from eight- to nine-tenths of their existence men roved about killing wild game and gathering wild roots with implements of stone, bone, shell, and wood. Humanity's progress may be likened to that of an aged pupil who has dawdled away most of his life in kindergarten and then with lightning speed rushes through school and college. This appears clearly from a table of the chief stages of culture, with their approximate earliest dates.

Not even the most hard-boiled optimist can glance at this table and credit man with a natural tendency toward rapid progress. A forward spurt must be the result of altogether peculiar conditions. What these may be, becomes clearer when we compare the more backward with the more pro-

CULTURE HISTORY
(Read up)

4	IRON AGE	2000 B.C.
5	BRONZE AGE	3000 B.C.
6	COPPER AGE	4000 B.C.
12	Age of Pottery and Farming	10000 B.C.
	STONE AGE	
100	Pre-Ceramic	100000 B.C.

gressive peoples. Among recent races the Tasmanians, who became extinct in 1877, were as low as any. They had miserable screens in place of huts, knew nothing of pottery, and even their stone tools were no better than the Neanderthaler's of, say, 30,000 years ago. Why did they lag behind other groups by tens of thousands of years? A look at the map proves that it was not because of a torrid climate. Tasmania lies about as far south of the equator as Philadelphia lies north. But the map also shows that when the ancient Tasmanians had once reached their historic home they were cut off from intercourse with the outside world. For neither they nor their nearest neighbors, the Australians, had boats that favored communication. Contrast this with any of the complex cultures of history. Ancient Egypt and Babylonia influenced each other, and the Babylonians were themselves a mixture of two peoples, the Sumerians and the

Akkadians. The Chinese had ancient contacts with these higher civilizations, and later borrowed inventions from the Malays, the Turks, and the Mongols. The Greeks built on the foundation reared by Egypt, and the Romans took over what they could from the Greeks. Our modern civilization is a thing of shreds and patches from every corner of the globe. Its repertory is rich and the Tasmanian's is poor because we have had innumerable contacts with alien peoples, and the Tasmanians next to none. For no one group has more than a slim supply of brilliant ideas. Isolated tribes, then, are backward for the simple reason that ten heads are better than one.

But that is true only if the heads are all more or less equal in wisdom. Now, on the whole, it is more likely that the startling contributions will come from men with an inborn capacity for original thought. Here again the Tasmanians are at a disadvantage. Even if they were roughly our peers, what chance had this handful of South Sea Islanders to bring forth a prodigy of genius? How many epoch-making discoveries or artistic achievements can be credited to Kalamazoo, Michigan? Yet its population is probably greater than that of Tasmania ever was. On the other hand, all the spectacular civilizations we know about had plenty of human material to draw from, and this yielded an occasional giant in intellect, as an occasional seven-footer will crop up among a million people.

With a large population these gifted individuals may further be relieved from the drudgery of keeping the wolf from the door and may specialize along the lines of their talents. Our textile experts today marvel at the fabrics woven by the Peruvian Indians. But how were they produced? By girls confined in nunneries and dedicating a lifetime to their looms. Had their efforts been spent mainly on digging potatoes, the art of weaving would not have developed as it did in western South America.

New ideas and improved craftsmanship may be expected, then, whenever peoples are sufficient in number to give birth to talent and to set it free for congenial tasks. Add plenty of opportunity for the alert-minded to draw profit from the thoughts of other communities, and a really complex culture may spring into being.

About all this, however, there is nothing inevitable. An intellectual prodigy may turn up among a million people, and again he may be crucified and his gift spurned. People may or may not chance to come into touch with other groups, and when they do they may or may not open their arms to the new ideas encountered. Thus accident plays a large part, and there is no royal short-cut to the history of civilization. That is sad, and some minds have accordingly been lured astray by one or the other of two will-o'-the-wisps, Geography and Heredity. Sign-boards must be put up to warn the wayfarer.

CHAPTER III

GEOGRAPHY

How did the Lapps come to breed reindeer? A well-known geographer has an answer ready-made: no other kind of animal could live on the vegetation of those cold regions, and nature furnished no crops that man can eat. This sounds plausible, but is wholly incorrect. Since man spent most of his career as a hunter and seed-collector, people are not obliged to turn to either stock-breeding or farming in order to live. The Eskimo have shifted tolerably well as hunters, and whenever the Lapps themselves lost their herds they fell back on fishing. On the other hand, if the Lapps had at any time happened to raise other stock than reindeer, they could have reared them even in the Arctic. It is not easy, but it can be done, for the Yakut are actually doing it in the colder parts of Siberia. In the thirteenth century these stock-breeders lived in the south of that country, around Lake Baikal. They were driven north by the Mongol invasion, and against great odds they managed to keep their domestic beasts. What is more, about 6 per cent. of them took over reindeer from their new neighbors and promptly beat these tribes at their own game of reindeer-breeding, since the Yakut were able to apply their past experience with cattle and horses.

The geographer's explanation thus turns out to be a sorry failure. It does not explain why the Lapp could not have gone on indefinitely as a hunter and fisherman. Nor does it explain why the Lapp could not raise cattle and horses, when the Yakut can do so in an equally forbidding country.

Our Pueblo Indians have likewise been a favorite butt of geographical "explanations." Take their stone architecture, for instance, "Any primitive people," says a famous archaeologist, "finding its way into this land of cliffs, rock-shelters, and ready-quarried building-stone, would soon be led under favorable stimulus to employ stone in building." Why, then, we naturally ask, have the Navaho been living in this very area for centuries without putting up anything in the way of masonry? The same writer goes on to tell us how the Pueblos invented weaving: there was little large game in their habitat; hence skin clothing was barred and they just *had* to devise the loom. But this contention is without rhyme or reason. In the same region the Paiute used to go naked in the summer, while for winter they simply twisted rabbit skins into ropes, sewed them side by side, and thus produced a warm robe without any pretense at weaving cloth.

The main trouble with this sort of reasoning is its misconception of human nature. Put man into any situation, so the argument runs, and he will grasp its possibilities. Accordingly he will at once adapt himself with a maximum of comfort to himself and of esthetic satisfaction for the beholder. The sad facts are otherwise. Not even in dress and habitation is man anything like so reasonable a creature. The southern tip of South America is in the latitude of Labrador, and even in the summer snow falls, while terrific squalls make life uncomfortable. Two of Captain Cook's men froze to death on a summer night in 1769. In the winter there are piles of snow in the woods and sheet ice in the open. Yet the Tierra del Fuegians have been unable to devise suitable clothing. Men and women often went naked and at best wore a cape of stiff seal or otter skin extending to the waist. North of them, in the Gran Chaco, the Choroti live in grass huts, where they are drenched by any heavy shower. A vast portion of Canada is occupied by members of the Athabaskan family. Strangely enough, the tribes living farthest north have no better shelter than a miserable tent or lean-to, while the southernmost representatives of the stock enjoy warm underground houses. How can geography account for such oddities?

Of course this is not the whole story. The physical environment has a good deal to do with group life, though not in the way often supposed. There are positive as well as negative cases. In the forest zone of Europe the peasants erect wooden houses. The King of Norway himself occupies a palace of timber when he stays in Trondhjem. On the other hand, in the Mediterranean area, stone is so plentiful that it is the obvious material for building. In Egypt, too, there is a pretty definite correlation between habitations and environment. Where stone is lacking and wood scarce we find mud huts. Where the sandstone plateau approaches the Nile, dwellings are excavated from the rock or built out of rock cubes.

Whether people shall fix their residence in a certain place or not may depend even more on nature than does the style of their houses. In the deserts of Turkestan travelers journey for weeks without catching sight of a single habitation. Then all of a sudden a densely peopled oasis bursts into view. Since man can live only where there is water, cities like Merv, no matter how many times they are destroyed in the course of ages, invariably rise anew on the selfsame spot. Here geography lays down an ultimatum, and man either conforms or goes to the wall. So the Australian must know every water-hole in his country if he wants to live, and the inhabitants of streamless Bermuda or Tonga *must* store the rain water. Adaptations like these are matters of life and death: they have survival value. By contrast, adequate dress in Tierra del Fuego or rainproof huts in the Chaco have mere comfort value. The Fuegians and Bolivians do not perish, they are merely abominably uncomfortable.

Unless it is literally a matter of life or death, nature thus prescribes nothing definite, but permits a whole gamut of adjustments. Some of them are elegant, others highly crude solutions of the same problem. Men may put up steam-heated ten-story apartment houses or get drenched in a grass hovel. They may defy the cold in Eskimo furs or go on shivering like the Fuegians, so long as they do not freeze to death.

In other words, geography does not *create* arts and customs: it merely offers opportunities or bars them. Why are the Gran Chaco Indians without stone tools? At some time in the past their ancestors must have had them, for stone-flaking is one of the oldest of human industries. The simple answer is that when they got to their present habitat they found themselves in a country absolutely devoid of stones. The same thing happened in Micronesia. The Oceanians who landed there lost their art of manufacturing stone adzes because the coral atolls yielded no suitable material. So there are certainly many things man cannot do because nature will not let him. Thus, he cannot begin to raise animals or plants that do not occur wild in his country. But the mere fact of their occurrence is never a sufficient reason for domesticating them. Were it otherwise, man would have been spared his lengthy apprenticeship as a hunter and root-gatherer.

Routes of travel seem to make a clear case for geographical influence. Any one who looks at ancient fist-hatchets from France and England will admit that they represent the same school; they are so similar that the knack of making them must have been carried from one country to the other. But how was that possible when there were no boats to cross the Channel in the Age before Pottery? Because in those days there was a land-bridge, so that Pre-Ceramic man could go back and forth dry-shod. Here geography is apparently the factor that counts. But *why* does it count? Only because the people affected had not yet become mariners. As soon as they developed navigation they could afford to smile at what was once a formidable barrier. Culture can thus triumph over nature, as it did in prehistoric Scandinavia. Sweden could never have had a Bronze Age unaided, for she had no tin. But by that time seamanship had reached a point where it was easy to import the metal, and accordingly ancient Sweden shared in the European culture of the period —not because of her natural resources, but in spite of them. Of course there are conditions no civilization can surmount. When the Scandinavians were smitten with a fruit-growing craze in the sixteenth and seventeenth centuries, a Lutheran bishop tried to raise vines in Bergen, and Danish kings experimented with almonds and fig-trees. Needless to say, their efforts came to grief.

Geography, then, decrees that such and such things shall *not* be, and that such others *may* be, but does not dictate what *must* be. To understand why things are what they are we must supplement geography with history. Just what does that mean? Let us go back to our Canadian Athabaskans. What makes their southern outposts live in warm houses that would seem so much more desirable for their northern brethren? The answer is simple. The southern members of the stock fell in with unrelated tribes whose substantial house types they were able to copy. Their northern kinsmen were less fortunate in their tribal acquaintances, so they continued to shiver.

All we have to do to see clearly in the matter is to look

at California. Social life there is not what it was under the Indian régime. The Pomo Indian, the Spaniard, the Anglo-Saxon, are not so much clay in the hands of environment. Each people had its own cultural standards; and these, with the limits set by nature, determined what they did in response to the same outer stimulus.

Japan is sometimes cited as a star example of what geography will do for a people. Nonsense could go no further. Japanese climate or landscape did not change all of a sudden in 1867. Her statesmen simply gave up the time-honored policy of isolation. The natives thus came into contact with our civilization and took over what they wanted. Even before that event the higher culture of the Japanese had been borrowed wholesale from China. The significant thing in Japanese development was the relationship with two alien groups—not Japanese geography, but Japanese history.

Geography, in short, supplies the brick and mortar of the cultural structure. But the *plan* of the building is prescribed by a people's past—by what they have previously thought and done, whether independently or in imitation of their neighbors.

CHAPTER IV

HEREDITY (RACE)

A CHIMPANZEE in the Bronx Zoo does not learn to speak English; a Negro in Harlem does. No amount of training will make the ape into the Negro's peer: he cannot share in the social tradition of any human group, because he is "not built that way." When Negro parents unite to form a new individual, their sex cells contain something the chimpanzee's lack, and that handicap the ape can never overcome. Heredity is all-important.

College students from the United States fail miserably when tested for linguistic ability alongside of Russian or Dutch age-mates. Have people in Russia and Holland a linguistic factor in their sex cells that Americans have not? That is impossible. For Americans of Northwest European ancestry are similar to the Dutch in heredity—certainly more like them than the Dutch are to the Russians. We also find that Americans raised in Europe are without the disabilities of their home-bred countrymen, and learn to speak French, German, and even English correctly. Experience, training, environment, is all-important; heredity counts for nothing.

So far it is all plain sailing: of living species, man alone has the inborn capacity for culture; and if human groups with similar heredity differ in culture, that difference, by definition, is not inborn. But are there not cases in between? Australians, Andaman Islanders, and Sioux Indians all have *some* culture, but its achievements seem meager compared to the Caucasian's. Some of these groups, it is true, are small in numbers and would be unlikely to yield a crop of great talents.[1] But in the United States there are millions of Negroes; yet no outstanding cultural feats can be traced to them. Why do they lag behind if not from inborn deficiency?

However, this is a two-edged argument. Massachusetts produces fifty times as many scientists as the South Atlantic states—a cultural difference with a vengeance. Do the Bostonian's sex cells carry fifty times as much of the research factor as the Atlantan's? The idea is absurd, because there is no appreciable difference in the heredity of the two. But if so enormous a discrepancy can be explained by environment, then Negro and white achievement, too, may differ on account of the social setting. I do not say that that is the real reason, but only that it *might* be so far as the argument goes.

Theoretically there is a direct way of settling the question. Psychologists can subject groups of distinct race to the same tests and compare the results. Those who have tried it generally come to the comforting conclusion that their own stock is superior to all others. Anthropologists challenge the fairness of the tests as being tinctured by the testers' cultural experience. The psychologist has no right to assume that his scores are a direct index of ability. If the Negro scores 90 where the white attains the 100 grade, we cannot simply write:

Negro Heredity = 90
White Heredity = 100

The equations should read:

Negro Heredity + X (Negro Environment) = 90
White Heredity + Y (White Environment) = 100

[1] See page 16.

Each equation contains two unknown quantities and accordingly cannot be solved. Anthropologists and psychologists are still painfully groping for some means to estimate the environmental influence and in some way to eliminate it. Up to date nothing positive is known.

In the meantime there are two important facts to be reconciled. Most colored races undoubtedly are backward in their culture; yet unbiased observers, such as Prince Maximilian von Wied, Alexander von Humboldt, or Delafosse, fail to find any striking mental differences between them and Caucasians. If the colored peoples had the same *average* endowment as the white but were less variable, all the data would be explained. The average Negro would then be in the same intellectual 5-foot 8-inch class as his competitor, but his giants might fall half a foot short of the white 7-footers. If this were so, the Negro could engage on equal terms with the white in the humdrum business of the workaday world, but not with his record-breaking sports of genius. This is the view expressed by Professor Eugen Fischer of Berlin, one of the foremost of physical anthropologists in Germany. He does not doubt for a moment that Negroes can learn arithmetic or foreign languages and qualify as mechanics and clerks. He is willing to concede that the average European peasant or proletarian may not excel the South African. But, he argues, Europeans are more variable—not only in sheer intellect, but even more so in respect to imagination, energy, executive ability. If a race should lack one or two of the hereditary factors that make for greatness, it could never or only very rarely produce leaders of men in science, business, or politics. This sounds plausible and cannot at least be ruled out of court as manifest nonsense. Up to date, however, it is merely a suggestive guess, for no one has proved that the Negro *is* mentally less variable.

Heredity-mongers are of course not satisfied with so modest a sop. They prefer to view the Negro as just a trifle better than a chimpanzee and as a rule see startling mental differences even among Caucasians. The tall, fair Nordic of Northwestern Europe, the stocky, broad-skulled Alpine of central France and South Germany, the small, swarthy Mediterranean of Spain, Southern Italy, and Greece, are each credited with a peculiar psychology. By *heredity* the Nordic is adventurous, combative, intellectual, idealistic, and at the same time imperialistic. The Mediterranean is clever, volatile, tricky, artistic. Both tower above the Alpine dullard, who has only the homespun virtues of thrift, patience, and honesty, and naturally plays the part of serf to a Nordic master. These picturesque contrasts are made to explain European culture-history.

All this is twaddle. Europeans have moved about and intermarried so much that not one region on the whole continent is purely Nordic or anything else. By general agreement Sweden is the most Nordic country in the world, but Professor Retzius, who measured thousands of her recruits, estimated that only 11 per cent. were pure Nordics. By this he meant no more than that so many combined tallness, fair hair, blue eyes, and long heads. A few years ago the Swedish State Institute for Race Biology made an investigation of 47,000 conscripts. A "purer [not pure!] Nordic type" was arbitrarily defined to include fair individuals over 168 cm. in height, the width of whose heads was less than 78 per cent. of their length. Even so this type embraced only 30.82 per cent. in the entire kingdom and in no district rose above 38 per cent.

But this estimate is far in excess of the figure of really pure Nordics in Sweden, for both Retzius and his successors are taking into account only a few outstanding features. If we consider more traits that may have characterized the fairly pure Nordic of 4000 B.C., the number of pure Nordics at once dwindles. Thus, Retzius found that well over half of his conscripts stood above 170 cm. (5 feet 7 inches), but barely 11 per cent. were likewise long-headed, fair, and blue-eyed. If he had reckoned as pure only those tall, long-headed blonds who were intellectual, imaginative, and capable as executives, how many would have been left?

There is another way of looking at the matter. If mental traits belong by heredity to racial strains, the laws of heredity ought to hold for them in much the same way as for physical traits. What, then, are these laws in the case of a mixed population? Modern science teaches us that each trait is inherited separately. By far the best-studied case is that of the Rehoboth colony in Southwest Africa. In the eighteenth century Dutch and other North European men began to marry Hottentot women, and their offspring have continued to intermarry. *Neither the Nordic nor the Hottentot race prevailed.* According to Professor Fischer's researches, the breeds are tall like the Nordic, but kinky-haired like the Hottentot; dark-eyed and dark in hair like the African parent, but never quite like him in skin color and rarely even approaching his yellow tints. Sometimes Fischer's subjects reminded him of German peasants in their cast of features. Some had very flat wide noses and kinky hair, yet at the same time were tall and thin-lipped like their European ancestors.

What is the bearing of these facts on our "Nordics"? Simply this: a man may be big and blond and yet be far from Nordic in his psychology. Not to go back before the

Viking period, the Swedish State Institute tells us that the Swedes then roved in all directions and brought back both women and slaves from foreign countries. In course of time these were absorbed in the general population. Later South as well as North German immigrants came, and in the early seventeenth century Walloon artisans from Belgium were imported. These Alpines were doubtless no more pure than any other recent European stock. Supposing, however, that a "pure Nordic" married a "pure Alpine," the children he begot might well inherit his Viking physique and their mother's dark hair, his executive ability and her frugal ways.

In short, *if* the Nordics of six or eight thousand years ago had peculiar mental traits, the time for determining them by mental tests or otherwise is past. Their psychology is unknowable and fit subject only for metaphysical speculation. Any statement about them has the scientific value of old wives' tales. There may indeed be *group* differences, but the groups that differ are not *races*. When psychologists test the mentality of persons born in Sweden, England, France, and Italy and assume that the differences found are racial, they are pitiably ignorant of history, anthropology, and biology. A naturalist might just as well weigh 365 elephants, 500 guinea-pigs, and 135 spiders and announce to the world that the sum exceeded that of 118 elephants, 620 guinea-pigs, and 262 mosquitoes. However flawless the arithmetic, the result would mean nothing. And this illustration is not too drastic; it is not drastic enough. For each of our beasts definitely belongs to a particular species, but with a given Italian we do not know the proportion of Alpine and Mediterranean, and possibly Nordic, blood. We do not know whether an adventurous Nordic disposition would be dominant in a cross with a Philistine Alpine one. We do not know whether Nordic dipsomania would truckle to reckless Alpine sobriety. Assuming that the several European races of, say, 6000 B.C. did differ, we have really not the slightest reason to suppose that their peculiarities were anything like those popularly ascribed to them.

As a matter of fact, there are powerful reasons for doubting it. According to the current scheme, the Walloon craftsmen transplanted from Belgium into Sweden were at least largely Alpine. Yet when surrounded by the purest Nordics of the world they did not at once sink to the humble place proper to them. Swedish anthropologists give them a very different character. "They have a lively, frank, talkative, polite and friendly way, rapid powers of perception, a fine sense of beauty, a warm inclination for music, and indisputable creative power in the fields of both literature and science. Their practical ability shows itself not only in the world's most excellent smith-work, but also in the achievements which many Walloon descendants have performed as public servants in advanced positions. It is obvious that these Walloons have proved to be a valuable acquisition."

How strange! Alpines—even though probably mixed with Mediterranean and Nordic strains—hold their own among the purest Nordics of the world. They even furnish them with statesmen. What becomes of that favorite dogma that the Nordic by the divine right of inborn fitness is the Alpine's lord and master, the ruler of all mankind?

That precious doctrine becomes a bit doubtful for another reason. If it were true, the purest Nordics should be the master imperialists. The Scandinavians are notoriously nothing of the sort; indeed, our foremost race theorist, Mr. Madison Grant, weeps bitter tears over the downfall of the Scandinavian countries. They have ceased to be "a nursery of soldiers"; today "all three seem to be intellectually anemic." We neither share that inference nor can we mourn because the descendants of the Vikings no longer pillage towns and ravish women but manufacture safety matches, redeem the heath, and discover the South Pole. But if they thus allowed the Alpinized Germans and the Mediterranean-ridden Britons to steal a march on them, it can only be because towheads are not inseparable from colonial empire.

Let us, then, leave the mental differences of the ancient European stocks to metaphysicians, to quacks, and to their dupes.

Even if inborn mental differences existed between races, they could explain only the tiniest part of our problems. For the history of culture constantly shows us cultural differences where the racial basis has remained identical. There is the case of our research men from Massachusetts and from the South.[1] There are the striking oscillations in British culture. Did the Elizabethans carry in their sex cells an extra dose of animal spirits that was blighted by a charge of gloom under Puritanism but revived by the Restoration? And what of Japan? There was no sudden influx of a new stock in 1867; there was a sudden change in culture because new *ideas* were allowed to enter. Neither geography nor heredity explains the difference between old and new conditions: the key is held solely by history.

There is an even stronger case. Those artists of the Reindeer Age, some 20,000 years ago, were at least the equal of any modern race. All anatomists seem agreed on this. In fact, their brains were considerably larger than ours. Did they soar to heights we have never reached? Not at all. They never got beyond the hunting stage, never molded a single

[1] See page 25.

pot. A high sort of racial heredity may thus go hand in hand with a Pre-Ceramic culture; it also goes hand in hand with our complex industrial civilization. Two things so far apart cannot be explained by a factor they share. Race cannot explain culture.

CHAPTER V

FOOD

Tomato soup
Breaded veal cutlets with fried potatoes
String-beans
Assorted bread (wheat, corn, rye)
Pineapple salad
Rice pudding
Coffee, tea, chocolate, milk

HERE is a bill of fare taken at random. It doubtless excels anything to be found in the primitive communities of the world. But how did it become possible? Not through any geographical or racial advantages of ours, but because we have borrowed food products right and left from the four quarters of the globe. Four hundred years ago our environment and our heredity were what they are, but three-fourths of the dishes at our command were beyond the ken of our forefathers. Improved means of transportation turned the trick. Could the Tasmanians voyage to America or China on their miserable rafts? (Figs. 5 and 6.) The Spaniards, the Dutch, and the English had sailing-vessels in which they could and did. But before the era of navigation and discovery the disparity between a European and a primitive meal was not nearly so great. The pre-Columbian chef in Madrid or Paris had no tomatoes, no string-beans, no potatoes or maize or pineapples at his disposal, for every one of them came from the New World. Imagine Ireland without potatoes and Hungary without Indian corn!

But let us analyze our menu more closely, beginning with

the beverages. Well, in 1500 literally no one in Europe knew anything about chocolate, tea, or coffee. When finally introduced, they were far too expensive to become at once general favorites. What is more, the oddest ideas clustered about them, so that their present place in our daily life is an extremely recent thing.

FIG. 5. TASMANIAN RAFT (*after Ling Roth*)

FIG. 6. PAVIOTSO RAFT OF TASMANIAN STYLE FROM NEVADA (*after photograph by Lowie*)

The Spaniards brought chocolate from Mexico, where the natives boiled a mixture of roasted cacao seeds, corn meal, Chili peppers, and other ingredients for a drink. They also used the pods as money, but the Spaniards did not adopt this custom and simplified the recipe for the beverage. From them it spread to Flanders and Italy, reaching Florence about 1606. In France Cardinal Richelieu's brother was apparently the first to taste it—as a remedy for an ailment of the spleen. Laymen and doctors alike vied with one another in ascribing to the newcomer marvelous qualities for good and evil. In 1671 Madame de Sévigné wrote about a noble lady who had indulged so immoderately while big with child that she gave birth to a little blackamoor (*un petit garçon noir comme le diable*). Some physicians attacked chocolate as a dangerous laxative fit only for the gross digestion of an Indian, but most of them took a kindlier view. One of them even advertised his own preparation of it as a specific for venereal disease. Divinity also took a hand. Was chocolate to be classed as food or drink? Upon the answer hinged its consumption during Lent. In 1664 Bishop Brancaccio published a Latin treatise, proving that chocolate was not *per se* food, even though it chanced to be nutritious. The qualms of the devout were silenced, and this convenient doctrine carried the day.

Tea was cultivated in China as early as the sixth century of our era, but Europe never so much as heard of it until about 1560, and the Dutch introduced it half a century later. In 1650 or thereabouts the English began to drink tea, and ten years later Pepys recorded his first experience with the new drink. But for a long time it was confined to high society. How many could afford to pay from 15 to 50 shillings a pound? Even in 1712 the best tea was still at 18, with poorer qualities at 14 and 10 shillings a pound, and the price did not noticeably fall until 1760. Just as in the case of chocolate, veritable miracles were claimed for the new commodity. French medical opinion advertised it as a remedy for the gout, and one writer made it a panacea: among many other afflictions it was guaranteed to cure rheumatism, colic, epilepsy, stone in the bladder, catarrhs, and dysentery. Daniel Huet, Bishop of Avranches, who had long been blear-eyed and dyspeptic, took to tea, and lo! his sight and his digestion were restored. No wonder his gratitude found expression in a Latin elegy of fifty-eight lines singing the praises of the beverage.

The story of coffee is not less entertaining. The tree is indigenous to Abyssinia. The Arabs used the beverage in the fifteenth century of our era and began to spread it. However, even from Constantinople it is not reported until the following century. It reached Marseilles in 1644, but except for a few of the larger cities France for several decades remained immune to temptation. Although Levantines and Armenians dispensed it in little shops where patrons could smoke and play cards, even Parisians failed to be interested until the Turkish ambassador who arrived in 1669 made it popular at private parties. The more pretentious cafés of modern type did not spring up until the latter part of the century. Then they rapidly turned into favorite haunts of all the upper classes of society—officers, men of letters, fine ladies and gentlemen, newsmongers and soldiers of fortune. About the same time the coffee house became an established institution in London—an exchange for news and political opinions.

By the eighteenth century coffee was a fixture in Germany, but violent protests were heard against the new habit. Husbands complained that their wives were reducing them to beggary and that many women would willingly forgo paradise if coffee were served in purgatory. At Hildesheim a Government ordinance of 1780 admonished the people to abandon the novelty and to revert to the tried custom of their forbears: "Your fathers, German men, drank brandy and, like Frederick the Great, were raised on beer; they were merry and of good cheer. That is what we also desire. . . . All pots, elegant cups and common bowls, . . . in short, everything that admits the epithet 'coffee,' shall be destroyed and smashed, so that its memory shall be annihilated among our fellows. Whoever shall sell [coffee] beans, shall have his whole supply confiscated. . . ."

Evidently prohibition is not an invention of the twentieth century and may be leveled against other than spirituous beverages.

Let us remember, however, that at first coffee, too, figured above all as a medicine. It was supposed to fatten the lean and to reduce the fat, to be effective against scrofula, hysteria, and toothache. With cream it was originally taken only as a medicine. Famous doctors regarded the combination as excellent for colds and lung trouble. At Lausanne physicians prescribed it against the gout. To be sure, there were not only skeptics but detractors. The Princess of Hanau had been a great coffee-bibber and had died in agony from a hundred ulcers caused by her harmful indulgence. A doctor's thesis in 1715 proved that the habit shortened life; a Dr. Duncan charged it with inducing not only nausea and cholera, but also barrenness in women and impotence in men. But a defender arose in the person of Philippe Hecquet, dean of the Parisian Faculty of Medicine, who conceded no more than that coffee allayed passion, put the relation of the sexes on a higher plane, and enabled monks to keep their vows of chastity.

Chocolate, tea, and coffee, then, are very recent elements of Western civilization. So is the sugar for sweetening these beverages. In India physicians and priests had indeed used it for centuries. But only after Alexander the Great reached the country in 327 B.C. did Europe first hear about a cane growing there which produced "a kind of honey without the aid of bees." For centuries to come the matter ended there. In 627 A.D. the Emperor Heraklius of Constantinople destroyed the summer palace of the King of Persia and with other booty seized a treasure trove of sugar. The Persians had got the cane from India, not much over a hundred years earlier. When the Arabs conquered Persia about 640 A.D. they at once took to cultivating the plant and introduced it wherever they went—into Egypt, Morocco, Sicily, and Spain. Now sugar began to be imported into Christendom on a larger scale, and after the discovery of the New World America rapidly became a great center for growing it. However, sugar long remained a table luxury and a drug prescribed for lung or chest trouble, against colds and coughing. In France the corporation of apothecary-grocers had the sole right to sell it, and "apothecary without sugar" was a proverbial phrase to denote a man without the essentials of his calling. In 1630 sugar was still so rare that at the largest hospital in Paris a monthly allowance was doled out to the woman in charge of drugs; and she had to declare on oath that she had used it only in preparing medicines as prescribed. But when tea, coffee, and chocolate had gained a firm footing in Europe in the seventeenth century a change set in, there was a sudden and ever-increasing spurt in the demand, and between 1730 and 1800 the consumption of sugar trebled.

To return to our bill of fare, rice also can be traced to India as its home and was brought to Europe by the Arabs. It, too, did not become a favorite dish until the end of the Middle Ages.

After cutting out the American tomatoes, potatoes, beans, corn bread, pineapples, and chocolate; the coffee that is native to Africa; the Chinese tea; the rice and sugar from India—what remains of our meal? Veal, wheat, rye, and milk. Of these, rye did not enter Europe until about the time of Christ. The rest are indeed very old there, but they are not natives. One and all they go back to the Near Orient: there cereals were first sown, cattle first reared, and cows first milked. *Western Europe does not deserve credit for originating a single item.*

This result is not due to a capricious choice of menu. Had we ordered chicken or turkey instead of cutlets, the Mongoloid's contribution would loom larger still. For poultry were first domesticated in Burma, and before Columbus' discovery the turkey was raised only in America.

Of course in France Baedeker would have warned us against slaking our thirst with water, and we should be dutifully ordering Bordeaux, Sauterne, or a bock. But that would not improve the claims of Western Europe, for long before any one there dreamt of viticulture the people of the Near Orient were busily fermenting grape juice. In southern France the vine was grown in 600 B.C.; Egyptian graves dating back beyond 3000 B.C. contain large wine jars with telltale sealing-inscriptions on their clay stoppers. Every king of the early dynasties had a special vineyard which provided the wine for ceremonial. However, the Egyptians did not limit it to sacred uses. After a meal the upper classes engaged in drinking-bouts, with fine ladies attending by no means as total abstainers. The tomb paintings of Beni-Hasan show us a gentleman carried away, stiff as a broomstick, on the shoulders of his slaves, while ladies are vomiting as a result of their carousal. We have records of the conversations at these banquets. A servant, carried away by the enthusiasm of the occasion, urges a reluctant guest to get drunk; a nurse bids her mistress drink and not be a spoilsport; one lady shouts at the porter, "Give me eighteen cups of wine, don't you see I want to get drunk? My insides are as dry as straw!" No wonder the people of the Nile were unable to supply their needs by home production. In the earlier period they eked out the demand with wine from such fruits as figs and pomegranates. The poorer folk, as in Babylonia, fell back on date wine as an excellent and inexpensive beverage. Later the Egyptians regularly imported grape wine from Phoenicia and Greece.

In short, viticulture was born in the Near East, and if it had not been for Syria and Egypt, no Frenchman would be enjoying his claret or Burgundy today.

The story of beer points the same moral. Brewed mainly from barley, it was the truly national liquor of the Egyptians. Peasant, fisherman, and shepherd drank it, but so did polite society; about 1800 B.C. the daily amount brought to the royal court was not less than 130 jars. Even the earliest texts list a variety of brands. So do the Babylonian records, which give us the very earliest recipes known, for they go back to 2800 B.C.

Professor Lutz has given us a lively account of Babylonian taverns. They had a most up-to-date flavor, being literally waterfront dives and brothels. No respectable gentleman could enter these saloons without loss of prestige. Their keepers were mostly women; at least, the code of Hammurabi, about 2000 B.C., never mentions men. The law dealt very severely with the publican. On pain of being thrown into the water she was not allowed to take money for a drink—only grain; and if she made her tavern the assembly of outlaws, she was liable to execution. When a lady thus harassed by the Government was also threatened by a falling off of customers, she naturally turned to religion. That is, she would pray to Ishtar, hoping that the goddess of love would help her retrieve her business.

The invention of dives is no doubt an independent achievement of the European mind, but the technique of wine-growing and of beer-brewing was quite as certainly borrowed from the Near Orient. Thus, once more we are led back to the same conclusion: our food and drink are at least predominantly not the creatures of our own culture.

But in the light of our vistas of civilization as a whole [1] we can go further. Some ten or fifteen thousand years ago even the oldest ingredients of our bill of fare were beyond *any* member of the human species, whether in Europe, Tasmania, or the Near Orient. Even wine and beer, old as they are, seem to be of the Copper Age; wheat, veal, and milk do not fall beyond the Age of Pottery as we go further back; and before that stretches the vast Pre-Ceramic, at least nine times as long.

However, the ninety-odd thousand years of hunting and seed-gathering were not a sheer waste of time. Man could not afford to squat on his haunches and wait for roast ortolan to come flying into his mouth. Roast ortolan indeed! How should you like roasted ants? I once declined a dish of them offered by Shoshone Indians in Idaho. Or what about roasted grasshoppers? That is what Indians in Utah took to when larger game failed, and a capital achievement it was. For naturally a single grasshopper does not make a meal, and it took joint effort to catch enough of them for a whole band. A hole was dug four or five feet deep, the members of the tribe spread out so as to surround a four-acre field, and by beating the ground with branches they frightened the grasshoppers into the pit. Other tribes near by organized such drives for rabbits, which were chased till they got entangled in nets. For larger game, such as antelope or bison, American Indians often used the same principle. They drove a herd into a large pen, where it was easy to kill them, or made them tumble down steep cutbanks.

In each of these cases the savage showed how immeasurably superior he was to the chimpanzee. Evidently he ac-

[1] See page 14.

curately observed the species he hunted, but he did much more: he planned the joint drive, organized it, erected a big pen or spread out his nets, and allotted posts to each hunter. All this was a work of the imagination that should not be underestimated.

These communal hunts, however, represent only a small portion of what man accomplished before he turned farmer. In these early days he learnt more about his particular flora and fauna than any but zoölogists and botanists among us

FIG. 7. BUSHMAN ROCK PAINTING OF OSTRICH HUNT (*after Stow*)

know about ours. He also added to his resources with astonishing ingenuity. It is not easy to hunt elephants with bow and arrow. But the South African Bushmen made pitfalls so that the unsuspecting giant tumbled into his prison as soon as he had stepped on the covering of a hole. These pygmies, who are among the crudest people of recent times, knew how to stalk game. A hunter would approach a herd of ostriches, covering himself with an ostrich head and imitating the movements of his quarry so as not to arouse suspicion; and when close enough he let fly his dart (Fig. 7).

Many of the simpler peoples *drugged* animals and fish.

While the Australians can stalk emus in Bushman fashion, they also know enough to put a decoction of the pituri plant in a waterhole used by the bird, which is thus stupefied and easily taken. The South American Indians systematically test their flora to find out what leaves will narcotize the fish in a stream.

Of primitive weapons, the harpoon goes back to the reindeer-hunters of France, which makes it about 20,000 years old; and an ancient Spanish rock-painting unmistakably shows an archer with bow and arrow. Until a few hundred years ago our ancestors still depended on a modified bow for their most effective instrument of war and the chase. Neither the Nordic nor the Mediterranean nor any other white race had been able to devise anything better, and only a little earlier the Chinese had invented gunpowder—*for fireworks.*

People grow expert by specializing. From the earliest times there was a characteristic division of labor between the sexes. Man concentrated on hunting and fishing. Thus it was woman who after myriads of years discovered that seeds accidentally dropped on the ground might grow. She began to plant them intentionally, turned her old root-digger into a hoe, and became the first gardener or farmer. Her husband's mind was fixed on animals; so he naturally did more to tame beasts that ultimately turned into our live stock.

But even after these fruitful ideas of tilling the soil and of breeding stock were in full swing, no one for thousands of years put the two together. Most primitive farmers have kept on wielding a hoe instead of lengthening it into a bigger cultivator that could be drawn by beasts. The African Negroes, for example, have plenty of cattle, but except when imitating the whites they never harness an ox to a plow. The Peruvians had llamas that might conceivably have served the purpose, but the idea never occurred to them.

Plowing is not essential to farming. Most of the American Indians lacked stock, so they were barred from our style of agriculture. This did not prevent dozens of tribes from growing manioc or maize, beans, and squashes. They passed directly from hunting to gardening or hoe-farming. *Man thus did not have to be a herder before he could become a tiller.*

In the Near Orient, however, people not only kept animals and scraped the earth but put the two notions together. The transition is shown in early Egyptian pictures. Hoes are figured as well as plows, and men as well as oxen are seen dragging at a plow. The plow was evidently not an easy thing to invent, for until the Copper Age man failed to accomplish this feat, and every people that ever used it seems to have got the idea from Egypt or Babylonia.

Of course man did not immediately drop his old food habits as soon as he had stumbled on new ones. It was a good thing he did not, for farming and stock-breeding are at best precarious occupations. Take a Lapp who had lost his reindeer in the old days. How could he have supported himself if he had unlearned to fish? So in East Africa the Baganda kept on hunting buffalo and elephants to eke out the food supply from their plantains and their cattle. So our Hopi in Arizona prize corn as the staff of life but also hunt rabbits. Even with us angling and hunting remain as sports, and what meat is superior to venison?

Man did not lose his ingenuity when he turned to herding or husbandry. A Hopi is able to dry-farm where a white agriculturist from Iowa fails. Our Eastern Indians fertilized the ground with fish. Negroes know that a cow will yield milk if her calf is present, and if it happens to die they cheat the mother by holding up the stuffed calfskin—a trick that never fails. In East Africa the Jagga dig irrigation canals, stall-feed cattle, and manure their banana groves. Observation through the ages has taught the savage how to grapple with insect pests and scant rainfall, where to pasture his flocks, how to milk, ride, and pack his beasts. In tropical South America he has converted a naturally poisonous plant, the manioc, into his chief crop. How could any one ever think up such an invention? Nordenskiöld has enlightened us. In the course of their experiments with fish-narcotics [1] the South Americans also tried out the bitter manioc. By chance they discovered that what was left after the removal of the poison had food value. By such devious routes ancient man scored most of his successes. He was very far from being a demigod. His very triumphs are shot through with incredible stupidity, as the story of domesticated plants and beasts will show.[2] Yet the fact remains that he laid the foundation of our economic life. *And with all our vaunted science, our soil chemistry and animal husbandry, we have not succeeded in adding one solitary species of importance to the stock handed down by earlier cultures.*

[1] See page 43.
[2] See page 57.

CHAPTER VI

FOOD ETIQUETTE

In making his tools, in gathering food plants, in snaring and trapping animals, the savage appears quite as rational as ourselves. That means, of course, that he is not quite rational. From the start his most matter-of-fact occupations had a way of getting mixed up with quaint conventions and superstitions. Milking a cow is a practical enough affair, but in South Africa a Zulu will not allow his women to do the work or even so much as come near the cattle corral. The idea may go back to that ancient division of labor by which males herded and tended stock animals. Woman's place is in the millet field; she does not "belong" in the cattle-raiser's universe. To admit her would be dangerous and immoral—much worse than letting our women smoke or admitting them to the bar a generation ago.

Eating is so important a part of human life that it naturally gets entangled with all sorts of notions; and the savage, who is often squeamish where we are indifferent, generally builds up a stately edifice of rules on the subject. Some of them cut deep and belong to ethics rather than etiquette. Thus, it is the unpardonable sin for an Eskimo to eat vension with his seal flesh. That, so the belief runs, always enrages a sea-goddess. By way of punishment she would keep all the big sea mammals from approaching the settlement and thus inflict punishment not only on the culprit but also on all his neighbors. No wonder they are wroth and insist on a confession of guilt to appease the deity. The Masai of East Africa have a similar taboo against eating meat and drinking milk on the same day. It would not only make the man sick, but—what is more important—the cow also.

Another type of regulation has a profound effect on social life. Men and women are often obliged to take their meals separately. When a Masai wants to eat, his wife departs from the hut. Neither will use the other's vessels to eat or drink from. In Greenland, in Hawaii, in Uganda, in Bolivia, and in Melanesia similar taboos are or were in vogue. Imagine the effect on our family life if spouses were never allowed to sit down for a joint meal!

Apart from such vital rules there are others that properly fall under the head of etiquette. In Uganda it was most impolite to greet people one found eating: only a boor would so much as look at them. Here a guest's duty was to eat heartily, thank his host, and belch audibly to show how much he had enjoyed his fare. A Masai was expected to click his tongue. When a Zulu boy went to a party, his parents admonished him to hold out both his hands when served; to do otherwise would be a reflection on his host's generosity. A common primitive rule is to set food before a visitor as soon as he arrives, regardless of the time of day. Such hospitality is a foregone conclusion among the Plains Indians. It is not obligatory to eat up everything that is offered. The visitor may even, without jarring the native sense of propriety, ask for a container to take home what is left. Sometimes the seating arrangements are fixed. Crow hosts and guests do not sit together, but each family forms a group by itself. Not so among the Hopi. Here everybody gathers around a big vessel and dips his wafer bread into the common pottage. Where rank plays a part in savage society, the natives are very finicky about the order of serving. In Polynesia cups of kava, the favorite beverage, were handed to the feasters with as much attention to precedence as has ever been shown at a state banquet in London or Washington.

In short, the savage rules of etiquette are not only strict, but formidable. Nevertheless, to us their table manners are shocking. It is not that utensils are wholly lacking. There are knives, spoons, ladles, gourds, coconut shells, and wooden bowls. But whatever may be available is used with a lofty unconcern for hygiene. A Bolivian Indian licks honey from an implement that looks like a shaving-brush and then passes it on to his neighbor. He helps himself to a lump of mashed fruit out of a big gourd, sucks at it, then spits it back into the common vessel. Why be fastidious about your neighbor's saliva?

In the great East African kingdom of Uganda savage etiquette probably reached the acme of refinement according to our modern standards. The natives wash their hands before and after a meal. A wooden bowl was handed around and somebody poured water over the guests' hands, or each received a sponge to wipe off the grease. There was great care not to touch another's portion with one's hands: it was passed in a leaf. However, forks were lacking. You broke off a piece of your food, rolled it into a ball, and put it into your mouth with your fingers. If there was gravy, you pitted the food-ball into a tiny cup with your thumb and then stuck it into the joint vessel. "It was quite an art to make the balls without being scalded, and it required some care not to spill the gravy when conveying the food to the mouth."

How ridiculous, if not beastly, all these customs seem! Well, let us look at the practices of our European forefathers.

When a Spanish nobleman of the tenth century entertained honored visitors, a magnificent cloth was spread on a table loaded with cut glass and plates; and one tempting course followed another. But there were no forks, so that knight and abbot needs ate trout, lamb, and chicken with their fingers. For soup and stew they had the savage's ladle and spoon. And like the East African Negroes they washed their hands before and after a repast. German custom was not superior. In the early Middle Ages every one ate out of a common bowl, and only people of quality used spoons. There were not even plates; and the idea of providing one for every person present did not become prevalent until the sixteenth century.

But what of France, the arbiter of elegance? She was ahead of Germany, but not very far and not on all counts. In genteel fourteenth century society soup was served in earthenware bowls—one for each *couple* of guests. Within the intimate family circle no one went to such lengths of nicety, but each member helped himself from the kettle that took the place of a tureen. For solid food each person received a *tranchoir*, which was simply a thick round slice of bread. When the carver had dissected the meat on a metal platter, each guest seized a portion with three fingers and put it on his trencher. After the meal the gravy-soaked bread was turned over to the poor. Plates did not wholly replace this primitive device until about 1650. Incidentally, it was quite proper to feed odd scraps to the dogs and cats under the table.

Forks were a rarity even among kings. They were costly affairs with glass or ivory handles. The wife of Louis X owned one, the Duchess of Touraine had two, and in 1418 Charles VI could boast of as many as three. Such articles of luxury were not lightly put to practical use. They were not intrusted even to the king's carver, who somehow shifted with knife and hands. What is more, their original purpose was to aid in cutting. In his *Arte Cisoria* (1423) Don Enrique de Villena describes a two-pronged *broca*, usually of gold or silver, and a three-tined *tridente*—both used in carving. The noble author points out that with these instruments one could convey cooked meat to the mouth without greasing one's hands, and he seems to have been the first Castilian to be struck by this happy thought. Of course it did not immediately take root in Spain, let alone elsewhere. Before 1600 even the highest French circles had not adopted the custom, and every one ate with his fingers. The middle class did not generally take to forks in imitation of their betters until the eighteenth century.

In the earlier period knives were proportionately more important, but not quite as one might imagine. In France two or three were held sufficient for a large party, and accordingly they were freely bandied back and forth. In 1560 a French writer describes the *whimsical* Swiss and German custom of providing each guest with a knife for himself alone. Thirty years later the great Montaigne noted the same practice in Switzerland. He himself used neither spoon nor fork and ate so fast that he sometimes bit his fingers.[1] But then even the world of fashion remained strangely crude. There were redeeming usages. In the sixteenth century a man drank to the health of his sweetheart as many times as she had letters in her name. Notwithstanding such refinements every one until about 1550 drank from a common glass. Over a hundred years later there was a lady in polite society who regularly served with her ten fingers. Another, in 1695, thought nothing of ladling out sauce for a guest with a spoon that came "fresh from her fair lips."

In short, two hundred years ago the most refined West Europeans were savages in their table manners. They had got as far as the East African Negroes in washing their hands before and after a meal; they had not got beyond that point.

[1] "*Je mors parfois mes doigts, de hâtiveté.*"

CHAPTER VII

FIRE AND COOKING

No CHIMPANZEE knows how to use fire or to cook a meal. All savages have mastered both arts. The knowledge of fire goes back very far. With the tools of Neanderthal man there are charred bones and bits of charcoal, proving that fire was used possibly 40,000 years ago. Many pursuits would have been impossible or difficult without it. For metal-work, pottery, and cooking it is indispensable. It aided the stone-worker to quarry flint and may have attracted the earliest animals that became domesticated. In large-scale hunting, when whole herds of bison or wild horses were to be driven into a pound or down a steep cliff, the easiest way was surely to start a fire and frighten the victims along the desired path. Small wonder that many tribes take no chances with so precious a possession and never allow it to go out. Nor is it strange that myths and cults cluster about it.

Early man could not of course make fire deliberately before knowing what it was like. He began by tending a flame due to some lucky fluke—a natural conflagration perhaps. The Andaman Islanders, when first discovered, did not know how to make fire but kept alive a flame secured no one can tell by what fortunate chance.

Among primitive peoples the most widespread means of producing fire is a drill. Many of them are able to make a hole in a stone by twirling a sharp shaft on it between the palms of their hands. Substitute a blunt stick on a block of wood, and the same process will separate a heap of wood meal from the block (Fig. 8). Gradually the fine particles are heated to the point of ignition, and if the spark is then caught on some dry inflammable material it can be blown or fanned into a blaze. There is a knack about all this, for when the hands get down to the bottom of the drill they must immediately be brought to the top again without a shift in the position of the shaft. Otherwise the dust has a

FIG. 8. PAVIOTSO DRILLING FIRE, NEVADA (*after photo by Lowie*)

chance to cool off, and all the previous labor goes for naught. For the inexperienced it is a difficult task, but I have seen Ishi, a Californian Indian, get a spark in twenty-two seconds, and under favorable circumstances ten will do. Arctic peoples improved the technique: a man revolves the stick by turning a bow, its string being twisted around the shaft (Fig. 32). In order to keep the drill in place, he holds it down with a mouthpiece between his teeth. It takes Eskimo jaws to do this with comfort, but the shaft can be held by an assistant, and in any case the bow-drill ingeniously saves labor. Like many clever ideas in culture-history, it has the merit of putting together two devices that were at first separate. The bow is very old,[1] and so is the drill. But using the weapon to twirl the shaft of a fire-making apparatus is a relatively recent invention shared by only a handful of peoples.

The Polynesians did not drill fire, but rubbed a sharp stick along a piece of wood to make a groove. In this hollow they kept on moving the stick until the pile of wood dust yielded a spark. The method was laborious, and whenever possible the natives preserved their fire by carrying torches.

Strangely enough, the crude Tierra del Fuegians had a better method than these more advanced tribes. They learnt to strike pyrites against flint and were thus abreast of our grandfathers with their strike-a-lights and tinder. Not that theirs was a method to brag about. Like Polynesians and other primitives, our forefathers treated fire-making as a grim necessity to be avoided and deferred as long as possible. To get up before dawn of a cold winter day, to strike a spark, catch it in some tinder, and then blow it into a blaze was a dreaded task. In order to get out of it the fire was often kept up all night, which of course meant consuming enormous quantities of wood. But that was expensive and hard to procure, especially in the cities. Peat was sometimes substituted. As for coal, even in England no one used it for household purposes before 1560. When the Queen Dowager of Denmark felt an urge to be extra charitable, she would send an old widow two or three cartloads of firewood. Until the French Revolution all the higher Parisian dignitaries had enormous fires blazing in front of their mansions during the winter time. There the poor were allowed to gather from

[1] See page 43.

six in the evening until one in the morning, to warm their hands, and to carry home a few live embers and lighted billets.

In northern Europe "borrowing fire" was a favorite makeshift. Troels-Lund gives a vivid picture of sixteenth century Scandinavians groping their way about pitch-dark alleys of a winter morning to beg fire from a well-disposed neighbor—provided he was not himself out on a similar errand. The custom was not only primitive, but fraught with peril, for all ordinances to the contrary notwithstanding, the citizens *would* carry the fire uncovered, and when a gust of wind blew the sparks into a thatched roof the prettiest conflagration was set going.[1]

Racial determination of progress? Fiddlesticks. Until a century ago Europeans were primitives in their fire-making. No new "luciferous" factor entered the sex cells of North and West European peoples at the beginning of the last century. But chemistry developed and was put to the solution of modern needs. In 1805 or 1806 a Frenchman coated splints of wood with sulphur and potassium chlorate. Dipped into sulphuric acid, they ignited. A little later our phosphorus match was invented, friction taking the place of immersion; and in 1844 was founded the great Swedish factory in Jönköping.

As for the preparation of food, all the important principles of cookery are known to savages. Even canned goods have their equivalent. Plains Indians could not always have fresh bison meat, but they had a way of preserving it in eatable condition. The meat was dried on racks, pounded up fine, and mixed with melted fat, marrow, and wild cherry paste. Stored in rawhide bags, this "pemmican" might keep

[1] See page 71 sq.

for years. The idea was by no means unique among primitives: in the Gran Chaco the women of a South American tribe roast fruit so it can be preserved for months, and the accomplishment is shared by Micronesians. The Polynesians of the Marquesas group dreaded famines and accordingly stored fermented breadfruit in pits so it would last a family for a year; sometimes a supply was laid in for whole tribes, and fruit of ten years' standing is said to be considered the best. In view of our own waste of natural resources nothing is more absurd than the popular gibe at the improvidence of savages.

Bread is a widespread phenomenon. Even mere seed-gatherers like the Central Californians can grind or pound acorns into meal, and a Hopi woman makes parchment-like "loaves" of corn bread. She grinds the kernels to flour on a stone slab and with a stone muller. Then she mixes the meal with water and spreads her batter over a slab of rock heated from below. A minute later she takes off a thin wafer-like sheet, and folds it or rolls it up into the right shape.

Baking was a specialty of the Polynesians, who prepared their fruit in earth ovens; and no one, according to a Swedish traveler, can rival a Chaco Indian when it comes to broiling fish. In Nevada a Paiute woman roasts seeds on a willow tray by rapidly tossing about red-hot coals so as to keep her basket from burning. With a deft movement she rolls the roasted seeds to one side and the embers to another. This sort of thing takes a lot of training.

But how was it possible to *boil* food in the era before pottery? Nothing is simpler, and any number of recent tribes have been caught in the act. The Vancouver Island Indians filled wooden boxes with water and meat, and threw in hot rocks, while the Californians substituted watertight baskets. Among the Plains Indians a paunch was suspended from four sticks above ground (Fig. 9), or they lined a pit with a hide and put in hot stones with the water and food. This ancient method still persists in Guipúzcoa, Spain, where the

FIG. 9. BLACKFOOT STONE-BOILING (*after Wissler*)

Basques drop hot rocks into wooden pails by way of boiling their milk.

Except for details the principles of our culinary art are thus known to rude hunting tribes and probably go straight back to Pre-Ceramic times.

CHAPTER VIII

DOMESTIC ANIMALS AND CULTIVATED PLANTS

PRIMITIVE man uses every wile at his disposal to kill a bear or whale, and then politely apologizes to the victim. He fusses over the corpse and implores the animal's soul to tell its fellows how hospitably he has treated it so that they, too, will come to be slaughtered. He out-Darwins Darwin; one clan is named after a bear, another after a snipe, and the members are supposed to be descended from these animals. Often they will not eat the flesh of their animal namesakes. When the Monkey clan of an East African tribe holds a wedding ceremony, the monkeys are formally invited to the feast. A South American woman suckles her infant at one breast and her puppy at the other. African Negroes have been known to commit suicide over the death of a favorite cow. A Kirghiz lover who wants to be especially complimentary to his sweetheart likens her to a filly.

All this is not the attitude of scientific animal husbandry, but it does represent the atmosphere in which the savage of long ago groped toward domestication. He did not scour his habitat and say, "There's an animal I'll milk," or "I'll keep that bird for its eggs," or "I'll shear that one for its wool." The plain facts knock such explanations into a cocked hat. Nature made udders for calves, not for men. Any aspiring dairyman who tried to tap the supply of a wild cow who had nursed her offspring would be cheated of his expectations. Actually millions of people are now raising cattle without tasting a drop of their milk. Jungle fowl do not lay eggs enough to pay for their board. Besides, chicken-breeding tribes often disdain the flesh and loathe the eggs of their birds. As for sheep, wild sheep have no wool, so *that* inducement was barred at the beginning.

Let us then make a complete face-about. Primitive man began to keep animals not with an eye to profit but for the uneconomic though quite human reason that he jolly well liked to have them about as companions and for entertainment. To this day South American tribes coddle parrots, cage birds of prey, and hang lizards by the side of their hammocks. In one village storks and ostriches stalk about as the children's playmates; in another there is a little menagerie of fawns, turtles, and mice. Yet none of these animals serves the slightest practical purpose.

Throw in the chance for sport, and the goad for raising beasts becomes as strong as any normal human urge. These motives are powerful enough on higher levels. What makes us train horses for the race-track, and Spaniards bulls for the *plaza de toros?* The Chinese taste runs towards insects and is less known but quite as instructive. In the eighth century of our era Chinese ladies took to catching crickets and beguiled the weary hours of the night with their chirp. Soon the vogue spread, and thousands were reared for their music. Wealthy owners hired experts to tend their pets; ministers of state wrote monographs for the instruction of fanciers; and poets composed odes to the insect. Under the Sung dynasty (960-1278 A.D.) the craze took a new turn. Crickets are pugnacious, so they were pitted against one another, and a favorite sport took shape. Keepers made a selection of battling insects, guarding them with the utmost care from smoke and heat. Large amounts were staked on the issue of a combat, and champion crickets had the satisfaction of having their names inscribed on ivory tablets.

Not that animals are never kept for serious purposes, but even these need not be a jot more practical. In East Africa the Wahuma disdain chicken flesh, are nauseated by the eggs (which they quaintly conceive to be excrements), and scorn neighbors who fail to share their queasiness. Notwithstanding all this nicety they raise poultry. Why? In order to dissect them and foretell the future from their entrails! And that comes very close to the original idea. For in Burma, where the bird was first domesticated, the natives use it for divination, as the Chinese chroniclers reported 2000 years ago. The diviner thrust a bamboo splinter into the perforations of a cock's thigh-bone, and the angle at which it projected served as a good or bad omen. Here, too, sport entered. Rival villages settled their claims by cock-fights, which thus were at bottom ordeals. As for modern farmyard methods, they are an altogether late by-product of these earlier customs.

But rearing a beast for companionship is only the first step towards domestication, and setting it against an adversary does not complete the process. The South American Indian's mice are not reckoned as "domestic," nor are the fighting kangaroos of circus shows. Even the elephant does not come under this head. He can be tamed and put to work, but every individual has to be severally crimped from a wild herd. In other words, he will not breed freely under human control like cattle and horses. Here, then, is the acid test, and by it most species taken at one time or another under man's wing have failed.

Domestication is altogether an incredibly difficult achievement. Savages unconsciously conducted experiments in it through myriads of years by keeping pets. A few of these were attracted to man for good and came to feel thoroughly at home in his society. Some little quirk in the make-up of the species might turn the scales for or against domestication. The reindeer has a passionate craving for human urine, and this has tied him firmly to his Siberian master. But the Eskimo never succeeded in attaching the animal. Is the American breed less avid of urine, or a bit shier than his Asiatic brother? A trifling difference of this sort may have proved all-important.

However this may be, the simpler peoples forestalled us, domesticating whatever species or breeds were fit. Consequently, with all our knowledge, we have added nothing to their accomplishment. Dogs were domesticated by 8000 B.C. or a little earlier; cattle, sheep, goats, pigs, probably by 6000 B.C. On a slate relief from Egypt dating back to about 3000 B.C. a scribe is shown reporting 760 donkeys as his master's property. The initiation of the ass as a pack-animal must then go back a good way further, for so large a herd would hardly come at the very start. Our earliest record of the horse is for Babylonia in about 2300 B.C.; however, characteristically it was not the civilized part of the population but the wilder tribes that introduced the beast. Thus the brunt of the task was literally borne by the ruder cultures in the case of all the important species of live stock.

Pet-rearing ultimately gave way to exploitation because man is not a total abstainer from common sense even if he indulges with fanatical moderation. He noted that the animals he sheltered from the struggle for existence came to differ from their wild brethren in point of size, hair, and other features. Some of these traits he prized as desirable and bred for. Thus trends that set in under the novel conditions were intensified: woolly and fat-tailed sheep, milch cows, egg-layers sprang into being. But this utilitarian frame of mind came last, not first.

True to type, early man evolved only a few ideas of basic

importance concerning the use of domestic beasts. Wherever he could he borrowed his technique from older breeders. In the riding-gear of the Plains Indians virtually everything came from the Spaniards who introduced the horse. A few trifling adjustments were all the natives added. Thus, they had formerly hitched dogs to a dray without wheels, and they now made a larger vehicle of the same pattern for horses (Fig. 10). Can we blame this want of invention on Indian heredity? Hardly; the Spaniards themselves did not

FIG. 10. DOG AND HORSE TRAVOIS (*after Lowie and Wissler*)

invent stirrups but borrowed them from the Arabs. Going further back, when the ancient Babylonians first got horses they acted very much like our Sioux Indians. They were accustomed to drive donkey-carts and simply broke in the horse in place of his gentler relative. They did not straightway, or indeed ever, invent the art of horseback riding. So we find the same story everywhere. The Siberian first had dog sledges; later he harnessed reindeer. Some Siberians encountered tribes of horsemen and took up reindeer riding by way of imitation. Again, the buffalo and the yak were obviously similar to the ox, and so the latter served as a convenient model. In India, where cows are milked, female buffalo are also milked; in Eastern Asia, where the practice is unknown, no creative genius thought of introducing it.

Milking is, indeed, a star example. It was invented just once in the history of humanity. No people dreamt of the idea unless they had been directly or indirectly influenced by the Near Orient. The Chinese had wandered away from the outskirts of that civilization before milking was in vogue, and even they with all their knowledge and patience did not conceive dairying themselves. Later they were too set in their standards to borrow it from their neighbors. On the other hand, where the custom took firm hold it was extended even to camels and mares. The nomads of Central Asia and thereabouts also developed churning and manufactured cheese. But here again the poverty of human inventiveness is borne in upon us. No people outside this sphere of influence made cheese, and while some Negroes churn butter, they use it only as a cosmetic to smear over their bodies.

Because man is what he is we can never safely guess that a particular people by their own toil brought their beasts and plants under control. Borrowing them from somebody else is so much simpler. Often it was not merely man's laziness but Nature that stood in the way by creating the species in some other part of the globe. Foreign trade now laughs at such barriers and has played fast and loose with the original distribution of the world's flora and fauna. Indian corn and manioc were unknown outside of America before Columbus, but nowadays they support millions of African aborigines, and Hawaii has become a famous center for pineapples, though their home is in the Antilles. Abyssinia is where the coffee tree naturally grows and the near-by Arabs made it popular; but later the scene shifts to Java and finally to Brazil for the world's main supply. Western Europe got its cattle, horses, sheep, goats, wheat, millet, and barley from the Near Orient; and except for the horse [1] this happened before that region was "civilized"—before writing and metal tools. Europeans may plead an alibi: the wild forms did not exist in their habitat. Yet the fact remains that for our food supply we are all indebted to ruder cultures. Even when the wild and the domestic form of a plant or animal occur together it does not follow that the people living there saw their opportunity and made the most of it. In 1492 most American tribes had dogs. The New World also had various wild members of the dog family, such as wolves, coyotes, and foxes. A naïve observer—one not specially warned against the "geographer's fallacy"—might guess that the Indians must have got their domestic animals by taming the related wild forms. No such thing. Every breed of dog from Alaska to Tierra del Fuego is descended from a wolf native to Asia. The ancient Indians brought it with them when they crossed Bering Strait.

So with the African banana. The family to which it belongs has wild members in Asia, Oceania, and Africa. In Uganda alone there are some dozen cultivated varieties of "plantain," as well as a wild species. Hence it might seem that the Negro found the plantain which Nature offered, saw that it was good, and began to grow it. But this is botanically absurd. Every cultivated banana in the world is seedless and must be grown from side-shoots. But the native African form has no side-shoots. Hence it cannot be the ancestor of the varieties intentionally planted in Uganda. These must have come from Asia, where bananas naturally do produce side-shoots. Africa's relations with Asia—a part

[1] See page 60.

of her *history*, then—explain why the plantain is a staple crop in Uganda. The environment merely allowed it to thrive after it was introduced.

Even where botanical hindrances are lacking people are not driven to cultivate an existing plant, let alone to make the most of it. Some scholars have pointed with glee at traces of olive leaves in old geological layers in Italy and exclaimed, "The olive grew here, so the ancient Romans must have raised it." However, the historical fact is that the cultivated tree was brought to them from Greece. Again, China harbors a wild vine. Surely the "agriculturists of forty centuries" saw its possibilities? Not at all. They would have remained vineless, perhaps to the end of their days, but for the initiative of General Čan K'ien. This famous traveler made a trip to Fergana and Parthia in 126 B.C. and introduced grape seeds into his native country. What is more, even the sophisticated Chinese were not able to fathom the possibilities of the new plant. They did not learn to make wine until 640 B.C., and then the secret was revealed to them by a neighboring people. What Egypt had achieved by 3000 B.C. the Chinese, with all their experience and mechanical knowledge, could not duplicate unaided thousands of years later. Such is the frailty of the human intellect.

Of course not all plants are cultivated for their food value. There are the great textile species—flax in the Mediterranean region, cotton in India and Middle America, hemp in China. There are the fig-tree of the Upper Nile and the paper-mulberry of Polynesia; the bark of both is beaten into cloth by the natives. However, as animals were kept as mere pets, so plants were at times grown without a thought of utility. Some Bolivian Indians are fanatical smokers of tobacco, and Northwest Californians, like the Crow of Montana, grow nothing but this useless weed. The Crow did not even smoke it, raising it solely for ceremonial ends. Similarly the Negroes of Uganda did not drink coffee, but chewed it or occasionally swallowed a bean or two as a religious act. When Dr. Stuhlmann and the King became blood-brothers, each scratched his skin near the heart, moistened the berry with the blood, and before swallowing it, took it from the other's palm with his lips.

The story of plants has many surprise kicks. Peruvian Indians chewed coca as a stimulant and found it helpful against fatigue in mountain-climbing; hence our cocaine as an anesthetic. Rye originally entered the European scene as a good-for-nothing weed, much against the farmer's will. In Persia and other parts of Western Asia he treats it as a nuisance that jeopardizes the true crops—wheat and barley. But in the mountain districts of the area he sows a mixture of rye and wheat. He has discovered that wheat is killed by an adverse winter, but that rye is not and will produce at least half of the expected yield. Thus a new staple was added to man's resources. So culture slinks in by the back stairs; it's a way it has.

CHAPTER IX

HOUSING

WHEN fig-trees bore fruit near Paris and elephants roamed over the neighborhood of Versailles, the people of France needed no shelter from the cold and lived in the open. But when a colder climate set in, they took refuge under overhanging cliffs or in full-fledged caves. There they built fires and made skin clothing for themselves. We *know* from the ashes of their hearths and from countless scrapers for dressing the hides of animals. This idea of using dwellings ready-made has come right down through the ages to the present day. Within the boundaries of New York City the Indians until recently inhabited rock-shelters whenever convenient, even though they were able to put up artificial huts; and the Vedda of Ceylon still live in caves.

FIG. 11. TASMANIAN WIND SCREEN (*after Roth*)

FIG. 12. MENOMINI WIGWAM, WISCONSIN (*after Skinner*)

What were man's earliest efforts at a real house? Probably much like the Tasmanian's of a hundred years ago. They planted a few stakes in the ground, placed strips of bark against them, and let it go at that. There was no roof, and the fireplace was in front of the structure (Fig. 11). Winter weather gets bitter cold in Tasmania, and this wind screen gave poor protection. The wigwam of our Eastern Indians was an improvement, for its poles intersected one another so that grass thatching or reed mats could be put on top as a roof (Fig. 12).

FIG. 13. YUKAGHIR TENT (*after Jochelson*)

Wandering hunters and herders invented a tent. From Lapland and Siberia into North America and as far south as Texas a similar form of this occurs—the conical shape with a cover of skin or bark. A photograph from northern Siberia would do equally well for northern Canada (Fig. 13). This tent looks very simple and easy to invent, but it is not. The Chukchi of northeastern Siberia are famous for their skill as mechanics, but when part of the tribe gave up the life of sedentary fishermen and turned reindeer nomads, they failed lamentably in conceiving a suitable lodging. Instead, they devised a most inconvenient contraption—hard to pitch and hard to take down. Why? Because of their past. To adopt stock-breeding was in itself progressive, but the Chukchi could not in the twinkling of an eye make all the adjustments that would logically follow from their new pursuits. They had always made a stationary house, and so they tried to make a tent that resembled it as closely as possible. If left alone, perhaps in another thousand years they might have hit upon a reasonable form of transportable dwelling.

Have we any right to sneer at primitive conservatism? Well, the Chukchi are, at all events, in good primitive company. The Hopi of Arizona are corn-growers and potters, and build square houses of sandstone. In short, they are a superior lot. But *where* do they build? On the tops of mesas. Every drop of water is painfully carried up the steep heights by the women; and the men have to walk miles to get to their cornfields. Nevertheless, very few families have shifted their quarters near the springs and gardens. Once there was a good reason for living high up, for it was safer. Nowadays, however, the U. S. Government would protect the Hopi against marauding neighbors. But man is not built so as to do a reasonable thing just because it is reasonable. It is far easier for him to do an irrational thing because it has always been done.

Conservatism is the burden of the history of architecture all along the line. Look at our state capitols: virtually all of them cling to the same style. Or, take a typical public building in Europe, say, the Austrian Parliament: its form is that of a Greek temple. And what, pray, is a Greek temple? A gable-roof on posts. First these were of wood, later of stone; and the columns that developed were based on Egyptian models (Fig. 14).

Indeed, when we consider how our ancestors of only a few centuries ago lived we can hardly afford even a smile at the backwardness of the Chukchi. On their travels in the Hebrides (1773) Dr. Johnson and Boswell entered a hovel which "for a window had only a small hole, which was stopped with a piece of turf, that was taken out occasionally to let in light." For that matter, many French peasant huts of recent years have been windowless. About 1550 A.D. not a single peasant's house in Scandinavia had such a thing as a window. At best a tiny peep-hole appeared in the gable. For illumination there was a sky-light half a yard square with a thin skin in a sliding-frame. Even in the towns our style of windows only slowly came in during the sixteenth century. In the beginning they were so rare that in 1521 a clergyman of Copenhagen, in drawing up his last will, made a point of disposing of his glass pane. For a long time openings in the wall were covered with wooden screens, especially in the shops. There they were lowered to form a counter, while the customer stood outdoors driving his bargain. At best the citizens might cover the wall-slits with strips of skin like the rural sky-lights. Their windows were on a par with those of Siberian savages, who make theirs of stretched eel-skin, the guts of animals, or split mica. "Such windows admit sufficient light, but they are not transparent." In 1554 when King Christian III of Denmark had a new wing built in his palace, he ordered that only a part of the windows should be provided with glass panes.

All of a sudden, there came a great change, and a few decades later glass was so common that roisterers staggering home from a wedding feast made window-breaking

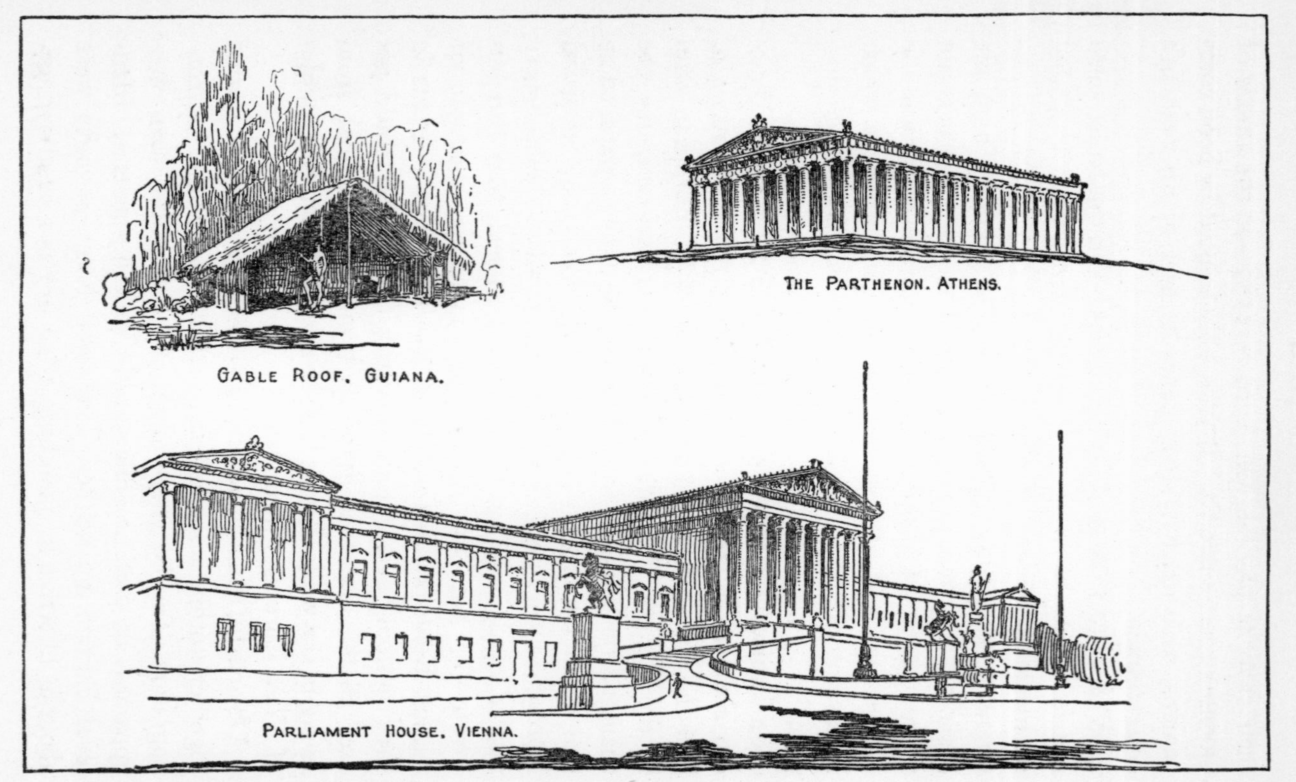

FIG. 14. GABLE-ROOF HUT, GUIANA (*after Roth*); PARTHENON; PARLIAMENT, VIENNA

their favorite pastime. On April 6, 1589—so the annals of Odense report—one Carl Bryske, ably assisted by boon companions, smashed fifty-four panes as part of his evening's entertainment.

What caused the progressive change? Did the Norse spirit rise in Viking wrath against opaque windows as a symbol of mental darkness? Troels-Lund, the great Danish historian, gives a more prosaic reason. According to him, the Scandinavians were purely passive. "The revolution was not a product of the people's native inventiveness; it was the lowered price of glass in the foreign countries from which it was imported that rendered the far-reaching change possible."

In comparing Chukchi progressiveness with that of Western civilization, we cannot, however, allow Scandinavia to bear the brunt of the argument. The rise of European cities in the Middle Ages provides a better test-case, for the change from rural to town life may be fairly compared to that from hunting to stock-breeding. Well, the medieval Europeans were not one whit readier to adapt themselves to altered conditions than the Siberians. Indeed, they had less excuse for loitering behind, for the shining example of ancient Rome was before them. But they were peasants in their outlook, and it took centuries before they could get used to the idea that living in towns was different from living in the wilds. Let us look at a few instructive examples of West European mentality.

Obviously, when hundreds of frame houses were crowded together within a narrow space there was danger of conflagration. The burghers might have improved their fire-apparatus or used noninflammable building-material. Medieval Europe did neither. The small hoses in vogue were about as effective in quenching a big fire as a nasal syringe.

In the North, water was not squirted at all but poured out of pails, which were sometimes ingeniously kept under lock and key in the town hall. Not before the seventeenth century did a resident of Nuremberg construct engines that were able to throw a jet of water to a respectable height. The municipal authorities recognized the danger and issued warnings against straw roofs, but the result was nil. In 1302 Thomas Bat was brought before the Mayor of London on a charge of not replacing his thatch with tiles. He offered to indemnify the City in case of any fire due to his thatch, and the authorities with incredible naïveté accepted this proposal. Even noblemen of sixteenth century Sweden lived in turf-roofed wooden houses and only gradually took to brick. In Denmark town-dwellers had begun putting up stone walls as early as 1500. However, with grim tenacity, they clung to the roof-thatching of rural days. Accordingly, their houses were no safer than the wooden structures of Sweden and Norway. Naturally, conflagration followed conflagration. Every one knew that in all probability his native town would be destroyed at least once during his lifetime. In fact, Aarhus was burnt down twice between 1540 and 1550; and Bergen suffered the same fate in 1561, 1582, and 1589. Within a space of sixty years thirty-six towns were thus destroyed in Scandinavia—some of them more than once.

In Denmark the Government heroically tried to remedy conditions. In 1496 the King requested the Viborgans to replace their straw with bricks. The residents thumbed their noses at the order, and when Viborg had been once more reduced to ashes in 1569, they merrily started to rebuild with thatch. Royal decrees rained down upon the towns of the realm, there were threats and fines, but all without avail. In Odense the old-fashioned roofs were removed in

1561; eight years later they were back again. They survived in Jutland well into the nineteenth century. "It took three hundred and fifty years and the governmental authority of thirteen kings to eliminate straw roofs from Danish towns." Yet there are those who believe that man has an inborn tendency to progress, and that it is strongest among North Europeans.

To lose one's faith in progress as a constant and inevitable thing it is enough to compare the cities of ancient Rome with those of medieval Europe. Imperial Rome had paved streets, exemplary highways, aqueducts and sewers. What is more, these blessings were spread over the entire empire: remote provincial towns in North Africa, like Timgad, had their public baths and comfort stations. But when the West European of the Middle Ages passed from a rural to an urban form of life he blundered as horribly as the Chukchi might have done in similar circumstances. For centuries the streets remained unpaved, and when it rained pedestrians had to wade through a bottomless morass. The house-owners were accustomed to the freedom of wide open spaces, so they would put up sheds, benches, and stairways in front of their dwellings, to the great discomfort of every passer-by. In fact, pigs were literally kept in the streets. In Berlin the sties were directly below the front windows as late as 1641. Not before 1681 did the Great Elector definitely put an end to the nuisance of hog-raising by the citizens of his capital. Other countries were not more enlightened in their policy. In 1131 a porker ran foul of a royal prince's horse in suburban Paris. The rider was thrown and died in consequence of his fall, but conditions did not improve. In Denmark the authorities strove against urban pig-raising as valiantly as against thatched roofs, and with about the same measure of success. In 1564 and 1576 King Frederick II.

issued a veritable declaration of war against the hogs. By way of reply a drove of them charged upon him and his retinue so that the horses shied. The struggle between the state and the pigs forms the theme of delicious mock-heroic pages in Troels-Lund's authentic history of the times.

As to sanitation, modern Europeans until the most recent times were on the savage level. Rather, they fell below that level. It did not much matter how wandering Australians or Indian bison-hunters disposed of offals and garbage. But it was serious business in seventeenth century Berlin to have refuse heaps piled up in front of Peter's Church. No better scheme occurred to the officials than the law of 1671, by which every peasant who drove to Berlin a-marketing had to do dustman's duty and remove a wagonload of filth.

Sewerage of course offered an insoluble problem. Some master mind hit upon the idea of digging a trench right in the middle of the house. Of course the air was tainted till the stench grew intolerable, but what was to be done about it? The outward pomp and circumstance of the period contrasts ludicrously with its handling of a practical task of the utmost importance. In 1183 the Emperor of the Holy Roman Empire held a diet in the magnificent hall of the palace at Erfurt. But the throng of lords and knights broke through the floor and many tumbled to an unheroic end—in the cesspool directly below. The Emperor himself barely escaped death.

By the sixteenth century most houses in Denmark had acquired privies of their own, but prudery made them as tiny as possible, and public sentiment decreed that no one might clean them except the despised hangman, who took relevant duties very lightly indeed. The whole town thus came to be dotted with centers of stench and infection. In 1583 a Hollander residing in Helsingör impudently outraged decency by personally cleaning his latrine when all attempts had failed to make town officials tend to the job. Such shamelessness could not be countenanced. In solemn assembly of the burgesses, the mayor and council asked whether one so forgetful of propriety should be allowed to live in their midst. Nordic citizenry rose to the occasion. It was unanimously voted that "they could by no means accept him as a fellow-citizen after his behavior in encroaching on the hangman's office and thus himself becoming a hangman."

But Helsingör was on the outskirts of European civilization! How, then, was the same problem tackled in its center? Paris in the thirteenth century already had a population of 120,000, which grew to 200,000 by 1600, and to half a million within another hundred years. Here, then, is a fair test of West European capability. The result is not creditable to Caucasian psychology. In the metropolis of Europe, the cradle of fashion, the streets reeked with filth. Montaigne found it hard to rent lodgings in which his nostrils could escape the stench from below. No wonder. For one thing, the Parisians freely emptied chamber-pots from their windows with little regard to the comfort of pedestrians. Those who were not nimble enough to dodge at the cry of "*Gare l'eau!*" were drenched—a favorite episode in the comedies of Molière and his contemporaries. But this was a comparatively harmless maneuver. The poorer classes were less finicky and eased themselves where they could, without the chamber or close-stool as go-between. In 1531, after a frightful pestilence, a decree ordered landlords to provide a latrine for every house, but the law remained a dead letter. Just before the French Revolution Sébastien Mercier complains of the men's urinating as a regular custom in the passageway that led into a house. "Coming home, you find at the foot of your staircase a man passing water who looks at you undisturbed. . . . This usage is very filthy and most embarrassing for women." By this time there were indeed privies galore, but they were kept in such condition that Mercier explicitly warns his readers against going near them. There were not many alternatives. A favorite one was to obey the call of nature on the terraces of the Tuileries, sheltered after a fashion by a hedge of yew-trees. The Count of Angiviller, who superintended the royal grounds, had the hedge removed, and established a comfort station in its place, charging an admission fee of two sous. The public revolted at so exorbitant a price and transferred their allegiance to the grounds of the Royal Palace. The Duke of Orléans hurriedly put up a dozen privies. Fortunately they somehow came to enjoy greater popularity than their forerunners. For in matters like these pre-Revolutionary France was strangely democratic. In the golden days of divine right, when the State was the King, the Louvre presented a sorry sight. People disburdened themselves freely in the courtyards and on the stairways, on the balconies and behind the doors—wholly undisturbed by the keepers of the palace and without any pretense at secrecy. But why marvel at such crudity on the part of the mob? On August 8, 1606, an order went forth forbidding any resident of the palace of Saint-Germain to commit a nuisance within the confines of the castle. That very day the Dauphin urinated against the wall of his room. In the more refined period that followed, dukes and even monarchs thought nothing of admitting visitors or secretaries to their presence while seated on their close-stools. Under Louis XVI Versailles boasted of a single, though comfortable, closet "after the English fashion," for the exclusive use of their majesties. Even royalty did not indulge in such luxuries anywhere else.

Were the Chukchi *very* slow in adapting themselves to a changed mode of life?

CHAPTER X

DRESS AND FASHION

WHY do we wear neckties? They protect neither our skins nor our virtue. And what is the use of hats? A Californian Indian puts on a cap because she does not want her forehead chafed by the strap of her burden-basket. But little can be said in defense of *our* headgear. More and more men in the United States and abroad are going about bareheaded and suffer no inconvenience. Take a detached view, and

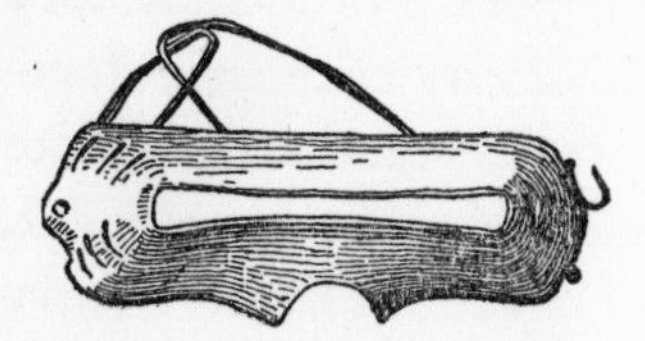
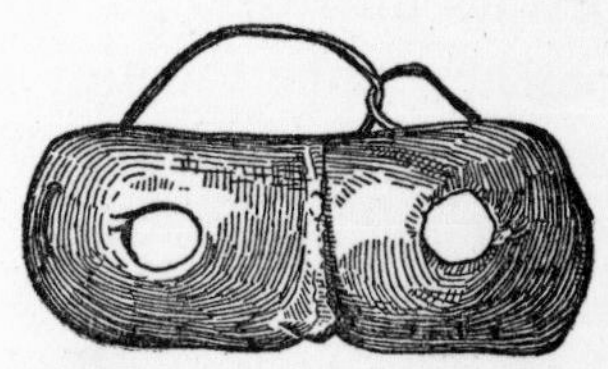

FIG. 15. ESKIMO SNOW-GOGGLES (*after Thalbitzer*)

only a tiny fraction of our apparel turns out to have any rational purpose.

The proposition holds generally. There are indeed cases on the other side. Footgear is sometimes indispensable for travel,[1] and the Arctic made master tailors and outfitters of the Eskimo and the Siberians, so that no white traveler can do better than to adopt their costume. The Yukaghir, whose country is the coldest in the world, have aprons, trousers, boots, summer and winter coats, leather mittens, fur scarfs and caps, and chin protectors. In the spring of 1740 Paul Egede, a Danish missionary in Greenland, was blinded by the dazzling white snow and had to remain indoors for a month. After this experience he was only too glad to wear the goggles the Eskimo carve from wood (Fig. 15).

[1] See page 116.

But compared with the sum total of man's raiment and trappings, such instances are few and far between, and unless Nature bullies man into a sensible adjustment he is likely to make a mess of the job. In Central Australia, for example, the temperature falls several degrees below the freezing-point, but the aborigines do nothing about it. They might make clothing from the furs of their kangaroos and wallabies, but they don't. The Tierra del Fuegians prove themselves equal bunglers.[1] Necessity is not the mother of invention. There is an alternative. If the climate of central Australia turned actually glacial, the tribes that discovered how to make fur coats like the Siberian ones would survive, and the rest would perish; that is all. Whether *any* of them would find the way out, it is impossible to guess.

Even the Siberians are not supermen. The Yukaghir have latterly altered their time-honored costume: their modern frocks no longer close over their aprons, hence wind and frost penetrate. Why this perverse change? Dr. Jochelson has revealed the secret: from pure coxcombry. For some reason the dress of their Tungus neighbors, who came from a warmer country, is considered smarter; so the Yukaghir sacrifice comfort to fashion. Why bother about living in the very coldest region of the world?

With all due allowances, however, we must admit that clothing has sometimes been invented for utility. It has probably never arisen from modesty. There is no instinct in man to cover his sex organs. In Japan both sexes mingle in the bath, as they once did in the public baths of Europe. Sixteenth century Scandinavians undressed in one another's company and went to bed stark naked—except for a night-cap. When a Polish visitor remonstrated, he was told that men need not be ashamed of what God had created. In a

[1] See page 19.

Swedish hotel the chambermaid will still offer to rub down a male patron in his tub; not to mention the recent prophets of "gymnosophy" (*Nacktkultur*).

Primitive communities not yet affected by alien conventions often exhibit the same happy simplicity. On one of his pioneer trips through our Southwest Major Powell stumbled upon a Paiute couple. It was August, and the man was "dressed in a hat; the woman in a string of beads only." More recently, in Brazil, Nordenskiöld saw Huari women running about completely exposed, while the men's sex organs were only partly concealed. The very covering sometimes used has precisely the opposite effect from modesty. When an otherwise nude Papuan squeezes his member into the opening of a gourd, he is throwing it into relief. This sort of concealment recalls the codpiece of European costume in the fifteenth and sixteenth centuries—that Rabelaisian sack, often richly ornamented, which hung down conspicuously between the tightfitting halves of the nether garment, and which in those pocketless days harbored one's purse, gloves, handkerchief, or even fruit.

Not that prudery is lacking, but it need not center in the sex organs. Oriental women veil the face, and under James I English ladies masked for public appearance. In the Middle Ages Spanish gentlewomen had morbid complexes about their feet, and an Austrian lady of the Victorian era has been known to boast that though she had borne her husband eight children he had never seen her breasts. The very Brazilian woman who unconcernedly stalked past Nordenskiöld in complete nakedness blushed violently when he bought the plug from her nose, and at once dashed off in search of a substitute. There is, then, such a thing as a sense of decency, and among the many possible parts of the human body the genitalia may be singled out for the scene of its operations. But there is nothing instinctive and inevitable about that, and with the *origin* of clothes it has no relations.

If neither chastity nor utility explains dress, the desire for beauty remains. This, indeed—often in the form of foppishness—probably counts for more than all the other motives combined. The rich embroidery on a Siberian fur coat and the marvelous feather cloaks of the Hawaiians had for their main or sole end esthetic pleasure. Men prinked before they shaped pottery or farmed: with burials possibly 20,000 years old there are perforated shells or teeth strung into necklaces. Even the Pleistocene reindeer-hunter felt the need for personal ornamentation. Whatever clothing he may have worn is lost. We can only *infer* that there was such; but his gewgaws have survived. Is not this fate symbolic of the relative part dress and decoration have played in human history? Certainly not one of the peoples ever described as naked lacked articles and methods of adornment. Powell's Paiute did wear a string of beads! And Nordenskiöld's Brazilians affected earrings, ear-drops, bracelets, armlets, shell necklaces, nose-sticks, and lip-plugs, while their sisters in a near-by tribe took endless pains grinding a bit of quartz into a nail they could thrust into the lower lip.

Naked or not, the savage lavishes enormous effort on personal decoration. Polynesians bleached their skin with plant juices, anointed themselves with coconut oil, and wore necklaces of fragrant flowers. Above all, they practiced tattooing —one of their fine arts. In New Zealand the same intricate spirals that figured in the carving of a canoe prow appeared on the face of a chief (Figs. 16, 17). The master craftsman dipped his comb into the pigment and drove the teeth into his client's skin with a little mallet. It was a painful operation—like our ladies' "face-lifting"—but the victim rarely winced. The workmen sang songs to cheer him, promising him the love of a wondrously fair maiden. In the Marquesas, where the whole body was often covered with patterns, the process might stretch over a span of thirty-five or forty

FIG. 16. MAORI FACE TATTOO (*after Elsdon Best*)

FIG. 17. MAORI CANOE PROW (*after Best*)

years. Only poor trash, like fishermen, who were unable to pay the artist, had to go through life untattooed. That not only advertised their lowly condition but also barred them from a highly coveted privilege: on pain of death they were not allowed to eat of human flesh.

Darker races, whose skins would not show tattoo, scar themselves. The Central Australians, who never thought of making a cloak out of kangaroo skins to screen themselves from the cold, are not so lacking in originality when it comes to useless disfigurement. They trace lines of ocher on their children's chests, and along these paths prick the skin with stone knives till the blood comes gushing forth. Then sand, fat, and bird's down are rubbed into the wounds. West African Negroes outline triangles, crosses, and stars in charcoal, gash the body to form these patterns, and deepen the marks with various irritants.

Such dandyism, however, often merges in another motive. As our women wear engagement and wedding rings, so a Hopi maiden shows her virginity by wrapping her hair round her ears in the "squash-blossom" style; and a Masai woman loads her neck with brass rings to announce her married state. Where bravery is prized, the warrior does not hide his light under a bushel but lets his apparel proclaim his deeds. When a Bagobo in the Philippines has killed two men, he puts a chocolate-colored band around his head, a second pair of slain enemies entitles him to blood-red trousers, and with a score of six goes a whole suit of that color. Distinguished Masai warriors were set off from the rank and file by bracelets and bells. In the Dog society of our Plains Indians there were officers with sashes slipped over the head by a narrow slit; they were pledged to stand their ground, come what might. Among these tribes even the wolf-tail dragging at the heel of a moccasin or the feather at the back of one's head was more than mere decoration, for it gave publicity to such and such feats of valor. And as we tell a Phi Beta Kappa man or an Elk by the ornament dangling from his watch-chain, so the member of the Dog society was unmistakably ticketed by his owl-feather headdress or a Buffalo Bull by his horned cap. Sometimes the several clubs of a tribe differed in dignity. Then the insignia by that very fact became a symbol of higher or lower position in the community. The horned cap was as good an index as a frock-coat and silk hat with us.

Tattoo, scarring, circumcision, and other mutilations may serve this same purpose of advertising social condition. The Australian scarifies his youngsters at puberty, or knocks out an incisor tooth, or circumcises them, or makes himself agreeable to them by other ingenious devices. Such disfigurements may be nothing but badges of age or status, or they may have a strictly religious meaning. The Polynesians did tattoo for embellishment, but not when they tattooed the tongue, where the marks could never be seen. That was done as a mourning rite. Tattoo was also used to ward off danger or to vow revenge. Often the motive was mixed. Our wedding rings also serve a double purpose.

The white man's fashions are as whimsical as the Polynesian's or the Negro's. Even when a change is rational, it is dictated by chance rather than reason. In the early nineteenth century, Galton tells us, no Briton was supposed to wear a mustache unless he were a cavalry officer; otherwise "it was atrociously bad style." But during the winter of the Crimean War it would have been a hardship to make the soldiers shave every day, so their beards grew and when they returned to England the custom changed through their influence. The beard now became a token of manliness, and at last even the clergy yielded "and forthwith hair began to sprout in a thousand pulpits where it had never appeared before within the memory of man."

The eighteenth century bristles with examples of what Caucasians will do in periods of superlative refinement. Under Marie Antoinette French ladies wore headdresses so high that a short woman's chin was exactly midway between her toes and her crest. No carriages could conveniently accommodate these towers of gauze, flowers, and plumage. When the Queen added to the height of her panache in 1776, its uppermost tier had to be removed as she entered her coach and replaced when she alighted. Ladies of the court knelt on the floor of a carriage, thrusting their heads out of the window. In dancing they were always afraid of bumping into the chandeliers. The heavily powdered and padded pyramids worn on the head came to teem with vermin. Discomfort was intense, but West European genius did not abolish the fashion. Instead it invented an ivory-hooked rod and made it good taste to jab at the itching spots with it. Many American tribes forbid menstruating women to scratch themselves with their fingers: they have to use a special stick for the purpose. Thus, the powerful intellect of *Homo sapiens* succeeded in twice inventing a head-scratcher. With the Indians it formed part of the sacred setting of an adolescence ritual. In eighteenth century France the device was sensible enough, if it proved effective —granted that powdered headdresses were indispensable. As a matter of fact, the remedy failed, but the vogue persisted. Were the French ladies more rational than their Indian sisters?

Europe had a counterpart to feminine folly. For some time past the men had been wearing wigs. Of course these would not stay on in active movement, so tennis and all violent exercises ceased to be genteel pastimes. Wigs started as a sign of distinction. At one time it was said in England that a doctor would as soon forgo his fee as his wig. But soon the lower ranks of society began to imitate their betters. Still there were differences in style and cost, and a man of quality had a varied assortment for different occasions. Pepys in 1663 bought perukes at two and three pounds sterling, but a dress wig came to cost up to sixty. No wonder English wig manufacturers were alarmed when about 1765 smart folk began to wear their own hair again.

Of course the wigs were powdered. In those gay days Parisian wig-makers were seen dashing back and forth in the streets with comb and puff. When the patron's head had been dressed he was taken to the landing of his floor. There the artist threw his puff against the ceiling, showering his customer's wig with a volley of snow—some of it often spattering over the clothes of an unfortunate visitor coming up the stairway. At a time when thousands of human beings were starving in France and England, immense quantities of flour were wasted on hair-powder. Yet philosophers sagely discuss *savage* improvidence! Finally Pitt's tax on powder put an end to this nuisance in the United Kingdom. In France it lingered on through the Revolution. The noble Robespierre himself always appeared in public immaculately powdered, and Napoleon gave up the custom only after his Italian campaign.

So fashion can survive even a popular cataclysm. But, being nonpartisan in politics, it may likewise defy monarchs by divine right. Even before Marie Antoinette tall coiffures had enjoyed a heyday under the patronage of Louis XIV's friend, the Marquise de Fontanges. Tiring of his mistress, the King conceived an antipathy to the tiers of starched frills that she had made popular. He recommended a low coiffure, but polite society balked. To be sure, when he expressly ordered the princesses to abandon the *fontange* it was discontinued, but only to return within a few years. The King remonstrated, harangued, raved, but to no purpose. All of a sudden there was a change about face. In 1714 the Duchess of Shrewsbury, the wife of the British ambassador, was presented at the French court. Her low coiffure was found charming by the ladies of fashion, who at once copied the style, flying from one extreme to the other—to His Majesty's intense disgust. He should have known better. Fashion is a rebel that has never known law.

CHAPTER XI

CRAFTS AND INDUSTRIES

NAILS create a sensation among savages. Eighteenth century explorers had their troubles keeping South Sea Islanders from ripping ships into smithereens to get hold of iron nails. No wonder. The natives formerly had to *lash* houses and canoes with cords of coconut husk fiber. Without being efficiency experts they saw that to nail boards instead of tying them saved infinite labor. Man to man, the savage was as good a mechanic as the white. He was merely worse off from ignorance of a particular device that filled a particular need. He was handicapped in the sense our ancestors were handicapped in the days of stage-coaches and tallow candles. Are our brains better than theirs because we can buy railroad tickets or switch on electric lights? The savage, too, learns to do that. Probably not one of the British tars who paid for a dusky bedfellow with a nail in Captain Cook's day could have invented it. On the other hand, the Polynesians were quite as apt at driving nails as our carpenters when they had learned how.

North American Indians know nothing of needle and scissors. In 1906 I saw a Shoshone woman in Idaho punching holes through her moccasin with an awl and pulling her sinew thread through the openings. Instead of the old-fashioned bone point she used a steel piercer, but the principles of her sewing were unchanged. She was only some 20,000 years behind the French seamstresses of the Reindeer Age, who had true needles with eyes. As for snipping a thread, that is a very recent accomplishment in human history. Ancient Greece and Rome had no true scissors, which only appeared several centuries after Christ. Even sheep shears—with a curved spring joining two blades at the top—did not come in before the Bronze Age. Notwithstanding her inferior equipment, however, a Californian basket-maker can sew her splints with sixty stitches to the inch, a record not many white women could equal.

The Eskimo are marvels of manual deftness, but they have no saws. The cutting of bone, says Boas, "was always done by drilling holes close together along the line on which the bone was to be divided. When enough holes had been drilled the parts were separated by a blow of a hammer or by means of a wedge." That is to say, the work was done ingeniously, though by a roundabout method.

Nails, needles, scissors, and saws eluded primitive man because they were hard to invent. Or, rather, he had a million tasks to perform and happened to fail in these particular ones. Building on his foundation, our ancestors gathered together inventions from right and left, and we are now enjoying the advantage of their wholesale loans. Ruder peoples borrowed less and possess fewer facilities because they had to rely more largely on their own insight. But they were not dunces: they were merely tainted with the original stupidity inborn in the whole of the species *Homo sapiens*. If they did not always and immediately do the most sensible thing, what about their supposed betters? Civilized and primitive peoples constantly display the same sort of mental inertia.

Around Lake Superior Nature furnishes copper in metallic form. The Indians availed themselves of the supply and worked it without applying any new processes to the new material. They hammered it cold, treating it as if it were flint. But the Egyptians of 5000 B.C. were not a jot more original in their use of gold. Altogether the Age of Metals crept in by stealth. Characteristically enough, gold was the earliest metal to be used at all, and of course it served solely for ornament. Copper came next, but at first it was used only for beads. When men later made tools from it, these were not much better than stone artifacts, for copper alone is too soft. Accordingly, many peoples would have none of it. However, not a single one had the intuition to divine that an alloy of 10 per cent. of tin with 90 of copper would mend matters and yield an ideal bronze. That was the result of long and painful trial with all sorts of proportions that gave inferior results.

Strangely enough, bronze came before iron even though iron ores are common and tin rare. Further, casting bronze is difficult, while a moderate charcoal fire of some 700-800° C. is sufficient to reduce iron ore. Yet the most civilized peoples reluctantly gave up the older for the more practical material. Homer, about 800 B.C., still mentions both bronze and iron implements. The Chinese had a long Bronze Age before they finally learned about ironwork from Turkish nomads to the north. In Egypt iron was certainly known by 1350 B.C., but the people were unbelievably backward in fully exploiting its possibilities. The Hittites, in what is now Armenia, were nimbler-witted, and, thanks to their iron weapons, they long held their own against the Nile-dwellers. Strangest of all, iron, too, was first used only for decoration. In the islands east of Greece it long ranked in value with gold. In South Germany the prehistoric natives originally decorated bronze articles with it, later wore iron rings and bracelets, and only in the last stage made their implements out of iron.

Like the Europeans, some primitives took to metallurgy, and except in the most recent centuries they did not linger far behind Western civilization. A Kikuyu blacksmith in East Africa lives near an iron quarry. Water is turned from its natural course to carry down the sand bearing the metal. The wives and children wash out a black mass, dry it, and carry it home. Now it is put into a clay-lined pit and heated, a goatskin bellows supplying the blast. The smith picks out pieces of fairly pure metal, heats them, and beats them out into standard two-pound lumps of wrought iron. That is the form in which a customer who orders a tool made buys the metal in the market and has to bring it to the artisan along with the charcoal needed. Even in this primitive tribe the equipment of a smithy is considerable. Besides the bellows it includes at least a spiked iron hammer and separate anvils for swords and spears. A similar arrangement is found among the Bakuba of the Congo (Fig. 18).

The Negroes thus make wrought iron, and that is as far as medieval Europe got. Cast iron was unknown there, as well as among the ancients. It requires a furnace and a high pressure of blast such as only developed in the fifteenth century of our era.

In short, it is not safe to twit an Indian or Negro with his shortcomings in the arts of life. This might provoke unflattering recriminations by his educated fellows about the plight of our own forefathers. It is more profitable to turn to the credit side and see what the illiterate races of the world have been able to accomplish.

Here the textiles of the Peruvians first come to mind. Without any of our modern appliances they produced virtually every kind of weave and textile decoration our factories put forth today. They made thread from cotton and the wool of the American camels—the llama, alpaca, and vicuña; and Mr. M. D. C. Crawford, a modern expert, declares that, at its best, Peruvian spinning was "not only in advance of the best machine spinning but apparently contains the application of certain principles that are unknown today." In evenness of size, in strength and fitness for the weaver's purpose, the ancient Peruvian yarns are considered

FIG. 18. CONGO BLACKSMITH'S SHOP (*after Torday and Joyce*)

perfect. The high-water mark of achievement was in tapestry: even the coarser samples are usually far superior to the French Gobelins. "The patience and skill indicated in the finest pieces," writes Mr. Crawford, "passes belief. Many contain nearly three hundred weft yarns to each inch. . . . A web containing 260-280 weft yarns to the inch was analyzed. It was impossible to count the weft in this fabric with the testing lens ordinarily used in textile analyses. It was necessary to clamp an inch of cloth on the platform of a dissecting microscope and pick off the weft yarn with a needle. The operation took three and one-half hours."

This is of course an extreme case. Looms were probably not invented until the Age of Pottery, and many of the simpler peoples lack them. But even they have other textile arts, and many of them know other ways of making cloth. All savages can make string. If they have no spindle, they can at least, like our Wisconsin Indians, twist fibers of bark together on the bare thigh and splice on extra lengths according to need. Almost equally general is the art of knotting such string into a fish-net. Civilization has done little to improve this savage technique; the gauges for making meshes uniform are much the same in Sweden and in the heart of South America.

Basketry is older than weaving. Most tribes ignorant of earthenware at least make baskets, which are thus probably of Pre-Ceramic Age. Technically the art is simpler than weaving, for the elements that are intertwined or sewn are neither spun nor stretched in a loom. Baskets may thus be distinguished from woven cloth as *hand*-woven fabrics. Simple as the industry seems, the savages have elaborated it by an infinite number of inventions. Indeed, some of the rudest tribes, such as the Californians, are among the very best basket-makers in the world, both as to technique and ornamentation. Some of the baskets in our museums are too tiny for any practical purpose and must have caused no end of pains in the making: they were doubtless produced mainly to show off craftsmanship. Larger ones from the same region are richly decorated with woodpecker feathers and quail plumes. They, too, are of no earthly utility. They were stored for their beauty, given away as presents, or—most commonly—*destroyed in honor of the dead*. Yet some writers will have it that man labors solely to fill his belly.

In the South Seas and other tropical areas the natives make cloth out of bark. This does not mean that they just strip off sheets from a convenient tree and proceed to drape themselves. In 1777 Captain Cook saw the Tongans in the act and described it. A woman removed the bark of the paper-mulberry and scraped away the outer rind. The inner bark was softened in water, laid across a tree-trunk, and beaten with a grooved mallet. The pieces so produced were pasted together into the length and thickness wanted, and for a glossy finish the cloth was dipped into some native juice. Often the Polynesians carved designs on wooden boards, put the bark cloth on top, and rubbed a coloring matter all over. In this way the patterns were mechanically printed, exactly as we can cover a nickel coin with paper, rub a pencil over it, and reproduce the bison or Indian's head.

All this was something of a feat, and so was the art of felting practiced in Central Asia. The nomads there make stuffs without spinning fiber; yet the process is anything but simple. A group of Kirghiz will stand round a heap of wool or goat's hair and beat it with long rods, then pluck it into fine bits, spread it in two layers, thoroughly wet it, and roll it up in a mat. This is fastened with a rope. Now ten persons face an equal number on the opposite side of the roll. Those of one group push it towards their vis-à-vis with their right feet; the others receive the parcel with lifted feet and push it back. This takes an hour and a half. Now the mat is untied and the women then beat out the stuff for another three hours. How did the myth of savage laziness ever take shape? And apart from the labor expended, how much experience, insight, and coöperation are implied by such a technique!

Nor did primitive man simply flay animals and hang their pelts over his shoulders. Even Neanderthal man did more if his numerous scrapers served their obvious purpose. Recent tribes have gone much further. Our bison-hunting Indians not only made bags of *raw* hide, but mastered leather-making, which requires some chemical process to soften the skin for good. Some peoples of the world have done this by working into the hide plant material containing tannin; others depend on animal fats, still others on salts. Our Redskins took the rawhide and rubbed into it deer or bison brains mixed with fat. They had adzes for taking off the hair of bison pelts and working the inside down to an even thickness. With a toothed bone chisel they hacked off the flesh. There was a stone for rubbing the hide, and deerskins were curried with a split leg bone (Fig. 19). At different stages the skin was dried, moistened, rolled up in a bundle, pulled with the hands, and sawed back and forth over a sinew rope. The Siberians also had a whole tool-kit and a complex series of processes. A Yukaghir removed the inner membrane with one type of scraper and used two others at later stages. To take off the hair the hide is soaked in water or urine, and the natives smoke tent covers or dresses to waterproof them so they will not shrink. That is likewise an Indian custom. In 1914 I watched a Ute tanner at her job. She sewed up a skin and hung it from a tripod over a pit, staking and weighting the bottom. A smoldering fire in the pit played on the inside for thirty-three minutes. Then the skin was turned inside out, and ten minutes was enough to give the reverse a lighter tan.

Craftsmanship like this, involving a knowledge of materials, tools, and processes, can be traced back to the earliest stages of culture. There is a world of difference between a chimpanzee shoving one bamboo into another to make a longer rod and a Pre-Ceramic stone-worker. The ape is not striving for a definite shape by a definite technique; the maker of a fist-hatchet had a pretty clear image of the implement he wanted before he began knocking off flakes from

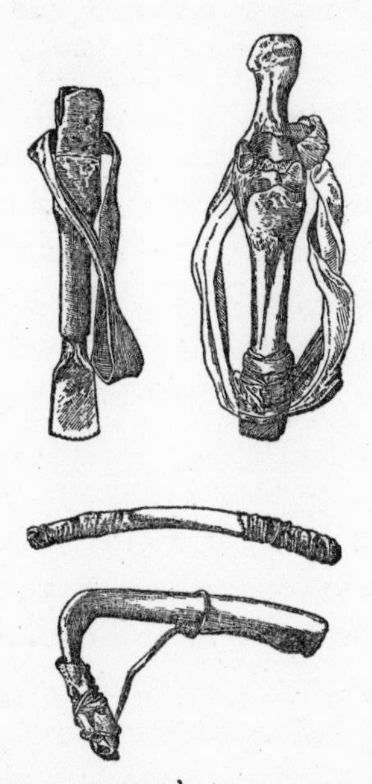

FIG. 19. CROW TANNER'S TOOL-KIT: CHISELS FOR FLESHING; BEAMING TOOL; ADZE-SHAPED SCRAPER (*after Lowie*)

his core (Fig. 20). For instance, he had no handle, but he made the butt into a grip by leaving it unworked. What is more, he acquired before long a practical knowledge of mineralogy. Not all rocks are equally suitable for all purposes. Obsidian and flint are excellent, while quartz and quartzite are refractory and with more labor yield poorer results (Fig. 21). In the course of the Pre-Ceramic Age man came to weed out the less adaptable rocks and to concentrate on the best kinds of flint. He acted exactly like the ancient Greek sculptors. They began carving limestone or any other local rock that was easily worked. Gradually they became

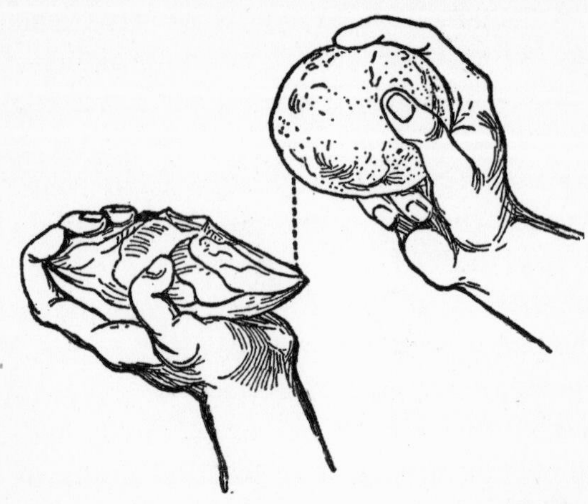

FIG. 20. CHIPPING A BOWLDER (*after Holmes*)

more fastidious, and finally they insisted on the finest marble from Naxos or Paros. The modern Australian savage, simple as his material equipment is, has a keen scent for such miner-

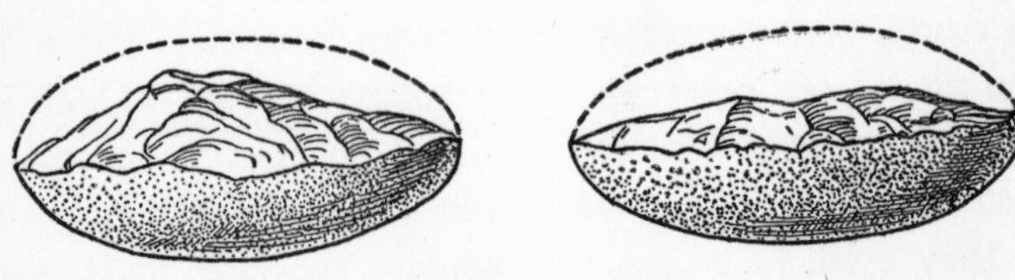

FIG. 21. FAILURE AND SUCCESS IN CHIPPING: THE FIRST SAMPLE IS NOT FLAT ENOUGH TO YIELD A THIN BLADE (*after Holmes*)

alogical differences. He does not attempt to grind quartzite but contents himself with chipping it. On the other hand, when he can get hold of diorite he manufactures axes with a ground edge. He sets great store by the proper varieties and asserts ownership privileges over the quarries. No one from an outside group is allowed to help himself to diorite without permission.

The invention of how to grind stone is not without its element of humor; it is so typical of what man will do. In the Age before Pottery there was no grinding of stone at all. The process was indeed known, but it was applied only to needles or other *bone* articles. Finally the prehistoric Europeans transferred the technique from bone to stone. Psychologically they were like the Asiatic buffalo-breeders who saw cows milked and tried out the same idea with females of another species. However, it took the early stoneworker thousands of years to make the transfer. When he once got going, in the Age of Pottery, he did not stop short with grinding an edge on his ax or chisel, but carefully ground the whole surface. The practical utility of this was exactly nil. An ax does not chop a bit better because it is highly polished on both sides. But it does look more beautiful.

This esthetic urge is almost as pronounced in the history of stonework as in that of dress. The earliest fist-hatchets are crude, heavy, asymmetrical, with irregular edges. But somewhat later the tools of this class become lighter and symmetrical, and the edges either straight or gracefully twisted (Fig. 3). They are made finer and finer at the top till they cease to be hatchets because the thin blade would shiver in chopping. All this, however, is nothing compared to a later phase of the Pre-Ceramic. The workers of that period no longer knocked off chips, but removed them by pressure with a bone tool (Figs. 22, 23). Before the Egyptians took to metal they excelled in this delicate chipping, and so did recent Californian aborigines. In 1915 I watched Ishi[1] turning a bit of bottle glass into an arrow-

[1] See page 52.

head with an iron nail. At every other moment I felt sure he would break the glass, but he never did. This sort of

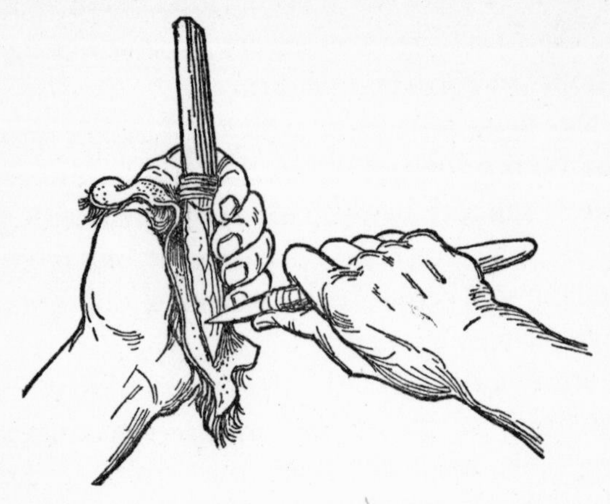

FIG. 22. CHIPPING BY PRESSURE WITH A BONE OR HORN TOOL (*after Holmes*)

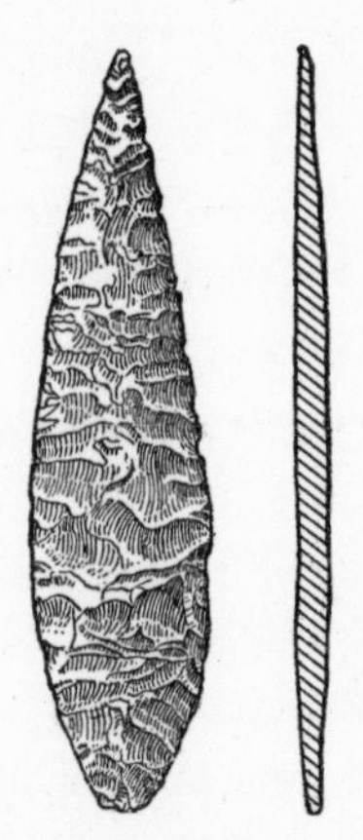

FIG. 23. LEAF-SHAPED BLADE, MADE BY PRESSURE-FLAKING ALL OVER BOTH FACES (*after Obermaier*)

work requires infinite nicety. The least false stroke or a shake of the hand proves fatal. An archaeologist who tried to duplicate Ishi's performance failed.

Oddly enough, this difficult type of flaking was invented before the grinding of stone. The point seems to be that this easier process takes more humdrum concentration. Man developed the finest precision before he could bring himself to spend hours in boresome drudgery.

About the same time man achieved another triumph of patience by boring through stone. He learned that he could wear a hole in the rock by twirling on it a stick with grains of sand. The drilling proceeded like that of our modern railroad tunnels: it was begun from both sides and continued till the wall was broken through.

Thus, stonework through the ages displays all the sterling qualities of the master artisan—industry, a knack at handling tools, resourcefulness in overcoming difficulties, a joyous love for the thing produced, and the desire to make it beautiful.

Pottery tells the same story. Using it to mark a new era of the Stone Age may seem like exaggerating its importance. At first blush earthenware vessels appear to be easily made, and they are not indispensable in cookery or anything else. The Californians used to boil food in baskets; [1] and in Utah water was stored and carried in plaited bottles pitched with resin.

Yet there are weighty reasons for considering ceramics of outstanding significance. Earthenware is *not* easily made. From the French reindeer-hunters of 20,000 years ago there have come down to us two skillfully modeled little clay figurines of bison, but of pottery there is no convincing evidence anywhere until we get to about 8000 B.C. The Australians never learned to produce it, nor did many people of higher rank, such as the British Columbians. If a native woman is asked nowadays to make a pot, she is likely to be

[1] See page 55 f.

fussy and insist that the only clay a self-respecting potter could use is fifty or a hundred miles away. If you wheedle or browbeat her into using clay near by, you discover that she knows her business, for the vessel forthwith cracks. In 1919 a young Swede, trying to live the life of the Stone Age under scientific guidance, attempted to manufacture pottery in the old way. Again and again he failed ignominiously because his vessels cracked in the firing. There is the rub: mere modeling in mud is not pottery. *That* can be made only from a clay of proper chemical quality, properly prepared and heated, for the minimum temperature of 400° C. is indispensable or the shaped vessel reverts into a lump of clay. And the final test is how it will stand the fire. When our Swede had learned to knead his earth, to mix it with coarse sand, to dry it thoroughly, and to apply uniform heat, he began to succeed.

In other words, to create even simple earthenware requires a knowledge of practical chemistry, physics, and geology, as well as not a little manual skill. Some clays are too sandy and cannot be shaped well; others are *too* plastic so that they stick to the maker's hands and crack under heat: that is why they have to be tempered with some other material. Thus, mica is added for greater plasticity in some parts of South America, while in the Amazon basin, where the clay was not sandy enough, the Indians added the ashes of bark holding silica. But there is a limit beyond which it is not easy to compensate, and so the manufacturer must know where to go for the best raw material he can get.

When the lump is ready for use it may be simply molded by manipulation of the clay. But another process is more common: the clay is shaped between the hands into a sort of sausage and wound in a spiral, continued by a second sausage, and so one bit of clay is coiled upon the next until the pot is complete (Fig. 24). The joints are evened out with the fingers, and the whole surface is smoothed and polished with a bit of gourd and a pebble.

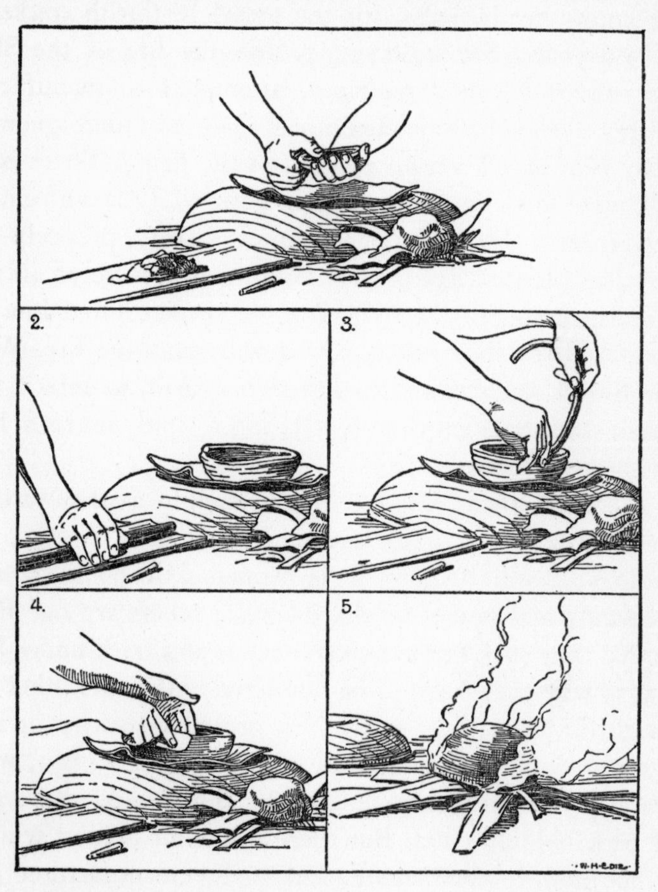

FIG. 24. COILED POTTERY, SOUTH AMERICA (*after Koch-Grünberg*)

Now practical science once more comes into play. The vessel will crack unless it is thoroughly dried before being heated, and it will crack from sudden shrinkage unless the drying is gradual. But the real trouble comes with firing.

Even if there are no untoward winds or showers, it is hard to heat pots uniformly, especially if they are large. Hence even skillful artisans spoil much of their earthenware.

Thus pottery is truly a technological achievement of the first order. Broadly speaking, it forms as true an index as any one activity can be of the general level of a people. In the first place, earthenware as a rule goes hand in hand with tillage of the soil, because nomads have little use for fragile containers. It is thus linked with a higher stage of food-getting. Naturally enough, tillers who abandon a settled mode of life generally lose the ceramic art. Further, an advance in the technique and artistic decoration of pottery generally goes with a superior status. The Northern Athabaskans of Canada make no earthenware at all and are rated lower in culture as a whole than the Eastern Algonkian tribes of the United States. These in turn do not equal the Iroquois of New York State either in pottery or in the richness of their social life. The Pueblo Indians with their stone architecture, almost complete dependence on farming, and wealth of ritual, mark a further rung in the scale; and their pottery is not only far more varied than that of the Iroquois but painted to boot. No one, however, puts them on the same plane with the ancient Mexicans and Peruvians. Well, the pottery of these highest of American aborigines was superior in both technique and beauty. They sometimes multiplied a particular form by using a mold—in other words, they hit upon the factory principle of production. But apart from this they also produced still more varied and esthetic effects than the Pueblos in their painting. Finally came the higher civilizations of the Old World, and all of these were technically ahead of any American culture because they had the potter's wheel, which the Egyptians invented possibly before 3000 B.C.

Exceptions there are, no doubt. Some peoples like the Polynesians, who must be ranked high on other counts, probably lost the art. Others, like the coastal tribes of British Columbia, never practiced it, though they are experts in other fields. But with a few exceptions of this sort the correlation holds. Pottery is a true, though only a rough, index of civilization.

How the first pottery originated, no one knows. Some writers suggest that since basketry is an earlier industry ceramics developed directly out of it. A basket was plastered with clay and accidentally burnt. This coating was thus turned into a pot, and the owner had his object lesson. We cannot disprove that this happened, but so many favorable conditions are necessary for the simplest true pot that an incident of this sort would hardly combine them all.

But a good deal is known about the history of that higher form of pottery called porcelain, and it sheds much light on how inventions are made. Porcelain is a special type of glazed earthenware. Glaze is a coating of fired glass applied to clay in order to make it waterproof, for even thorough heating will fail to do this. In porcelain this glaze penetrates evenly throughout the body of the vessel.

In order to understand the origin of porcelain we must therefore consider glass also.

Glass was invented by the Egyptians—not by the Phœnicians, as we used to be told. At an early period vases were manufactured in the Nile country, but what the Europeans of that era wanted and mainly imported was glass beads. The prehistoric Bavarians had got them by 1550 B.C. But for the longest time Europe remained purely passive: the first Italian workshops were not founded until our era. However, under the Emperors the industry went forward with a tremendous spurt. It all but perished in the Middle

Ages, when Venice alone preserved and revived it. There were glass window panes in Pompeii and in Roman settlements in South Germany. To be sure, they were only translucent, not transparent. The casting, too, was a bit inelegant, for the margins were likely to be twice as thick as the center. At all events, panes were not so rare as in the Middle Ages. Not before 1180 did even nabobs in Britain indulge in such luxuries, and as late as 1448 an Italian visitor to Vienna was amazed to find most of the houses provided with glass windows. How slowly these penetrated the North has been shown elsewhere.[1]

As glass traveled from the Nile to Europe, so it spread in the opposite direction until it reached China. But the Chinese did not adopt the new material in quite the same way as the Westerners. Imperial Rome reveled in glass bottles, bowls, goblets, and other vessels. The Chinese preferred to stick to pottery for household purposes, and used glass either for beads or as a hard stone to be cut and polished by the carver. Under the Han dynasty (206 B.C.-220 A.D.), however, the potters began to glaze. Their ware has been analyzed by chemists; it was already like porcelain in composition but not in its physical properties, for it was still porous and the glaze was too thick, so that it would run in the kiln. But from now on the Chinese haltingly, but quite independently of the rest of the world, coped with these difficulties; and by the beginning of the seventh century they finally achieved a true white porcelain.

The outstanding steps, then, are as follows. In China, as elsewhere, simple hand-made pottery goes back to the Stone Age. Some time after 3000 B.C. the wheel reached her people from the Near Orient, and much later they engrafted upon their ceramic art another Western idea, that of glaz-

[1] See page 69.

ing. But they were not mere imitators. As the Greeks were not content to borrow the Egyptian column, but developed an original style of architecture, so the Chinese created something quite new. There is nothing discreditable about adopting a fruitful idea from a foreign source. All complex cultures are built up of borrowed elements, and those which like the Chinese are goaded into active labor by their loans have produced the spectacular results.

In Europe the word "pourceline" or "pourcelaine" often figures in the Middle Ages, but only to designate such substances as agate, mother-of-pearl, and chalcedony. True porcelain from China was introduced by the Portuguese in the sixteenth century. In 1607 the French Dauphin took his broth in a china bowl, but only kings and lords could afford such luxury. At least as early as 1518 European potters and alchemists tried to duplicate the Chinese invention. Many of them pretended to succeed, but not one of them ever did. The King of Saxony came to take an interest in the matter, and at last, about 1710, true chinaware was produced in Meissen and marketed in 1713. That is to say, with samples of Chinese ware before him, with all the advantages of Western technology and royal patronage, it took the Caucasian craftsman a couple of centuries to catch up with the benighted Mongoloid.

Often a tribe attains supreme skill in one industry and executes mediocre work in other crafts. The Plains Indians were good tanners but made few baskets, and the very tribes in California who rank highest in basketry are quite ignorant of pottery. The Pueblos, on the other hand, excel in earthenware but are not to be compared with the woodcarvers of British Columbia. In civilized countries there is often similar specialization. The Germans of the old Austro-

Hungarian monarchy did fine carving, while the Slav peasantry went in for textiles. In Sweden the province of Västergötland stands out for the quality of its woodwork. Heredity can hardly account for this, for there is nothing to show that the farmers of neighboring Östergötland belong to a different race. If this holds for Sweden, it ought to hold elsewhere too: the Pueblos are not potters because their sex cells carry a clay-shaping factor that is absent from the cells of Californian and Plains Indians; and so forth.

But geography is not more helpful. Shall we lay the inferiority of Hopi carving to the dearth of timber in northern Arizona? Doubtless their juniper is too brittle and crooked to be used for anything but firewood, so that they have to fall back upon cottonwood. But is this the real reason for their want of skill? In the Atlantic region of the continent there is plenty of good pine wood, but the Eastern natives did not turn into expert joiners. They chose to exploit the birchbark of their environment. As usual, nature offered alternatives: *they* happened to select *one*, and the British Columbians *another*.

Well, then, was it the Hopi's ignorance of the wedge that kept him down? Certainly it was a drawback not to be able to split wood into plane surfaces. But the wedge was not responsible for the Northwest Canadian's craftsmanship. If tools made the artist, the African Negroes with their iron implements would all be far ahead of any Stone Age peoples. Some of them, in the Congo, for example, do make admirable boxes and goblets. But this is far from general. As a rule the African clumsily fashions a block of wood as a sculptor might work marble. A Herero in the Southwest dawdles for weeks over a simple milk pail. When a Pangwe on the west coast wants a powder flask he rough-hews a solid bottle, halves it, hollows out each half with an adze, and finally joins the pair by sewing a skin over them. Notwithstanding his iron knives, chisels, adzes, and saws, he halts woefully behind the Canadian with his shell, bone, and stone outfit, or the Polynesian with his mounted shark's tooth.

The plain fact is that neither tool-kit nor race nor environment accounts for tribal craftsmanship. *Individual* aptitude certainly enters, but why it found scope in carving on the Pacific coast of Canada, in basketry further south, and in pottery among Southwestern tribes, remains a mystery. It is a fact, as it is a fact that water runs downhill and is composed of hydrogen and oxygen.

Shakespeare's father was a glover and tanner. As such he was expressly forbidden by statute to sell raw meat, and in some towns he would have been barred from so much as buying hides before they were removed from the beasts. So rigidly were the lines drawn between different occupations. In France nothing would have amazed a Parisian of the period more than that a time would come when any one might open shop and sell goods without responsibility to his fellow tradesmen, without having served a set apprenticeship and undergone an examination of his fitness. Not before 1791 was a Frenchman legally free to carry on whatever business he pleased. The practice of medicine is still hedged about with regulations of the same order.

This scheme of watertight compartments developed in the Middle Ages, but not all at once. In the earlier medieval centuries the peasants merely practiced some craft as a hobby in leisure hours. When they migrated to the city where farming was impossible they naturally made a regular pursuit of what had once been a mere avocation.

Some sort of specialization developed very early in human

history. In some recent tribes it rests merely on individual ability. Citizeness X has a knack at pottery, and her ware is prized above all others. Y makes first-rate bows, and his fellows pay him handsomely for them. A parent naturally teaches his tricks as trade secrets to his sons, and so a dynasty of potters or weavers arises. The occupation may be more or less highly regarded than others, and so this is one way in which social classes or castes come into being.

Even when there are no fixed trades, specialization may go to weird lengths. In West Africa the Pangwe do not make a business of carving and weaving; all such work is done on the side in the intervals of fishing and farming. But in so far as a man does carve he is the narrowest of experts. He will manufacture stools but leave bows to his neighbor, and a spoon-carver would never attempt a ladle. This frame of mind makes for technical skill, and also for barter. Often whole villages or tribes specialize in this way, and then foreign trade is fostered. Thus only sporadic settlements in New Guinea devote themselves to pottery, but their earthenware output is carried by boat 400 miles from the place of origin. In northern South America one tribe builds canoes, another weaves hammocks, a third supplies both of its neighbors with cotton, while still another has the monopoly of manufacturing curare, the arrow poison.

These are extreme cases of specialization. But one form is absolutely universal. In every tribe the tasks allotted to men differ from those which fall to woman's share.[1] There may be some overlapping, but for the most part there is very little. In Bolivia the Yuracáre, for example, fish, garden, and beat out bark cloth irrespective of sex. But only the men manufacture weapons, plait baskets, and build houses or canoes; while the women cook, sew, spin, weave,

[1] See page 43.

make pottery and fish-nets, bring home firewood and water, and serve as porters on the march. Some of these occupations may seem to be "naturally" masculine or feminine, but that is only because we are biased in favor of our own scheme of dividing labors. The Samoan men are no mollycoddles; yet they think nothing of doing their own cooking. Spinning and weaving strike *us* as proper pursuits for a girl. In the Odyssey, when Telemachus sends his mother to her chamber, he falls in line with European tradition when he bids her mind her "own housewiferies, the loom and distaff." Yet even in Western civilization men have been weavers, and in alien cultures there is every possible variation. I have attended a spinning-bee of Hopi men, who logically enough do the loom-work too. But among their next-door neighbors, the Navaho, both tasks belong to the sphere of women. There is no logic about the whole business. In Nigeria the women spin, and their husbands weave; in the Congo the men make the cloth, and their women add the fine plush-like designs. Hence, even when vast areas practice an industry in one or the other way, that does not prove their custom to be natural. As a rule, one can easily find an equally large region with exactly the opposite usage. Thus, in the South Seas the women beat out bark cloth, and if one has been there or has read only about Oceanians, this seems in harmony with the eternal fitness of things. A glance at East Africa is enough to teach us otherwise. In the huge kingdom of Uganda a husband grew a particular species of tree and pounded out its bark into cloth. It was quite as definitely his duty to clothe his wife in this fashion as it was hers to raise plantains and feed her menfolk. Again, the tanning of leather appears an eminently masculine business until we find that among most North American natives it is invariably one of a woman's accomplishments *par excellence*. Among the Plains Indians a hide-scraping male would hardly escape the suspicion that he was homosexual.

All this must make us very cautious about declaring that any particular activity is either natural or unnatural for men and women—whether it be cooking, or smoking cigars, or healing the sick. That men should hunt, fight, and wield a sledge-hammer is natural enough; but when no primary or secondary sex traits are directly involved it is sheer convention which sex shall perform such and such tasks. In the Trobriand Islands off New Guinea the father assumes the dry nurse's job and does very well at it. In short, in discussions of this topic, "natural" almost always means "conventional."

Primitive man has us constantly hovering between admiration and contempt. He has laid the basis of our own knowledge and arts, but he never fails to do sensible things in whimsical or even ridiculous fashion. In Uganda there are many things a blacksmith must do and avoid doing that, as we see it, have no bearing on the success of his work. He must shun his friends while engaged in his trade, must eat by himself, and abstain from intercourse with his wives. As soon as his son has given the first proof of his skill at the craft, the tool made is handed over to the boy's mother for safe-keeping. Then the smith jumps over her "to confirm the boy in his work." For this bit of conjugal acrobatics is firmly believed to insure good luck and to ward off evil on any important occasion of life.

Rather more important than such quaint associations of ideas have been the political and social distinctions that go with occupation. One thing is quite certain: the value a society puts on a man's business has rarely anything to do with its utility. The peasant of continental Europe has always been looked down upon, and upper-class Europeans still find it hard to grasp the social difference between an American farmer and a Polish or French tiller. A true aristocrat feels besmirched by the thought of useful work and is degraded even by carrying a small parcel, let alone a valise. The bluebloods of East Africa also have strong feelings on the subject and spurn anything in the way of manual labor. There is just one exception: they herd and milk cattle not merely with industry but with fanatical devotion. So in the Middle Ages a French gentleman suffered no loss of dignity as a glassblower. Again, tanning is surely a worthy enough occupation in the abstract, and in North America a woman expert in dressing skins was a highly prized mate. Yet in various parts of Africa the tanners form an outcast class.

More surprising still is the way most East African societies despise the blacksmith. He represents the important advance towards a Metal Age and provides his community with all their indispensable tools and weapons. But human psychology is above such sordid considerations. Among the Masai, for example, the smiths form the pariah class, and they are tolerated only as an unavoidable evil. The trade is inherited from father to son, and no one can climb out of his status by not being bred to the craft. The smiths are compelled to dwell apart, for otherwise they would bring calamity to other folk. No Masai proper entertains them or expects hospitality from them. They are not allowed to join other warriors on their raids, and whatever spoils they get on their own expeditions may be confiscated at will. A Masai not only will not marry into a smith's family; he even disdains sex relations outside of wedlock. A Masai who should disobey this law will become insane, it is said, and is likely to be killed in the next campaign. The issue of such unions would be sickly. At night the very word for "smith" is not uttered; it would lure lions and enemies into the camp. The craft is literally outlawed. If a Masai is killed, his kindred receive compensation from the murderer and his family, but no indemnity or other penalty follows the murder of a smith. On the other hand, if one of the outcasts were to kill a Masai by sheer chance, a gang would immediately swoop down upon his settlement and slay several of his fellows by way of revenge. Even the tools manufactured by the hated group are tainted. Indispensable as they are, every ax, knife, razor, sword, or spear from the workshop has to be purified with grease before use.

The reason alleged for this attitude is ingenious. God has forbidden bloodshed. The wicked blacksmiths manufacture weapons and thus tempt the Masai to transgress the divine commandment; hence they are accursed. Every one can see that the smiths are poor; hence God cannot love them. The argument recalls modern eugenists. They, too, prove to their own satisfaction that the needy are born inferior.

The Masai treatment of a harmless group plying an honest trade seems silly and cruel, but . . . In the early Middle Ages all wayfaring entertainers were outlaws, devoid of honor and without claim to compensation for injury or even death. The Swabian code put the point with fiendish sarcasm. "Whosoever has injured them and is to suffer penalty shall step in front of a wall with the sun shining on it. The player shall go thither and strike the neck of the shadow on the wall. This revenge shall be reckoned his indemnity." According to the oldest municipal law of Brünn a woman of the strolling actor class might be raped with impunity, and any one depriving the ravisher of his property was himself liable to punishment for theft or robbery. The Spanish revision of the Justinian code decrees that a son may be justly disinherited for associating with actors and acrobats. Berthold of Ratisbon, the great preacher, denounced actors and musicians as the human counterpart of Lucifer and his rebellious horde. For a long time they were excluded from Holy Communion. Only gradually their position was improved. The musicians came to follow the example of the crafts and organized in fraternities of their own, such as the St. Nicolai guild of Vienna (1228). British law long classed players with "rogues, vagabonds, and sturdy beggars." But in Shakespeare's time they could elude the disgrace of their profession by putting themselves under the protection of a nobleman. Like Shakespeare himself, they might even buy a coat of arms and become gentlemen. On the Continent, too, lords and kings patronized the formerly despised caste. In 1508 the Bishop of Strasbourg went so far as to free the musicians of his diocese from their disability. The "beloved pipers in Christ," as they were now dubbed, gained access to Holy Communion—provided they abstained from playing for five days before and after.

CHAPTER XII

TRAVEL AND TRANSPORTATION

BY 2700 B.C. the Egyptians constructed seagoing vessels with double masts and steering-oars and space for twenty passengers. Later they cut a canal connecting the Nile with the Red Sea and enabling ships to go to what is now Somaliland or even to the Indian Ocean. This was an enormous step in advance of the Tasmanians, who never ventured more than a few miles off shore on their cigar-shaped bundles of rushes (Fig. 5). It was also a great improvement on the dugout canoe of many modern savages (Fig. 25),

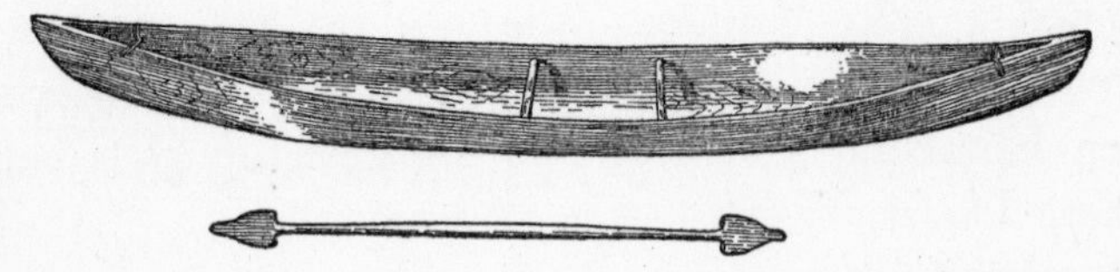

FIG. 25. DUGOUT CANOE, YUKAGHIR (*after Jochelson*)

which was already known to the Stone Age people of Switzerland.

But when the Caucasian had got that far, he promptly proceeded to rest on his laurels. The Phoenicians were active sailors who even managed to reach the British Isles, but they added not a single new principle to the mariner's art; neither did the ancient Greeks or Romans. For all these nations the Egyptian ships served as models, and they handed the old pattern down to medieval Europe. In what respect were our ancestors of 1400 A.D. better off than many of their savage contemporaries or the seafaring Egyptians of old? The Indians of British Columbia could build dugouts sixty feet long and holding fifty passengers. In New Guinea, boats were carrying pottery 400 miles from their place of manufacture. Polynesians made still longer voyages and knew that a log parallel to the boat, the "outrigger," safeguards it in a heavy sea. Some of these South Sea Islanders had sails, whereas the Nordics of the Bronze Age never got beyond rowing. Nothing Europe achieved in navigation before Columbus and Magellan was above the powers of a Polynesian crew.

A new era was ushered in by the mariner's compass. But who first conceived the idea of a compass? Apparently the Chinese, who had a magnetic pointer as early as 235 A.D. They mounted a figure on a chariot and by connecting it with a lodestone made it point south. However, long after Europeans had come to use the compass in voyages, travel remained a risky business. When a Swedish princess set forth from Calais in 1565 in order to pay her respects to Queen Elizabeth, she made two unsuccessful trials before reaching Dover. It was not at all uncommon in those days for becalmed passengers to finish a Channel trip in a rowboat.

At all events, for such navigation as there was, Egypt and China paved the way. After the improvement of the steam engine by Watt it was doubtless a clever idea to let physical energy do the work of wind and oar. But it was not in principle more remarkable than for an ancient Siberian to harness a reindeer to his sledge in place of a dog. The earlier attempts of engineers with steamers were modest enough. Fitch ran his boat at three miles an hour, Fulton achieved five, and the *Savannah* took twenty-five days to cross the Atlantic. From such humble beginnings came the records of our ocean liners. They represent no new principle of locomotion. Science has been putting at the disposal of an intelligent engineer a mass of theoretical and practical knowledge which the Egyptians, Greeks, and Europeans of a hundred years ago lacked. What is more, society puts a premium on time-saving inventions and thus gives inventors a powerful incentive. As a Philippine warrior tries to outdo his fellows in head-hunting because of the prestige he gains, so a modern technician deliberately casts about for means to cut down an hour of the record or to perfect a safety device in order to pocket *his* reward of pelf and glory. The individual ability required is rarely out of the ordinary. If the results are spectacular, it is because dozens of minds have contributed.

What holds for voyages holds for travel by land. The truly epoch-making inventions from a long-distance view of humanity are not trains at a mile an hour. Pre-Ceramic man's improvements of travel afoot, the use of beasts in the Age of Pottery, and the invention of the wheel in the Copper Age—these make everything subsequent trivial by comparison.

Even before he had learned to control animals man rose above the chimpanzee level. Any one who tries to walk on a patch of cactus will understand why Arizona Indians wear sandals. Footgear, in moderate and hot climates, is first of all a means of travel. In biblical times the Syrians dispensed with it altogether in everyday life, but donned sandals for a journey; and for the same purpose modern South American Indians put tapir hide on their soles when crossing thorny or rocky country. It is no mere chance that the British Columbia Indians, who travel mainly by water, are of all North American aborigines the most generally unshod. In Siberia and North America, where the winter snows are heavy, the natives put on snowshoes, and for speedy journeying the Northerners of the Old World have skis. On these thin wooden boards an East Siberian can keep up with a reindeer.

Stilts are not merely a boys' pastime, but still help French mail carriers and shepherds to walk over marshy soil and to survey their flocks in the Landes district. In the seventeenth century Austrian peasants used them to ford streams in Carniola. But among primitives an element of unconscious waggery enters. In West Africa stilts are sacred, belong to secret fraternities, and no woman is allowed to watch a performance on them. So in the Marquesas the Polynesians ran on stilts and held contests on them during memorial festivals in honor of a dead priest; and here, too, women were excluded.

Before man had domestic beasts he had to carry his goods himself, but even then he hit on ways of making the job easier. No chimpanzee ever puts a burden basket on his back, claps a cap on his head to protect his forehead, and then passes a tumpline over it. A Paiute woman did all of these things. Canadian Indians dragged loads on the runnerless sleds known as toboggans, with or without the aid of dogs. This sort of thing did not disappear with civilization. In ancient Egypt and Assyria immense blocks of stone were moved on sledges pulled by scores of slaves. It looks like a strange survival when we see carts in the very same picture. Why were not these vehicles used to convey the rocks? But the waste of energy is not so wanton as it seems. The ground was rough, and though there were wheeled conveyances, none of those available to the ancients could have transported such huge weights.

Human traction still lingers on. In the Far East there are the rickshaw and the sedan chair. In 1908 I was towed up the Athabaska River by seven or eight Canadian half-breeds harnessed to a line in the good old way. And standing in front of the Hamburg railway station of a summer morning in 1924, I watched the processions of vegetable venders pulling their carts to market, shoulder to shoulder with their dogs.

However, letting the dog do all the work is more convenient, and in several regions man had the wit to break in his first domestic beast for the task. The Plains Indians crossed two poles, fastened their front ends to the dog's back, and allowed the butts to drag along the ground. A netted frame could then be lashed to the spreading sides, and to this the load was tied (Fig. 10). The Eskimo and the Siberians travel on sledges drawn by dog teams.

By breaking in larger animals during the Age of Pottery, man revolutionized his system of travel, and in the Copper Age the job was virtually completed. Oxen could not only pull plows, but also carry loads on their backs. Muddling along in his usual fashion, man tried out new species when old ones failed him, and thus chanced to make momentous discoveries. A horse as well as an ox could be harnessed to a plow; or, like a donkey, to a cart. Adjustments became necessary, and so simple inventions were added. Reindeer can be ridden like horses, but not *all* reindeer. There are breeds with weak backs that would break under a rider. But some clever Siberian tried sitting over the animal's front legs, and it worked.

Primitive man did not travel as a sight-seeing tourist. Improved means of transportation meant that he could make war and scour the country for game as never before. When the Plains Indians got horses from the white man, their economic life was not directly changed: they did not begin to eat horse flesh or to milk mares like Turkish nomads. Yet they were now able to surround a bison herd with little trouble and could easily swoop down on a hostile camp. The

Asiatic nomads developed cavalry tactics and finally worried the Chinese into copying their technique and everything that went with horsemanship. The Chinese of 300 B.C. were far superior in civilization, but they borrowed from their lowly enemies as we borrowed potatoes from the Indians. It was precisely through such intelligent borrowing in the past that they had become superior.

By 3000 B.C. the Babylonians had the wheeled cart, that is, the principle of our automobiles and railway coaches. The wheel looks simple but was a very hard thing to devise. American Indians slid canoes over skids, spun spindle-whorls, and played at a hoop game, but the idea of the cart never occurred to them. Even the Peruvians and the Mexicans never invented it. In fact, no people ever used it who did not, directly or indirectly, learn about it from Babylonia.

But as soon as a tribe had once put some animal before a cart, it was as well off in point of transportation as any North European in 1800 A.D. An Englishman of that period enjoyed no advantages over an Egyptian of 1700 B.C. who had just got horses to draw his chariots. For several thousand years humanity accomplished next to nothing.

The Romans, to be sure, built marvelous roads, but they did not add new principles of conveyance; and the Middle Ages did not so much as continue the Roman tradition. Incidentally, even the Romans did not solve the problem of urban traffic after the fashion of supermen. While hundreds of wagons and carriages were driven back and forth over the magnificent highways of the Empire, even the upper classes had to travel in sedan chairs within the cities. For cabs and coaches were tabooed by law; only at night trucks were allowed to pass to and fro. This was not a perverse police regulation, but an inevitable consequence of the narrow streets. Ancient Rome had its parking and traffic problems exactly as we have. When a new condition suddenly confronts man, his way is to flounder awkwardly before he discovers a halfway tolerable solution.

Whatever may be said on behalf of ancient Italy, North European travel in 1700 A.D. and later was a costly and dangerous adventure. Apart from highwaymen, the roads were such that coaches often stuck fast or were upset; in some districts in England they were pulled by oxen. In 1765 the Bath coach started from London in the morning, stopped overnight at Andover, and arrived the following day, making a hundred miles in twenty-nine hours. Thirty years later it was still something of a feat to start at four in the morning and get to Bath by 11 P.M. On the Continent travel was no more expeditious. In 1665 it took ten days to go from Paris to Lyons; in 1760 the time was only cut down to five or six. A traveler leaving Paris in 1681 arrived in Brussels on the eighth day. Two centuries later an express train covered the distance in four and a half hours.

Our modern railway systems were not struck off by a sudden flash of insight, but developed by quite the same mental processes as similar improvements in savage communities. The earliest British railroads had timber rails and were worked by horse traction. They did not convey passengers or even general freight, but only coal from the pits to the nearest river. There boats were relied upon to take them to their destination. As a Plains Indian substituted the horse for the dog to pull his wheelless dray and later harnessed it to a wagon, so the managers of British collieries first had only wooden rails, then plated them with iron, next made them altogether of metal, and finally used steam traction. Their tramways for decades were restricted to coal mines and quarries, and no one dreamt of using them for ordinary merchandise.

In putting together ideas from different compartments the European was as much of a dullard as the savage. Not to speak of earlier models of the steam engine, James Watt's improved form had been patented by 1769. But as primitives tilled the soil and bred cattle without immediately hitting on the scheme of cultivating with plow and draft-oxen, so for nearly half a century no Nordic thought of using anything but horse power with the railways. R. Trevithick tried a steam locomotive in 1804, and ten years later Stephenson built another, which drew an eight-wagon train at the rate of four miles an hour. Yet as late as 1824 the *Encyclopaedia Britannica* pooh-poohed railways except for short distances and considered navigation a superior means of transportation for general trade. Nor was that so silly as it sounds today, for most trains were still being run by animal power.

Our means of travel *are* infinitely superior to the savage's. But they became such by the same devious routes and against the same sort of mental sloth that characterize the whole story of human progress. They are a thing of yesterday, and relatively to the whole white population very few individuals played any part in their development. Unless we are all born superior to Newton and Galileo, who—poor dears—had nothing better than stage-coaches, riding on express trains is no sign of a higher mental development.

CHAPTER XIII

SEX AND MARRIAGE

PRIMITIVE society does not allow its members to gratify their lust at will; hence there is no such thing as real promiscuity. Parent and child are never permitted to mate; brother and sister, very rarely. Often the rules are stricter than with us: fifth cousins are prohibited, and by sheer fiction even unrelated individuals rate as kin. About some unforbidden forms of sexual intercourse savage society is merely indifferent; others are positively approved, and stable unions of this sort may be called marriages.

An Australian was killed if he cohabited with a woman of the wrong group. No one cared if he slept with a woman of the right group. From the latter the elders of the tribe allotted to him a girl he *married.*

Western civilization also approves, tolerates, and condemns, but profession and practice do not tally so well as among savages. Until recently cohabitation was sanctioned only by a religious ceremony, which normally created a lifelong bond. However, bachelors were not outlawed for sowing their wild oats; and Dr. Samuel Johnson, devout churchman and moralist that he was, considered a married man's amours mere peccadilloes. On the other hand, single women became outcasts by losing their virginity, and so did wives by unfaithfulness to their husbands. That natural children should be regarded as bastards was a foregone conclusion. In practice, only those suffered who were without influence. A king's mistress was not treated as a street-walker: the virtuous Empress Maria Theresa stooped to write polite letters to Madame de Pompadour and admonished Marie Antoinette to be nice to Madame du Barry. Humane sentiments also tempered behavior towards the bastards of princes.

Present custom in civilized countries varies and is in a flux; hence no general statement can be made to hold for all. Some substitute a legal for the religious rite. Divorce and remarriage are common. There are European states which ignore the difference between legitimate and natural children. In some circles equal freedom for both sexes is preached and practiced; others in the same countries cling to the old standards. What we nowadays call conservative and radical positions as to sex both occur in different primitive societies.

Among the Northern Plains Indians the double standard of conservatism held sway. Parents encouraged their sons to be gay young blades and bade their daughters beware of philanderers from other families. In a woman chastity was highly prized, though hardly expected. Girls who fell were not beyond the pale. But they would not fetch large offers of horses from a suitor, and some rites in the Sun Dance could be performed only by absolutely pure married women. There was surely more illicit intercourse than in the middle-class homes of Victorian Europe; there was perhaps less if we take into account the customs of the countryside and the prostitution of the cities. Real differences existed: a Crow or Blackfoot might be legal husband to two or more wives, and divorce was common, being in no wise hindered by authority. But in the *ideals* of sexual behavior there was much similarity: men were to be red-blooded Lotharios, and women saints; and stable unions ranked higher than loose ones.

But in other regions we find the radical pattern of free love. Off the coast of New Guinea lie the Trobriands where a girl is never a virgin at marriage. From a child she plays at the sex game; when older she sleeps with the youths of the village in the bachelors' hall; she becomes a particular boy's sweetheart; and finally the two set up a permanent household. Similarly, among the Masai of East Africa the young braves, to the number of fifty or a hundred, sleep in a dormitory of their own, the hut being shared by the young girls. Each warrior has his own mistress, who remains loyal so long as he is about. Should he go off for a single day, she takes up with another lover. Pregnancy, however, is a disgrace, which is staved off by artificial means.

Is this not promiscuity? It is not. For even this free and easy life has its limitations. One of them is not less quaint than the recently abolished British law forbidding a widower to marry his wife's sister. Though a girl mates with almost any other bachelor in the neighborhood, with her fiancé she must *not* sleep, and to prevent that she is sent to another dormitory. Further, both in youth and later there are fixed limits to license. Blood-relatives do not consort with each other, nor do people in the same subdivision of the tribe. A man may not mate with his foster-sister or wed two women in the same clan. He is further restricted to his own age-class and must not stoop to the daughter of a blacksmith.[1]

In short, there is not promiscuity. But there *is* license, before, in, and outside of marriage. For the Masai are not like some other tribes that allow free love in youth, yet limit it in wedlock. Husbands exchange bedfellows; a host turns over his wife and hut to a guest; widows and divorcées live out of wedlock, but uncensured, with men of their husbands' age.

However, the Masai clearly distinguish between marriage and licensed fornication. Here, as elsewhere, the object of

[1] See page 111.

marriage is not indulgence of the flesh but a home and children. Of this, more anon; let us first see how one gets a spouse.

Primitive tribes generally dispose of their daughters at puberty. This explains why girls are often not consulted as to their marriages. At fourteen or thereabouts they do not know what is good for them. (Their parents do not either, but they can hardly be expected to realize that.) When it was the European custom to marry off daughters young, their inclinations counted for little. Experience shows that neither arrangement by parents nor free choice guarantees happiness, but that is immaterial for every one but the couple in question.

With us and with savages what counted was other considerations, in some respects alike. Marriage took care of the daughter's sex life; it gave the husband the children he coveted; and it cemented a bond between two families. There was a difference, however, imposed by economic conditions. Primitive woman was an economic asset; why then give her up gratis? Compensation could be secured in several ways. In Australia and New Guinea two households having each a son and a daughter swap girls; each youth is thus provided with a wife in the least troublesome way. Elsewhere the suitor goes to live with his parents-in-law and for a year or more plays the part of servant to them. Or instead of such service he may offer a bride-price.

On the primitive level there is nothing degrading about the purchase of a woman. It was the highest form of marriage recognized by the Crow—the one most honorable for a girl. In a love match the man was trying to get something for nothing, he was "stealing" his sweetheart. Such unions were not likely to last long. But when a man paid ten horses for a girl, it was proof that he esteemed her for not being a spitfire or a gadabout; and then the marriage was likely to be stable. Northwest Californians stressed purchase even more, for the offspring of an unbought woman were reckoned bastards and excluded from the men's club.

Because marriage was a contract of *families*, certain customs naturally sprang up. When a man in north central California got his bride, his brothers and cousins usually chipped in to make up the "purse" required. Nothing more natural, then, than that if the husband died, one of his kinsmen should inherit the widow. On the other hand, if a woman died, her family would send a sister or cousin to take her place. Often two or more sisters might be wives at the same time: a Plains Indian paid for the eldest and married others as they came of age.

Interesting consequences flow from the idea of women as economic goods. They come to form the main part of a Negro's estate, so that his eldest son will inherit all wives except his own mother. Divorce logically implies return of the price paid. Adultery becomes trespass on property rights, calling for indemnification. Again, there is a logical development of the ruder Australian system of exchange, by which a youth obtained a wife through a trade of sisters. In the more complex African conditions, the same result is achieved by storing the amount "pocketed" for a daughter in order to pay for a son's spouse. Finally, though there is no end to legal possibilities, a father can get a loan on the security of a small daughter. He can borrow a heifer and a bull even on the merest prospect of having his wife bear a girl.

Marriage, then, is a contract. But the conditions implied in it vary. When a Kai in New Guinea pays for his wife, she becomes his property, to be inherited by his heirs and punishable for infidelity. But he gains control neither over her chattels nor over her issue: both belong to her and her kin.

Contrast with this the common Negro idea of purchase. Here what the husband craves and secures is progeny. When he has paid the full price, he is entitled to children, and barrenness becomes the chief cause of divorce. The views of the Lango on the upper Nile are typical: "Infecundity brings more shame and disrepute on a woman than the most riotous living." But it is the recipients of the bride-price that are responsible, having failed in the implied contractual obligation. Hence the payment is returned, or a sister of the wife's is given to the husband gratis. Further, the price paid for a wife entitles the husband to *all* her offspring thereafter. Hence, in flat contradiction to our ideas, the results of adulterous matings are legally children of their mother's purchaser. Their blood-father has no claims upon them whatsoever. This is a common principle of African law. The Masai, for example, cannot always know who begot a particular infant. That, however, does not matter, for its legal relationship is fixed by payment for the mother.

Where women are bought, a rich man naturally buys two or more wives. Polygamy is hardly ever founded on masculine lechery, which can be satisfied outside of wedlock. But a Siberian with several herds of reindeer needs a wife for each, and a Negro with large tracts of land to till can put several women to hoeing. Sometimes a sexual reason also occurs: a Lango is forbidden to sleep with his wife until her child is weaned, and since it is nursed for nearly three years he turns to other wives. In no case do the natives consider the practice degrading. Generally the first wife herself twits a man with being a miser if he fails to buy her an assistant, and thus goads him into getting a second spouse.

However, considering that about an equal number of male and female children are born into this world, polygamy can never be common in a community unless there has been tampering with the normal ratio. For instance, if men are regularly killed off in war or on dangerous seal-hunting expeditions, an excess of women results. Or, as in Africa, the chiefs and wealthy men may seize an undue share of the females, letting the rest of the men go hang. These others prefer, however, to seduce the married women of the land. In most savage societies polygamy is not forbidden; yet most unions are monogamous. For wherever people are more or less on a level of equality, the tendency will be to follow the natural ratio of the sexes.

A rarer form of polygamy develops when infant girls are killed in large numbers—usually because of the hard struggle for existence. Then there results an excess of men, as in southern India; hence a woman will have several husbands. But since blood-fatherhood matters as little here as elsewhere,[1] it is easy to assign children to their *social* fathers.

Primitive monogamy need not be any more "moral" than polygamy. Marriage is rarely sacramental; hence divorce is easy and frequent. The Greenlanders, though not forbidding polygamy, are mostly content with one husband or wife; but Captain Holm found a girl barely twenty years old who had just left her sixth mate. The Hopi prescribe a single wife, but the partners are constantly shifting: it is "progressive" or "brittle" monogamy. Characteristically, however, unions always become more stable after the birth of children.

To sum up. The sex life of all civilized and all savage peoples is at bottom amazingly similar. What varies quite as remarkably is the emphasis on this or that feature, the appraisal of the same behavior. Modern prostitution enables a man to cohabit with an indefinite number of women, each having a similar range of partners. This, then, combines the two forms of polygamy that occur among savages. How

[1] See page 127.

does the Masai plan differ? It differs in that *all* the girls of a community share the experience of multiple sex relations, that accordingly none of them is outlawed, and that their favors are not for sale. Here it is the legal wife that is bought, and not mainly for sexual purposes. The traditional European father spurns the bastard foisted upon him by an adulterous wife; the African insists that all her children, begotten by whomsoever, shall be his.

There is not a single custom, a single sentiment, connected with Western marriage that cannot be paralleled from some savage people; and not one that is not proved conventional by the practice of other societies. Some tribes sanction male jealousy: a Blackfoot had the right to slice off his wife's nose to punish adultery. But the Masai share wives with age-mates, and some tribes regard infidelity as irrelevant to divorce. There are always prohibited degrees, but the lines are differently drawn. The Lango forbid marriage with any one no matter how remotely related on either the father's or the mother's side. Some West Australians, on the other hand, insist on a man's marrying his maternal uncle's daughter. So there is endless diversity on the basis of the selfsame instinct of reproduction. Yet again there is likeness, not in the concrete sex behavior or philosophy, but in that everywhere without exception some modes of intercourse are lifted above the rest as more dignified because bound up with the maintenance of society.

But what of love among savages? Can it flourish in the midst of such looseness and prudential considerations? Passion, of course, is taken for granted; affection, which many travelers vouch for, might be conceded; but Love? Well, the romantic sentiment occurs in simpler conditions—as with us—in fiction. A Plains Indian story shows the Sun himself smitten with the beauty of a maiden and luring her to the sky. Heroes set out to achieve deeds of derring-do "all for the love of a lady." Orpheus-like, a husband follows his beloved wife to the land of spirits; and even in historical tradition a young woman braves a long trip through hostile country to rescue her crippled lover. In frigid Siberia a love-

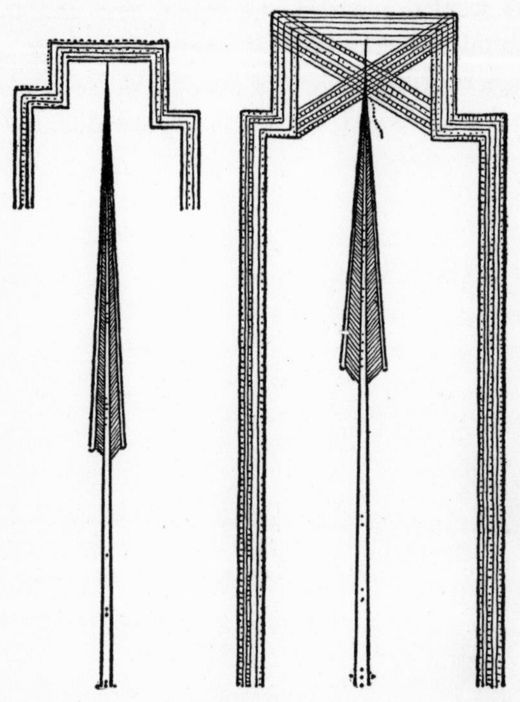

FIG. 26. YUKAGHIR LOVE LETTER (*after Jochelson*)

sick Yukaghir maiden scratches her desires on a sheet of birchbark: it is the only outlet society allows. The symbols are oddly conventional (Fig. 26): a figure like a folded umbrella represents the youth; a wider sample of the same design, the artist herself; crossing stripes above her betoken grief, connecting bars indicate love; and an incomplete house means desertion. So the girl can utter her plaint—"Thou goest hence, and I bide alone. For thy sake I weep and moan."

Yukaghir women are no better than they should be, but there is more than fleshly lust in these birchbark letters faithfully transcribed for us by Dr. Jochelson. They breathe the same wistful longing one meets now and then in the primitive tales that register the tellers' outlook on life. So Love exists for the savage as it does for ourselves—in adolescence, in fiction, among the poetically minded.

CHAPTER XIV

THE FAMILY

THE family, then, is a universal institution. But not *our* family. In fact, what does "our family" mean? It is not today what it was a century or even half a century ago. The relations of husband and wife, parents and children, have changed. In some Western countries even the state now views these relations differently; so vital a matter as divorce is not regarded in Nevada as it is in South Carolina or New York. What, then, is common to all human societies is not the way in which the duties or rights of family life are defined, but *that* they are defined at all. A Kai in New Guinea freely cohabits with women he meets, but he owes them nothing; his wife, however, has claims for support, as he has claims for her services. In other words, the *sanctioned* forms of intercourse imply a continued relationship, though it need not be permanent. Spouses may separate on little provocation, but they do not fly off immediately after mating; and a mother does not abandon her child after weaning. *That* is what the universality of the family means. Apart from that, there is infinite diversity; even the same group alters its standards at different times. Let us look at some of them as regards the main relationships.

Marriage is a contract. The terms have been found to vary, but even when not expressed they are clearly understood within a particular community. An unfaithful Victorian wife, a barren East African one, a Uganda husband who fails to beat bark into cloth for his woman's dress, are not playing the game. In the overwhelming majority of

Western marriages practical considerations have been not one whit less prominent than among savages. This is obvious in the arrangement of royal marriages, but not less so among European gentlefolk and peasantry with their settlements and dowries.

The average Caucasian attitude through the ages is well illustrated by Benjamin Franklin. "That hard-to-be-governed passion of youth" had often led him "into intrigues with low women." These, however, were expensive, inconvenient, and risky. So he paid court to a tenant's kinswoman, "the girl being in herself very deserving." After a while Franklin let it be known that "I expected as much money . . . as would pay off my remaining debt for the printing-house." When the sum was not forthcoming, he broke off negotiations. The notion of matrimony, however, would not down; so he "made overtures of acquaintance in other places." He discovered that printing was held a poor sort of business that did not warrant an expectation of dowry. So in the end he turned to an old flame of adolescence, who turned out "a good and faithful helpmate" and "assisted me much by attending the shop; we throve together, and have ever mutually endeavor'd to make each other happy." As he remarks, "it was lucky for me that I had one as much dispos'd to industry and frugality as myself."

Among savages, too, such pooling of interests concerning the household and the children born into it leads as a rule to mutual tolerance and even sympathy where the mates are not incompatible sexually and temperamentally. Thus, contrary to what is sometimes alleged, the average husband of aboriginal society does not abuse his wife. The division of labor is generally fair, and there is no beating without due cause as recognized by the particular social tradition. In this intricate relationship, however, much depends on the individuals concerned, who may snap their fingers at the most firmly rooted conventions and theories. Chinese philosophers may think of women as inferior and as allied to the evil principle of the universe. Nevertheless, as everywhere else, stories and popular prints are full of reference to henpecked husbands. On the other hand, in the United States women vote, can be elected to the governor's chair, and are socially on a par with men. All this to the contrary notwithstanding, they are sometimes beaten up by their husbands. What is more, irrespective of equality, many wish to be coddled, and some hanker after rough treatment.

So far we have been looking at what makes all societies alike: the general psychology of the sexes, varying within more or less the same limits everywhere; and the universal tendency to hallow stable mating arrangements that imply obligations and claims. But these can doubtless be influenced, though not wiped off the slate, by the *special* rules laid down by a particular community. Among the Hopi of Arizona a husband always takes up his residence in the home of his wife's family. No matter how sadistically he may be inclined, as a mere lodger of his mother-in-law's he has to check his impulses. The wife's kin will shield her from undeserved thrashings, and if there is a divorce she holds the field while the man departs. On the other hand, where a woman dwells under the eagle eye of her husband's relatives, she has to mind her p's and q's, especially as regards unallowable flirting.

Thus, customs of residence vitally affect each spouse's position; and no matter what may be his or her inborn bent, it makes an enormous difference whether that disposition is balked or is allowed free rein by society. Rules as to domicile may produce other effects. In Melanesia adult men often sleep, eat, work, play, and dance in a club house apart from the women's huts. This arrangement does not *destroy* the family, for each sex still fulfills its distinctive tasks on behalf of the other: the father pays occasional visits to his wife, and the mother rears the children till the boys are old enough to enter the club and the girls to marry. But such an institution does not allow the companionship some Western nations consider essential.

Another social condition that affects the relations of the spouses is the division of labor. The modern washerwoman or factory drudge is self-supporting and casts her vote. Is she better off than a pampered harem beauty or than the sheltered middle-class Victorian housewife? I do not know, but her status with reference to her husband is different—more like the Uganda plantain-grower's or the Crow Indian skin-dresser's.

For reasons explained, polygamy is less significant in this context than one might imagine. Often the wives are sisters or cousins and live quite amicably with their joint husband. Or each may have her own hut, so that a wealthy South African with eight or ten wives is like an overseer or headman of a small camp. Also, since the first wife so frequently urges her husband to get additional mates,[1] she has little cause for grievance. In fact, her status is improved, since she becomes the mistress of a maid or more. Occasional jealousies arise, of course, as happens wherever human beings are brought into close contact, whether on a camping trip or in wedlock. But these outbursts are no more serious than the extra-marital amours of Europeans: they fail to disrupt society or the family. Deeper discontent probably arises mainly when a woman feels that her children are slighted on behalf of another's.

Though polygamy has not the lurid effects popularly sup-

[1] See page 127.

posed, it nevertheless changes the aspect of the conjugal relationship. Or, to be more precise, the institution is connected with a set of circumstances all of which differ from their equivalents in modern society. For instance, how many men in the United States today can support six wives? A Zulu is better off with twice that number because they largely support him. But since their value is known, he has to pay for them, and that he may not be able to do till he is an elderly man. Then he will no longer satisfy them and they cast about for intrigues with the poor bachelors of the tribe. Inasmuch, however, as the children all belong to the legal husband, who is further entitled to damages from the adulterer, all is well from the native point of view, though not so well from ours.

We should not forget that the law of Christian nations has during certain periods connived at concubinage, that is, given legal status to the concubine. This holds for the code of thirteenth-century Spain as revealed in *Las Siete Partidas*. Elsewhere, indeed, the Age of Chivalry also treated a knight's *amie* with all possible honors.

In no society do parents lose interest in their children as soon as they are weaned. Incidentally, the suckling period is usually very long in savage communities. I have seen a four-year-old Navaho boy run to his mother's breast, and the Rev. Hr. Gutmann has made similar observations in East Africa. Mothers are passionately fond of their children, and so are the legal fathers, whether they have begotten them or not. This seems strange to us only because the traditional notion of paternity has become an obsession. Primitive folk are constantly adopting children and lavish upon them as much emotion as upon their own issue. It is natural for an adult male to like children; he takes a special interest in the offspring of the woman he has protected during her pregnancy; and when these grow up in his company, association deepens the emotion. Indeed, the second link in the chain is unnecessary, as when the Negro husband wants his runaway wife's children even if they are obviously not the issue of his loins.

With all this love of progeny, why do some tribes kill infants at birth? The reasons vary; they are sometimes discreditable to native intelligence, rarely to native feeling. For instance, there is the case of twins. They are a bit out of the ordinary, and what is unusual readily assumes one of two aspects in the primitive mind: it is either hailed as auspicious or feared as ominous. Both attitudes may be found in the same race, indeed. In the Congo, the Bakuba rejoice over twins, and their fathers are honored by having a delegate at court. But the East African Jagga put one of the infants to death to ward off a calamity. If triplets are born, all three are killed, and their mother is despised as a moral leper. This reminds one of the medieval notion that multiple births must each be due to a distinct father.

Then there is the notion of sacrifice. In Tahiti the Polynesians had a society called the Areoi, whose members throttled their children at birth—on pain of being expelled from the organization for failure to do so. Even this, however, was not callous murder, but merely the offering of a precious gift to the god Oro—an act of renunciation.

Another cause of infant-killing is grim necessity. On March 28, 1726, Hans Egede, the Danish missionary, was immeasurably shocked when a Greenlander put his three-day-old infant into his wife's grave; the woman had died in childbed. But what was the poor man to do? There was no baby farming in Greenland. In a small settlement it was not possible to find a woman who could give suck to another's offspring, and the available food was quite unfit for a newborn infant. The alternatives were starvation or burial with the parent.

Again, as in part of the Eskimo country, the provisions may be so scarce that a number of newborn children are put out of the way—females, because here the getting of food falls on the men's shoulders.

Invariably the babies allowed to live are treated more affectionately than in the average white family. To deny a child anything he cries for impresses the crude savage as incredible callousness. This feeling is not confined to their own offspring: a missionary in Africa had difficulty in keeping the blacks from upsetting his son's stomach with sweets. There is rarely any form of corporal punishment; in many tribes, never. In a New Guinea village the natives came near lynching a white trader for beating his own child! Compare this point of view with that of civilized Europe until a few decades ago. Dickens' *Oliver Twist* and *Nicholas Nickleby* might be barred as exaggerating the facts, but truth is weirder than fiction. Dr. Samuel Johnson praised one of his masters as a good teacher because he had flogged him well. Was not the pedagogical wisdom of the ages boiled down into the proverb of "Spare the rod, spoil the child"?

Well, the rod was not spared. When knighthood was in flower, the youthful aspirant to chivalry was soundly thrashed for disobedience. In much later times both sexes in all circles of society were raised on the same principle. If Marguerite of Valois spoke correct Latin, it was because her instructors had beaten it into her. Henry IV expressly ordered his son's governess to whip the prince, since "there was nothing in the world more profitable to him" (*qu'il n'y a rien au monde qui luy face plus de profict que cela*). The dauphin's floggings are accordingly registered with touching fidelity. There are such entries as:

October 9, 1603. Woke up at eight o'clock. He was stubborn and was flogged for the first time. [He was born on Sept. 27, 1601.]

March 4, 1604. At eleven o'clock he wishes to dine. When the dinner was brought in, he had it taken out again, then brought back. Troublesome, severely whipped [*fouetté bien fort*].

On May 14, 1610, he was proclaimed king, went to Parliament, received a delegation, and what not. But even after his coronation as King of France he was not exempt. The nine-year-old's reflections on the subject are not without a note of pathos: "I should rather do without so much obeisance and honor, if they wouldn't have me whipped" (*J'aimerois mieux qu'on ne me fist point tant de révérences et tant d'honneur, et qu'on ne me fist point fouetter*). Louis XIV was not favored with so careful an education; nevertheless as a prince he was by no means spared, and his eldest son was cowed and beaten into imbecility by his tutors. In the second half of the eighteenth century Chateaubriand, the son of a haughty nobleman, was freely reviled by his penmanship teacher, who would pommel him with his fists for good measure. The old count, whose very presence froze wife and children into statues, was not likely to object to such sound pedagogy.

Education will be discussed more fully later on. Suffice it now to point out that much of it is given outside of the family circle. Even with us the child is far more intent on the approval of his playmates than on his parents'. This is easily observed in any American immigrant home, where neither bulldozing nor bribery will make the children learn their parents' tongue, because they *will* be like other boys and girls. This tendency is often emphasized among primitives; young boys are set off by themselves in a separate encampment, and so are the young girls. The constant association with one's age-mates thus throws their influence into relief, to the detriment of the effects due to the parents' home. Even when a Melanesian boy enters his father's club house, he is not *with* his father, but in a separate compartment of lower rank; and had he trespassed on a higher one in the old days he would have suffered death. With the mother there is an even greater break, for henceforth the adolescent never more sleeps or eats in her hut. This separation need not destroy the family bond, but it certainly modifies its nature. Imagine once more an American family in which father and son, say from his twelfth year, regularly dine and sleep out.

But even where the children are not so separated, social conventions may give a flavor to family relations such as is quite foreign to us. Let us return to the Hopi.[1] The father's status with reference to the children is different because he is not master of the house, which belongs to his mother-in-law and her daughters. His home—the one to which he returns if divorced and upon whose shelter he has a moral claim—belongs to his mother and sisters. His children, then, growing up with the children of his wife's sisters, become more closely associated with them than with other cousins. Also they have more constant intercourse with their maternal than with their paternal uncles and aunts. Even after marriage a mother's brother will stroll into his old homestead to loaf with his nephews and nieces and perhaps instruct them in religious beliefs. Here it is also customary for a man to pass on his priestly office not to his sons but to his sister's sons.

In such conditions the father's control of his children is of course limited by his wife's kin. As a matter of fact, there are many tribes without the Hopi rule of residence which

[1] See page 134.

nevertheless confer authority on the maternal uncle rather than the father. Often a girl cannot be married without his consent, and the lion's share of the bride-price may go to him. Also, not only office but wives and material goods, too, will be inherited by a man's nephew (through his sister) and not by his own sons.

This may lead to dramatic conflicts. From the Tsimshian of British Columbia and the Trobrianders near New Guinea come similar reports of divided loyalty. The maternal uncle educates and controls his nephews, and it is his duty to protect their interests. Yet sentimentally he is more strongly attached to the children he has fostered from infancy, his wife's children whom he treats as his own, whether they are or not. Inclination prompts him to neglect his duties and to favor his wife's children whenever their welfare is contrary to his nephews'. This situation could not arise in our modern Western civilization, where the "paternal instinct" has unhindered leeway instead of being balked by a legal convention. Family life cannot be the same in the two instances.

On the whole, brotherly feeling is more powerful among primitives than with us. Brothers share one another's possessions, revenge one another's grievances, and protect their sisters, who in turn cook and make clothes for the boys. The girls help one another at gardening and in the housework. This general picture nevertheless does not do justice to many relevant facts. When the lust for property and power grows, the savages display the same frailties as civilized whites, so that in Africa, where autocratic institutions prevail, there are as many family brawls as in medieval Europe, and one brother is quite as likely to banish or slay another in order to gain the throne.

Certain marriage rules [1] fundamentally alter the char-

[1] See page 126.

acter of this relationship in ever so many tribes. When a man inherits his elder brother's widow, while a girl is her elder sister's probable fellow spouse or successor, these relationships bear another meaning than with us. Of course, that meaning is only part of a larger whole: the conception of the individual as a member of the family. A modern American treats wooing and marriage as personal matters and expects no help from his brothers when he sets up a new household; hence they stake no claim for their sister-in-law's person. Again, where a man regularly gets the bride-price from the sum his own sister fetches in the market,[1] a peculiar relation is set up between the two. No wonder that a West African parent exhorts his son not to abuse his sister: she might be driven into suicide, and what would then become of his chances of matrimony?

But one arrangement cuts deeper still. In Melanesia an inexorable law separates brother and sister from early childhood on. They must neither speak to each other nor have any intercourse whatsoever; indeed they are often raised in different settlements to forestall such an event. In North America there are similar rules, though not quite so severe. A Crow Indian regards our customs in the matter as singularly shameless. He would protect his sister and expect her to make moccasins for him, but they would never freely chat together. If he comes to a tent and finds his sister alone, he says anything vital he has to convey to her and then withdraws forthwith. In neither of these two areas is the confidential intimacy between brother and sister conceivable, let alone possible. Certainly, the Crow and the Trobriander have a family life; but it is not *our* family life.

The pattern of avoidance which in Melanesia holds between brother and sister is far more widely applied to

[1] See page 126.

parents-in-law. This has nothing to do psychologically with our mother-in-law jokes, for the reason a man shuns his wife's mother, and vice versa, is not hostility but mutual awe. Moreover, in some regions the same rules separate a daughter-in-law from her husband's father. In one form or another the custom exists in all continents.

A Crow will not ask his wife's mother the simplest question if she is two feet away, except through her daughter or some other go-between. In East Africa the Jagga forbid the two to see each other until a child is born. Should a man chance upon his mother-in-law on the road, he conceals himself. If she appears unexpectedly at his house, he finds a hiding-place and sneaks off as soon as he can. The Lango along the upper Nile go still further. If a man wishes to pass through the village in which the mother-in-law lives, he sends word ahead to prevent her getting into his way. If she seeks refuge in his village, she has to be carried there on a litter, the bearers covering her with a cowhide until her daughter's husband has prepared a hut for her and has left the settlement. On one occasion a woman invited her mother without telling her husband, who thrashed her severely for this outrage on decency and was upheld by her own kin, although the old woman had left before her son-in-law's arrival. To break the taboo is said to cause death to the old woman, the husband, the wife or her child!

Often the child-in-law is prohibited from uttering the parent-in-law's name or any word that forms part of it, so that odd circumlocutions are invented. For instance, a Plains Indian woman might be named "Yellow-buffalo"; in that case her son-in-law would have to call yellow something like "the color of autumn leaves" and the buffalo "the big humped animal."

But not all connections by marriage are treated after this

fashion. At the opposite pole from awe-inspired avoidance stands unbridled familiarity. A Blackfoot bandies the vilest jests with his sister-in-law. A Crow will shun his wife's mother and be very circumspect when her brother is about; but with her sister he can do much as he pleases. I have seen a middle-aged man handle in the freest manner the body of his wife's sister while his wife and adult son were looking on and evidently considered the procedure quite proper.

Whatever the reason for these practices, they imply notions of family life very far from ours.

Is the primitive family looser than ours? It might seem so because divorce is commonly easier. Also the strict division of labor, the disabilities imposed on women socially, the bachelors' camps apart from the married couples, such laws as the Melanesian brother-sister taboo—these and other institutions all tend to separate husband and wife, parent and child, brother and sister. But in reality none of these customs interferes with the discharge of certain traditional duties. A Trobriander never sees his sister, but he plants largely to support her household and rears her sons. That is as firmly established a regulation as that American parents must provide for their offspring. The norms vary, but there *are* norms, there is a certain stability.

Nevertheless, the savage family *is* loose because the family in the nature of the case is a loose type of social unit. Or, to put it in other words, the *type* it represents is permanent, but any particular sample of it must be loose. For the only way of founding a family is to marry, and that means that one partner at least severs in some way his connection with the house group of his past. This evidently changes both families concerned, no matter what rule of residence is followed. Either the young couple set up a house of their own; and then both families suffer a loss; or the bridegroom goes to his parents-in-law; and then his own kin lose him and his wife's household receives an addition not related to the other inmates by blood. And in the reverse case there are corresponding changes. There is thus an unavoidable shift. Civilized society favors the newly forming family unit in making the wife inherit from her husband. Most savage tribes favor the old family unit by disinheriting the spouse and affirming his and her union with the kin among whom they were born. Neither the primitive nor the civilized form can be said to be looser or more stable on that account, and neither can get around the inherent difficulties of the situation.

These are often wrongly blamed on modern industrialism. But let us go back to Benjamin Franklin again, who lived before the machine age. His father, Josiah, had seven children by his first wife, and ten by his second; Benjamin remembered thirteen sitting together at one table, all of whom married. Allotting to each of the twelve other couples five children each, Benjamin would have a minimum of two parents, twelve brothers and sisters, as many brothers- and sisters-in-law, and sixty nephews and nieces, in addition to his own wife, her children, and all his cousins. Nobody could maintain intimate relations with that number of human beings. It is clear that he didn't and that no one else in the family did. Even the narrowest circle of kindred did not remain united. One of the sons broke away and went to sea. Benjamin was apprenticed for nine years to his brother James, a printer, who beat him and treated him exactly like any other apprentice, "which I took extremely amiss." So Benjamin ran off, whereupon James went to the other printers in town, warning them against giving the rebel employment. The father sided with the older son; so Benjamin quietly slipped away to New York and Philadelphia, his whereabouts being known only to one of his friends. After seven months' absence he turned up in Boston, but instead of tarrying went back to Philadelphia, sailed for London, and returned to Philadelphia after an eighteen months' stay in England. "After *ten* years' absence from Boston . . . I made a journey thither to visit my relations, which I could not sooner well afford."

In what sense was the unit into which Franklin was born a permanent one? How did it correspond to our ideals of family solidarity? Shall the brother who escaped to sea be reckoned a member of the group? If so, why? And in what sense was Benjamin a member during that ten years' absence? And what kind of *family* relationship is it by which a brother is formally apprenticed to another? The conditions of life a hundred and fifty years ago were not more likely to preserve the individual family than modern conditions. The more mouths there were to be fed, the more urgent was early separation; real understanding among all the members grew impossible, wholesale estrangements inevitable. Nothing is more instructive than the polite concern Benjamin expresses over this or that sister's illness or death, or his casual reference to "my sister Lydia, who I hear is lately married."

CHAPTER XV

CLAN AND STATE

FATHER, mother, and children, then, cannot be held together for good, certainly not with the same force as when their relations begin. This holds for us today, for our ancestors 200 or 2,000 years ago, and for savages. But a less intimate bond *may* last and take in more people. Suppose Mrs. Josiah Franklin, born Abiah Folger, to have been the only wife married by Benjamin's father. Further, imagine her to have married on the Hopi plan—with her husband and her sisters' husbands all dwelling under the roof of Mother Folger. The offspring of these unions would not be ticketed by their fathers' names or homes. These would not furnish a common denominator; while Benjamin's father would be a Franklin, his aunts might have wedded Browns and Smiths. On the other hand, the mothers share the Folger home and pass it on to their daughters. There is thus a line of landladies, all descended from one ancestress, who form a stable core of relatives for any child born and raised in the house, while there is no telling how soon any of the husbands will be divorced and leave. Naturally, then, boys and girls take their mother's rather than their father's name. However, only the girls pass it on to the next generation by the Hopi law of female descent.

For several reasons the Folgers feel differently toward one another than even close relatives in the real Franklin household. A Hopi does not run to sea or wander off for years, like young Josiah and Benjamin, respectively. Even when he lives with his wife, he comes in regularly to visit, to pet the children, in the old familiar mansion. He is bound to its inmates by a common ceremony and sacred bundle that go with the house. Then there is the common name, which in itself means much more than with us. A Folger owes Folgers service and protection, and he can expect them in return. He may not feel toward a remote namesake as he does toward a beloved brother. But civilization palsies even a brother's affection: James Franklin beats Benjamin as he would any other apprentice. The loose family bond snaps; the less personal tie with a house, a lineage, a ritual, endures. No Hopi would treat his remotest fellow Folger as though he were *not* a Folger. Thus dozens of individuals may be leagued together for offensive and defensive purposes.

Exactly the same sort of result is brought about by the reverse arrangement. If the men own the houses or bring their wives to their settlement, the children born in one mansion or locality will have a stable core of male relatives. The grandfather, father and father's brothers, brothers, sons and brothers' sons, would then always be with the Franklin home or hamlet. A common name and any other common interest would cement the group into a solid unit as in the Hopi case. Only now the girls would leave the old home, and only the men would hand down their name to posterity. This is what happens among the Miwok of central California and some of the southern California tribes.

Such one-sided bodies of kin, whether through maternal or paternal descent, may be called "clans." Actually, most clans are composed of more than one lineage of genuine relatives. How this comes about may be studied among the Hopi, where some clans are made up only of blood-relatives through the mother, while others are formed by several such lineages. What has happened is simply this. Some lineages became reduced in numbers and felt the need of tying up with a larger group; or perhaps mere sympathy or common religious interests made two lineages join to make a single one. In course of time people forget that some of their namesakes had a different origin from their own. Those who were admitted as Folgers by courtesy come to be considered true descendants of Grandma Folger. By this sort of adoption ultimately hundreds of people may be united as a body of blood-kin where the real lineage would only number dozens.

The fiction that unrelated people are kinsfolk has a widespread consequence: persons bearing the same clan name are forbidden to marry. A Crow Sore-lip would be jeered if he married a woman of his clan, even though no one could prove a relationship; people would say that he had married his sister. Indeed, savages commonly addressed clansfolk of their own generation as brothers and sisters. The Australians were stricter than the Crow. If a Kangaroo man mated with a Kangaroo woman even of another tribe, he was guilty of incest and liable to be knocked over the head.

The clan thus formed a social and political unit that was larger and also more stable than the family. By legal fiction it could expand far beyond any family group. It is not indispensable to human society, for the simplest and the most complex cultures lack it. But it appears on intermediate levels and seems to pave the way for firmly-knit states. In America the ruder hunters have only the family; higher hunters and hoe farmers have clans as well; the advanced Peruvians and Mexicans (like the ancient Chinese, Greeks, and Romans) still had at least clear traces of clan systems but they were eclipsed by another form of political organization, the state.

The state is the central power that controls the people within a given area. In Southern California the clan coincides with the state, because it owns land and acts as an independent political unit in war and peace. But such a clan cannot expand indefinitely without trespassing on land of other equally sovereign clans. It could, of course, conquer these, make itself the ruling class over a wide stretch of country, and degrade the other people into commoners or even slaves. That is how states have been founded in other regions, though not in California.

Far more commonly two or several primitive clans share a tract of land. Then the clan may come into conflict with the larger state idea. A Crow Sore-lip kills a Whistling-water man. The murderer's clan protects him, while the Whistling-waters clamor for revenge. In this pretty how-de-do the Crow tribe is liable to go to pieces, separating out again into its component clans.

That is, however, only what *would* happen if the thirteen clans all felt like so many independent states. In reality, the clan tie merely overshadows the broader loyalty, but the latter exists in weaker form. Were it otherwise, a Sore-lip would kill a Whistling-water in the same spirit in which he kills a Cheyenne or Sioux, and the more the merrier. There would be scalping and gloating over a victory. But of all this there is not a trace. A Crow has been taught from infancy that even a brawl with a fellow citizen is disgraceful. So the Sore-lips are greatly put out over their clansman's deed. They rally, indeed, to protect him against revenge. But they feel jointly responsible and are willing to make amends by paying an indemnity. A peace-pipe is smoked and there is a reconciliation. Neighborliness prevents the threatened rupture.

The machinery falls short in that everything is left to the parties at odds. If the criminal's side were not conciliatory, a feud would certainly break out and there might be a real schism. The Hidatsa of North Dakota made a further step. A police society took the initiative. They did not, indeed, arrest or punish the criminal. But neither did they leave reconciliation to mere chance: filling a peace-pipe for the wronged party to smoke, they gathered together property for them, and with gentle words tried to turn away their wrath. That is to say, the Hidatsa had an official go-between. They saw that the possible feud was not a mere private quarrel of two clans, but touched the life of the "nation." Hence, the police had authority, not to coerce but at least to play the part of moderator.

Even a people with still less government, the Ifugao of the Philippines, have a device of similar type. They have been described as true anarchists, with every family in a village (they have no clans) the possible enemy of every other. Yet even they are not without the milk of neighborliness. A thief from another settlement is killed when caught; a pilfering fellow villager merely pays a fine. It's the story of the Crow Sore-lip as against a Crow Whistling-water or against a Cheyenne. Here, too, a feud is not treated as a private affair between two families. The community *is* interested, and go-betweens, though wholly without authority, try to make a peaceable settlement.

In short, everywhere a man owes *something* to his neighbors as well as to his kin. It is this local tie that lies at the root of the modern state and warrants us in saying that the germ of a state is as universal as the family.

Even among the Plains Indians it becomes much more than a germ. Under ordinary conditions an individual there was free to do much as he pleased so far as compulsion went. But when the tribal buffalo hunt came, this personal liberty vanished in thin air. The police force, which had merely advisory powers in case of murder, now assumed complete control. Any false movement might endanger the food supply of the people; so no one was allowed to give chase until the order was issued. The police held the camp in the vise-like grip of a wartime government. If any one disobeyed, they gave him a drubbing and took away his property; if he offered resistance, they might kill him.

In other words, murder was not considered a crime, that is, an offense against the state; it was merely a lamentable personal wrong. But disobeying the rules of the hunt *was* a crime, and the state rose in all its majesty to smite the culprit.

What loomed in the Plains as an occasional phenomenon due to the stress of threatening starvation was the normal condition in many parts of Africa. There was a strong permanent central authority, often a king with unlimited power over life, death, and property. The Kaffir in the Southeast had no feuds; the king would not tolerate it. Every case had to be brought before a magistrate, that is, the local chief, who represented the monarch. Further, injury to a person was a crime against the Crown, while cases involving property rights belonged to civil law. With this there went the taking of evidence and an elaborate court procedure. In some of the African monarchies several million people were thus governed by the all-controlling force of a ruler and his ministers.

How advanced all this appears alongside of the lowly Crow system! What, however, does it mean in simple human terms? When a Crow was slain in a fight, his relatives received compensation. But a Kaffir king owned his subjects' bodies; so he alone had claims on the indemnity paid. The humbler Crow knew no punishment but fines and personal chastisement. In the great kingdom of Uganda justice introduced a refinement; offenders could be put into the stocks, which often crippled them for life, since the rubbing of the wood against the foot soon made a terrible sore. The Crow had next to no legal procedure, while the Africans reveled in taking evidence. But evidence meant making the defendant swallow a poisonous bean: to clear himself all he had to do was to survivc the test. Doubtless, too, a subject of Zululand or Uganda in their palmier days was less likely to be robbed and murdered by foreign raiders than an Indian of the Plains. He had the superior privilege of being ground under the heel of a native despot. Wealth was not hoarded in Uganda, for the King would seize it "on some trifling pretext." In other African countries it was easy for the chief to present a charge of witchcraft against a man he envied. The public, crazed with fear of sorcery, always inclined to favor a conviction. That could be easily secured by proper attention to the poison ordeal, and the criminal's property naturally reverted to the Crown. There were other advantages in living under the protection of a powerful monarch. At the bidding of an oracle the King would decree that dozens of human beings were to be sacrificed to the gods, and his chief of police directed the executioners. "The party conducting these prisoners was one to be avoided; no sooner did they leave the royal presence, than they began to loot and plunder wherever they went. If they caught any one, he would be added to the number of their victims, unless he promised them a reward for being set free; women would be enslaved, and property plundered on all sides." In West Africa, too, hundreds of victims were massacred to take messages from the King to the ghosts of his forefathers.

Of course, we must not imagine that the Negroes viewed such matters from our angle. Being human, they preferred life to death; but there was rarely any whimpering. They were much like conscripts drafted into a civilized army as part of their patriotic duties. "The victims went to death (so they thought) to save their country and race from some calamity, and they laid down their lives without a murmur or a struggle." This romantic loyalty of Negroes has been tested more than once. South Africans will blindly obey the chief who orders them to catch a crocodile or a lion. They are almost pathologically fond of their live stock, but in 1857 they destroyed cattle by the hundred at their ruler's bidding. In 1851 the British governor set a bounty of five hundred head of cattle on the king's head, but not one of his subjects betrayed him.

The same frame of mind crops up in the South Seas. There a chief might take what he wished of the commoners' possessions and earnings. The German pre-war officials tried to stop such outrages, but the people submitted to them as before. They were not citizens of a civilized country evading an income tax. Rendering to Caesar what Caesar exacted was a sacred duty, and no force was required to keep up the custom.

Is the institution of strong organized government a progressive or a backward step? When we consider the brigands of China holding up travelers and defying the city and provincial authorities we are tempted to cast our vote for centralization of power. But let us take a few examples from European history. On behalf of public safety Louis XIV founded the police organization of Paris in 1667. At once prying stool-pigeons began to invade private life, and suspects were clapped into the Bastille without legal formality. To get back to fundamentals, the rise of nationalism is commonly described as a marvelous thing. In the early Middle Ages, noble was pitted against noble as one Crow clan might be against another. The King's peace seems a great advance. But practically it meant that while hitherto the barons had abused the commoners, a powerful autocrat now despoiled and executed at will both barons and people. According to the early crude Germanic law the judges were laymen, and since, as among the Crow, most offenses were not crimes against the state but personal grievances, no magistrate could proceed unless a plaintiff preferred a charge. The defendant was then allowed to defend himself publicly and could not be convicted except by his own confession or the testimony of eyewitnesses. But as the central power grew, all this changed. The judges were now professionals steeped in Roman law. As agents of the state they might prosecute without a complaint and without giving the accused a chance to clear himself. The result of this professionalism was to perfect torture in order to wring confessions from the defendant and to inflict barbarous penalties for trifling offenses. Evidence continued to be taken as before, on the principle of Negro witch ordeals. Burning and quartering remained as forms of punishment. Witches were condemned to death after 1750. In eighteenth century England a pickpocket was hanged for a theft above a shilling's worth.

Man swings back and forth between two alternatives. Sometimes he tries to establish order, sometimes he lusts for liberty; to combine both seems beyond his powers. Has our society solved the problem? Alas! we have not even solved that of order pure and simple. Theoretically, of course, we have accomplished miracles. The state is absolutely sovereign within its own borders and controls all of its citizens. In practice it has never ceased to bungle its foremost task. For proof all we have to do is to look at the headlines of any metropolitan newspaper. In 1750 London was infested by robber bands in league with an organized army of fences. Historians put the blame on such conditions as the darkness of the streets and the lack of policemen. Our streets are well illuminated today, and every city of consequence has a large police force; nevertheless gangsters in New York and Chicago arm themselves with machine-guns and defy the officers of the law. And that measures our success under normal conditions. When the police go on strike, as they did in Boston some years ago, bedlam turns loose.

Let us now go back to our Crow camp. By taking murder for an illustration of how their law works, we have really done an injustice to the Indians, for normally nothing of the sort occurs. Without jails, judges, or a coercive police (except during a tribal hunt) they manage to live together in amicable relations. How is this possible?

In order not to be unfair to complex civilizations, we must note that one chief goad to crime is wanting on the Plains. The food problem exists, but equally for all. So long as there is a supply, no one is allowed to starve. Commonly primitives do not consider food "property" at all, and it seems sheer Caucasian callousness to them that a white butcher or trader should *sell* meat. On the other hand, objects of dress may be freely borrowed from one's kin, and really valuable forms of property like sacred bundles are safeguarded by the ideas about them. It would not help any one to steal one of these fetiches unless he knew all about its history, the song linked with it, and the precise way it has to be treated. Indeed, possession might be dangerous, for even a slight error would bring down a calamity upon his head.

But superstitious dread is not the greatest single cause of the normal peace in a primitive community. That is public opinion. Primitive man wants, above all, to shine before his fellows; he craves praise and abhors the loss of "face." There are, of course, unsocial beings and defectives everywhere who flout the standards in which they have been raised, but in primitive groups they are exceptional. What sort of behavior is approved, of course, differs in different areas. A Melanesian dreams of getting to the highest grade of the men's club house; a Crow warrior, of accomplishing the four feats of bravery that earn the title of "chief"; a Cheyenne woman, of embroidering thirty robes with porcupine quillwork; a South African, of buying plenty of wives and getting a brood of children. And as there are things to be striven for, so there are deeds to be shunned, no matter how tempting. When a Fox Indian boy in Illinois was taught not to steal and never to abuse his wife, his elder did not hold up to him any tangible punishment here or hereafter nor any abstract rule of morality. The clinching argument was: "The people will say many things about you, though you may not know it."

Gossiping sometimes took special forms of ridicule. An Alaskan youth thus reports his experience: "If you do not marry within your village, they joke about you—they joke so much that it makes it disagreeable." The Crow sang songs in mockery of a miser, a bully, or a man who should take back a divorced wife—the acme of disgrace. Certain kinsmen had the privilege of publicly criticizing a man for breaches of etiquette and ethics, and there was nothing he would fear more than to be thus pilloried. This system was developed by the Blackfoot along slightly different lines. "For mild persistent misconduct, a method of formal ridicule is sometimes practiced. When the offender has failed to take hints and suggestions, the head men may take formal notice and decide to resort to discipline. Some evening when all are in their tipis, a head man will call out to a neighbor asking if he has observed the conduct of Mr. A. This starts a general conversation between the many tipis, in which all the grotesque and hideous features of Mr. A.'s acts are held up to general ridicule, amid shrieks of laughter, the grilling continuing until far into the night. The mortification of the victim is extreme and usually drives him into temporary exile, or, as formerly, upon the warpath to do desperate deeds."

A primitive man sacrifices half his property lest he be dubbed a miser; he yields a favorite wife if jealousy is against the code; he risks life itself if that is the way to gain the honor of a public eulogy. That is why savages of the same tribe are not forever cutting one another's throats or ravishing available women, even if they lack written constitutions, jails, a police force, and revealed religion.

CHAPTER XVI

PRESTIGE AND ETIQUETTE

MAN is a peacock. He likes to flirt, to smile, to wallow in riches, but he will play the ascetic or the spendthrift if it gives him a chance to strut. Mere power and material profit are not romantic enough; they do not make life worth while without the tinsel of prestige.

Why, for instance, did an Indian chief on the British Columbia coast amass blankets by the thousand? To give them away at a public feast and show how little such a princely gift meant to him! That was the way to gain fame and to score against his rivals. For the same reason he would destroy a valuable boat or kill a slave in cold blood—just to show every one that such a loss was a mere trifle to so great a man. Even the money-mad Yurok further south were not *so* crazy for pelf as to sell food. "It wasn't done" by a gentleman. If any one stooped to such baseness, a patrician of the old school would sneer, "May *he* do it, he is half poor." In the same vein these misers would not stint themselves in buying a wife, but mortified their greed. It was reckoned honorable to pay a lot, and to offer a small amount disgraced not only oneself but made bastards of one's children.

Much the same spirit is shown in Melanesia. A Banks Islander cheerfully pays higher and higher initiation fees as he gets promoted from one grade in the club house to another.[1] For the higher he gets, the better his social position; and if he manages to climb to the top rank, he becomes a

[1] See page 157.

chief. But the lust for praise will not let him rest on his laurels. Some one *might* say that he was stingy, so he goes on giving lavish entertainments, slaughtering countless pigs for the people at large. Doubtless he would rather eat them himself—but he would rather not eat them than lose his standing.

If there were some practical end to be gained by all this self-sacrifice, we could explain savage conduct so much better on rational grounds. But over and over again there is nothing of the sort. Polynesian nobles were not much troubled by the proletariat, who were pretty well ground under the heels of their betters. Would it not be sinful to disobey these descendants and fosterlings of the gods? No, what a Polynesian blue-blood worried about was not the class-struggle, but whether some fellow patrician was going to have kava served before himself. *That* would have been an affront if the man favored was not more directly in the line of descent from the gods.

Are democracies more sensible? Alas! there are no egalitarians. The society that really swallows up the individual exists only in the imagination of sociologists. The Plains Indians had no hereditary classes, yet the individual tribesman had an insatiable hankering for recognition. The right to sing a little ceremonial chant, to decorate the face with a simple design, or to put up a sacred lodge, was considered a highly honorable privilege. Hence, in order to rank above his peers, a man was quite willing to buy the "copyright" with a horse or a load of blankets. Above all, the Plains Indians loved to advertise his deeds of bravery. When a Crow stole a horse from the enemy, he often gave it to an old man, who would go through camp and herald the donor's good qualities in a song. But publicity work was not left to others. Whenever people were gathered together, the braves began to count their exploits in war. Every tribe had its own code, and generally the senseless "stunt" ranked higher than an effective blow against the opposite side. A Crow got nothing for killing an enemy, but if he dashed up and was the first to "tag" the corpse of a foeman killed by a comrade, that counted as a real feat. So you might steal a whole herd of horses and get no prestige for your pains, but if you risked your neck cutting loose one picketed horse, that was something to boast of in public assembly. A Crow or Cheyenne was always ready to perform some foolhardy and useless deed in order to be talked about. He resembled the people who tumble down Niagara Falls in a barrel or jump off Brooklyn Bridge. But the savages also resemble us in their fondness for badges of distinction. An Indian brave with wolf-tails dragging at his heels to show that he had struck a foeman was very much like a European decoration-hunter. Or shall we rather compare him to members of our American orders strutting about with outlandish headgear, medieval swords, and other fantastic insignia?

Prestige has strange and varying relations with power. The two naturally go together, yet by no means always do. Among our central Californian natives the political chief was often eclipsed by the "shaman," that is, the doctor-priest or medicine-man, who had no official authority whatsoever but a great deal of influence with the people. In our American cities the mayor may be a mere puppet compared with the machine boss who created him. On a higher level, the prestige of a personality like Theodore Roosevelt's sways millions and gives him even as a private citizen power greater than an office-holder's. On the other hand, a British premier may be the strongest single person in the Empire, but unless he has social status apart from office he must yield precedence to the humblest peer of the realm at a state banquet. Similarly in Tonga, a hundred years ago, King Finau was master of the island, but Polynesian etiquette made him bow before the spiritual lord of the group as his superior. In the early Middle Ages the French kings of the Merovingian dynasty became mere tools in the hands of their ministers. So, among the latter-day Bakuba in the Congo the King is in theory an absolute monarch, and every one treats him with supreme reverence. But actually the reins of government are in the hands of his grandees.

Prestige does not beget etiquette, but it fosters it as its outward symbol. In Europe even a university professor enjoys some esteem. An American scholar traveling abroad thus finds himself unexpectedly a person of consequence, with younger colleagues prancing to and fro at street corners to give him the right-hand side of the road. Plains Indians reserved the rear of a lodge for the host and a specially honored guest. In more complex societies, etiquette becomes elaborate and rises to its acme in the ritual of court life.

The presentation of a French lady under Louis XVI may serve as a sample. First of all, her pedigree had to be approved as sufficiently exalted. Then royalty announced the time of day—always a Sunday—on which the ceremony was to take place. The novice betook herself to Versailles on the eve of the great event, accompanied by her sponsor, and paid official visits to the lady-in-waiting, the lady of the bedchamber, and various princesses. When presented, she wore an enormous hoop-petticoat and a detachable train of incredible length. At the door she made her first obeisance, having been carefully drilled in the proper style. After several steps she made her second, and when close to the Queen a third. Removing her right glove, she stooped and seized the hem of the Queen's skirt to kiss it, but the Queen forestalled the act by pulling back her dress and stepping backward: the will was taken for the deed. The Queen uttered some gracious remarks, then bowed to indicate that the audience was over; and the happy initiate withdrew backwards, skillfully pushing her train aside as she offered her farewell curtsey. A duchess was above the feigned kissing of her Queen's robe; instead she presented to the sovereign her right cheek and had a light kiss imprinted on it.

Even French royalty was subject to the etiquette it had created. The King could not befuddle himself at his own board were he so inclined. For the rules prescribed that as soon as the King had drunk the glass should be taken back to the cupboard. Marie Antoinette loathed dining in public, but once a week she submitted to the ordeal.

The difficulties that hampered the great have not always been fully appreciated. In 1699 the Princess Palatine Elizabeth Charlotte, sister-in-law of Louis XIV, wanted to visit her daughter, who was to be confined in Lorraine. Though her heart was set on the trip, it proved impossible. For the Duke of Lorraine insisted that he was to be treated like an Elector in the presence of "Monsieur," the King's brother, and "Madame," the King's sister-in-law. That is to say, he was to sit in an armchair, since the Emperor himself allowed him that privilege. Louis XIV replied that the imperial code was different from the royal: the Emperor, for example, granted armchairs to cardinals, who were never permitted to sit down before the King of France. The Duke's ancestors had been at the French court and had never laid claim to an armchair. One of them never sat on anything but a footstool before his own sister. Louis was willing to grant a high-backed chair (*chaise à dos*), but never an armchair. His brother proposed an ingenious compromise. Why not follow British precedent? The King of England pretended not to grant Monsieur and Madame an armchair in his presence, while they laid claim to that honor; yet the problem was happily solved by His Britannic Majesty's seating himself on a mere stool (*derowegen setzt er sich nur, wen wir dar sein, auff ein tabouret*) in receiving his near-royal visitors. Monsieur and Madame might do likewise. But Louis would not suffer such abdication of dignity, and the Princess was prevented from seeing her daughter.

Primitive etiquette, however, was not less irksome to the elect. A Samoan chief had all manner of prerogatives. He might appoint a favorite girl relative to the coveted position of village princess. He had to be addressed with a special set of verbs and nouns. His speakers provided him with food and did him honor on every public occasion. Yet a young man's imagination is not fired with the thought of the office. A twenty-seven-year-old chief thus unbosomed himself to Dr. Margaret Mead: "I have been a chief only four years and look, my hair is gray, although in Samoa gray hair comes very slowly. . . . But always, I must act as if I were old. I must walk gravely and with a measured step. I may not dance except upon most solemn occasions, neither may I play games with the young men. Old men of sixty are my companions and watch my every word, lest I make a mistake. Thirty-one people live in my household. For them I must plan, I must find them food and clothing, settle their disputes, arrange their marriages. There is no one in my whole family who dares to scold me or even to address me familiarly by my first name. It is hard to be so young and yet to be a chief."

So in Africa. The poor king of the Bakuba is not allowed to walk or sit on the ground. He rests on a skin or on a slave's back and travels on a litter. He must not address the Queen Dowager but waits till he is spoken to. He may not eat in the presence of women. On state occasions knives of special shape serve as his scepter and he must wear two rings on his big toes. The grandees of the court watch his every move and are not backward in scolding him with studied disdain for a breach of the rules. In West Africa Benin was for a long time the most powerful state, and the ruler was treated as a god. "When his noblemen are in his presence," writes a sixteenth century observer, "they never look him in the face but sit cowering, as we upon our knees, so they upon their buttocks with their elbows upon their knees, and their hands before their faces, not looking up until the king commands them. . . . When they depart from him, they turn not their backs towards him, but go creeping backward with like reverence." However, this divine monarch could not do quite as he pleased. He was never allowed to see his mother so long as she lived, and he never went outside the palace walls except on the occasion of a particular festival.

Perhaps least enviable of all was the lot of a prince in Unyoro, East Africa. He was lucky indeed to survive his father, for the news of the King's death at once precipitated a free-for-all fight among the princes, and the victor took pains to put all his brothers out of the way. But the new monarch was hardly master of his own soul. His diet was rigidly prescribed. He was not allowed to partake of vegetables or of mutton. In the morning and at noon he drank milk, for dinner he ate beef, and before retiring he had to take another ration of milk. He was not permitted to touch food, but was fed by a cook. At midnight one of his wives woke him up and led him to another house, and before dawn he was roused again to resume his slumbers in a third residence. In the morning his wife rubbed his body with butter. As soon as he was seriously ill or lost his virility, his chief wife appeared with a poison cup, and he was obliged to commit suicide.

A comparison of savage etiquette with ours is most encouraging. We are holding our own. Being illiterate is not in itself a safeguard against folly.

CHAPTER XVII

EDUCATION

UNTIL recent times European schoolmasters were wont to lash seven-year-old boys with leather thongs so that they bore the marks as long as they lived. In the seventeenth and eighteenth centuries young counts, princes, and even kings were brutally beaten by their tutors.[1] Primitive peoples, on the other hand, pretty nearly always go to the opposite extreme. There is almost a direct ratio between rudeness of culture and gentleness with children. The Semang, a group of pygmy hunters on the Malay Peninsula, are always seen fondling their offspring and never chastise them. In Ceylon Dr. Seligmann saw a petulant little Vedda hurl an ax at his father, which hit him in the leg. "The man was obviously annoyed and threw the ax from him into the jungle, but he did not attempt to scold or punish the child, who was now howling with rage; indeed, after a little while some food was given him to pacify him." An Australian has been known to beat up his wife for daring to strike her child. In years of South American travel Baron Erland Nordenskiöld met with only one case of corporal punishment by Indian parents: a refractory girl got three light strokes on her calves, buttocks, and back, respectively. Dr. George Bird Grinnell, after studying Plains Indians for decades, writes: "Indians never whip their children. . . . Sometimes a mother irritated by the resistance of a yelling child will give it an impatient shake by one arm as she drags it along, but I have never witnessed anything in the nature of the punishment of a child by a parent."

[1] See page 138.

Negroes perhaps indulge in severity more frequently than the Indians: among the Kaffir a boy who does not take proper care of his father's herds may be soundly thrashed, and West Africans rub pepper into a young thief's eyes. But such instances are exceptional. Of this race, too, observations such as these are more typical: "An attractive feature in the Akambas' nature is their love for children, especially small children. A person who sees any one treating a child brutally will rush wildly to its help, even if he has not the slightest idea whose child it is."

This sort of thing goes very far indeed among the Turks of Central Asia. An only or favorite son is a privileged character in a Kirghiz household. The father will take a three-year-old tenderly into his arms and encourage him to call his mother names, teaching him a varied assortment of vile terms. Whatever we may think of this pedagogical technique, it does not smack of callous brutality toward the young. That sets in when one gets to higher levels. Where an illiterate Crow would at most pour water down an unruly boy's nostrils, an ancient Egyptian scribe relied mainly on flogging to teach his wards how to write. It is the old story of human culture. As soon as conditions get complex, man fumbles, muddles, and bungles. Hieroglyphics are forbidding, and one way to impress the juvenile mind forcibly with their importance is evidently to associate them with a thorough drubbing.

According to the uniform report of travelers, the unflogged children of savages are far less naughty than the children of whites who enjoy the superior advantages of Caucasian sadism. Says Mr. Dudley Kidd of the South African Bantu: "Obedience to parents hardly needs to be taught, for the children notice how every one in the kraal is instinctively obedient to the old men; the children catch this spirit without knowing it. I never remember seeing a small child distinctly and definitely disobedient to its father." Every visitor to the Eskimo marvels at the goodness of their children. "They grow up," writes Holm, "in the most untrammeled liberty. Their parents cherish an unspeakable love for them, and never punish them, however refractory they may be. In spite of this it is wonderful to see how well brought up the little children are. . . . The grown-up children cherish great affection for their old parents, and often display great thoughtfulness and self-sacrifice." In Montana, Cheyenne boys play the roughest games with a minimum of bickering. Of the Bolivian Chimane Nordenskiöld reports, "The children never strike one another." In Arizona Professor Leslie Spier was astonished at the good behavior of the little Havasupai. "They are docile, not forward, reserved before their elders, and, I judge, are never long the topic of their parents' conversation, at least while they are present. Children rarely cry, and this is not frequently for anger or to gain their desires."

Whence this uncanny goodness, largely remains a mystery. One possible factor is encouraging to a mere Caucasian, for otherwise we might blush with shame. The savage makes considerable use of a device we can not sincerely approve—to wit, bugaboos. Any and every kind of bogy will do—a mother will imitate a hooting owl to cow a squalling brat or point at a visiting anthropologist as a likely ogre to kidnap the offender or inflict damage on him. The Pueblo Indians call an owl to pick out the offender's eyes and impart to the child their own abject fear of witches.

At Zuñi, New Mexico, there is even a set ceremonial for impressing naughty children. During one of the native festivals a pair of mummers, one of them disguised as a woman, make the rounds of the village. They chase any youngsters they meet and solemnly enter particular houses. There "they berate and lecture the terrified and often wailing children. The children who have not yet been initiated, children under seven or eight, are terribly frightened and even the older children may be upset. 'You must not mock your parents,' all are instructed. 'You must mind your mother.' 'You must not soil the floor after it has been swept up.' A boy is told he must learn to look after the horses, a girl that she must look after the baby, she must learn to cook and to grind." Then the pedagogical tactics become more strenuous. The "woman" drags some little girl to the stone hand-mill and pretends to grind her up, while her companion with a knife throws his hair back from over his mask and threatens to lop off the children's ears. The masqueraders even mimic cannibalism. If one of the boys has been uncleanly, the clowns who have come with the mummers seize him, take him to the river, and either wash his face or souse him. At last the elders pacify their uncanny guests with presents of food and make them go away.

Another weak spot in savage educational practice must be admitted, although here they are quite on a par with ourselves. All human experience goes to show that formal moral instruction will bore the recipient into rebellion and thus defeat its end. This has never prevented old wiseacres from pouring forth interminable streams of pedantic counsel for the orientation of the younger generation. A Pangwe Negro in Kamerun gives daily lectures to his son, setting forth such gems as these: "Listen to your father's speech, for when you marry later on it is your father that will pay for the girl. If your sweetheart brings you food, do not immediately devour it all, but modestly take two or three spoonfuls lest the girl think you are a glutton and cease to love you. . . . Treat your sister well. If she should abuse you, do not reply in kind. Do not beat her, for the money she fetches in marriage will purchase a wife for yourself. If you beat her, she may commit suicide and you will have neither money nor wife, and people will have no respect for you."

This particular tirade is not so bad in point of effectiveness, for the appeal is evidently to the boy's self-interest. In a more complex culture, that of the Aztec, the advice was naturally more prolix and less likely to do the least good. One of these Poloniuses would lavish a flood of verbiage on a defenseless son. The adolescent was to work industriously, be humble in social intercourse, emulate the example of a distinguished relative, be moderate in fleshly indulgence, and to follow the golden middle path in dress, avoiding alike extravagance and squalor. A girl was treated to a double dose at puberty. First her father admonished her to learn weaving and other domestic accomplishments, so as to do honor to her parents. Suitors were to be treated with proper humility. Then the mother stepped in and laid down the law: a young woman was to be chaste, must bear herself properly in walking, and ought not to use cosmetics, the symbol of sinfulness.

Ridiculous as many of these reported sermons appear, *one* really vital point is often made—the effect of conduct on public opinion. An old Winnebago in Wisconsin would say to a son aspiring to become a doctor, "The people will make fun of you publicly (if you fail). 'A holy man, indeed!' they will call you." Similarly, the Pangwe preacher says, "Be not niggardly with food. Otherwise people will laugh at you and when you visit others you yourself will lack food." [1]

But at adolescence many tribes have much more than

[1] See page 170.

speechifying. This is the time for something like a real school with formal teaching and strict supervision. In some places there is nothing but discipline. In Guiana youths and maidens were not allowed to marry before undergoing a painful rite—exposure to the bites of ants. Within the same region the elders scratched a boy's chest and arms with a beak or a boar's tusk, while a girl menstruating for the first time was soundly flogged or was forbidden to laugh or eat meat.

Elsewhere there is a good deal more than mere discipline. In British Columbia, as soon as a Shuswap lad's voice showed signs of changing, off he went by himself to fast as long as he could stand it, and tried to get a vision. He drank through a tube and scratched his head with a special stick. But apart from these fanciful rules there was real training. Much of the period was spent in shooting at targets and in gymnastic exercises. An adolescent girl was more restricted, but she also got more definite preparation for the tasks of life. She fasted for four days and for a whole year had to use a drinking-tube and a head-scratcher. She never left her hut until dusk. Then she roved over the mountains, bathing at daybreak and praying to the Dawn. Before daylight she had to be back in her retreat, for no one was allowed to see her except her instructor and her nearest relatives. If she met a stranger, she had to shield herself with a screen of fir twigs. On her return she ate some breakfast and lay down to rest, but her guardians did not allow her to sleep too much. While on her ramble she was supposed to practice running, climbing, and carrying of burdens. She also dug trenches as a preparation for root-digging in the future. Every morning she had to fetch a load of firewood. Then her teacher made her do little bags, baskets, and mats, sewing and embroidery, and taught her to tan skins. As an exercise she plucked fir needles from the branches so as to give nimbleness to her fingers.

This sort of thing is arranged on a much bigger scale in Australia. There an initiation ceremony for boys is a gigantic undertaking. Several friendly tribes take part—at least the male portion of them, for the women are not allowed to come near. The old stagers who run the show select all the boys old enough to be initiated as responsible male fellow citizens. In some tribes the novices have a tooth knocked out, in others they are circumcised. The entire ceremony takes weeks, and in the meantime there is much and varied instruction. The boys go on hunting trips during the day, but above all they get religious and moral teaching. They are told to obey the old men, to leave married women alone, to share food with their friends, and under no condition to reveal the secret proceedings to women and the uninitiated boys. They learn how wicked it is to eat a male opossum or honey and other choice morsels reserved for the aged.

In Africa both sexes have their schools, but they are not co-educational. The boys and the girls are carefully kept apart, each group under the direction of a special instructor. In the eastern part of the continent Yao boys between eight and eleven years of age are segregated for three months in a lonely hut. Here they are circumcised, and while recovering from the operation hear sermons about sex relations, about duties to parents and parents-in-law, and about dietary rules. The girls of the same age have each a female mentor, while a mistress of ceremonies presides over the whole flock. Thus they get their first lessons on sex hygiene, to be continued as soon as they menstruate, when their mothers turn them over to the former teachers. In the same way a woman who is pregnant and one who has just given birth to a child receive further instruction. A young mother is told to get up early, to air her infant, massage it, wash it with lukewarm water, and rub it with oil. She also acquires amulets to ward off disease.

In ancient Peru there was vocational training of a different sort. Girls of noble families were kept in "nunneries" at Cuzco, where they learnt to spin and weave garments for the ruler and his wives.[1] It was a lifelong job, for they were considered wives of the Sun and were not allowed to marry a mortal husband.

Aboriginal New Zealand also had schools not connected with puberty or sex instruction. One kind was open to the common herd during the winter season and was held in a building large enough for a hundred people. The pupils were allowed to eat nothing but roasted fern root and had to eat and sleep in fixed places. The course was strictly practical: it had to do with the native crops, fowling, and fishing. Not so in the "sacred college" for the nobility, where only the first-born sons of the patricians were normally admitted. Here there was a three to five years' course in nothing we should consider of the slightest use. For about four or five months each year the pupils, who were admitted in batches of twenty or thirty, learnt all about the myths of their people, the native philosophy, and the magic formulae. They slept during the day and studied until midnight. Every one was pledged to secrecy, and whoever breathed a word to a sweetheart or a friend about what went on inside was at once expelled. The curriculum started with Maori "history," that is, with the mythic traditions about the gods. Then came a seminar in magic. Every detail had to be learnt letter-perfect, for the slightest mistake might spell disaster for every one. None of our college finals can compare with the examination these noble youths had to undergo before graduat-

[1] See page 16.

ing. First a candidate had to throw a little stone at a larger one, and if it broke he failed and had to go back for another term. Next he had to sing one of his spells and by the mere power of his chant cause a hard stone to shiver. If successful, he was expected to use his magic against a dog or a flying bird. If the youth passed this test, he was admitted to the supreme ordeal. The examiner picked out some individual whom the students had to kill by uttering a deadly spell against him. If the victim fell dead at once, all was well; the candidate merely went through some rites of purification and was honorably discharged as a full-fledged alumnus. By what tricks or legal fiction these examinations were ever passed remains unknown.

Maori wizards of less lofty rank were taught essentially similar things, but with not so much ceremony. They, too, acquired a vast number of spells for every imaginable emergency and graduated when they could kill beasts and men or make trees topple to the ground.

Man being what he is, these institutions for imparting legendary lore and magical incantations naturally ranked infinitely above the humble agricultural schools. It was in the same spirit that sixteenth century Europe exalted the superstitious Latin-spouting doctor above the deft barber-surgeon.[1]

As usual, complex conditions mean a clouding of counsel. When the savage gives formal education, he stumbles into the pitfalls of civilized pedagogy. So long as he relies on his inborn common sense, he is abreast of advanced educational theory.

A Plains Indian lad got his bow and arrow at the earliest possible age and was giving chase to small birds or rabbits at eight or ten. When he shot his first deer, the Crow had a

[1] See page 255.

big celebration, and some clansman of the hunter's father went about camp advertising the boy in a song of praise. There was target practice with one's comrades, there were sham buffalo hunts and mock-battles. The players organized into clubs and imitated the ways of their elders. Grown-up braves struck foemen in order to score honors; the youngsters treated buffalo, wolves, or mountain-lions as if they were enemies. In their fraternities they mimicked the style of the men's societies, with all their regalia and offices, so that by the time they were out of their teens they knew enough to fit into one of the genuine tribal organizations. Children played at camp life, the girls pitching miniature tents and packing dogs like their mothers. Since a camp needed food, the boys went foraging, both alone and in groups, so that there was training in coöperation also. "The care," says Grinnell, "with which they twisted and wound in and out of cover when approaching the game, and of the clumps of rye grass, was precisely what they would have to practice when hunting later in life."

All this was capital vocational training. In the same way an Australian lad goes with his father on a hunting trip; while he is enjoying his jaunt, he casually picks up the rudiments of woodcraft, learns to hurl a spear, and gets practice with the boomerang. In the same easy-going fashion the South African Negro child grows into the obligations of later life. The adults are experts at making traps and snares, and tiny children master this technique while they are watching the ripening corn to scare away birds. A slab of stone is propped up at an angle of forty-five degrees; grain is placed so that to disturb it means touching a trigger, which immediately releases the stone so that it crushes the bird. Or, a long flexible stick is planted in the ground, with a slip-knot cord at the free end. This end is bent over so the noose can be fixed to a trigger on the ground. As soon as the quarry puts its head through the noose, the trigger is released, the rod flies up, and the victim is carried into the air in the tightening noose. The Kaffir lads are adept at this sort of contrivance. "No farmer's boy in England," says Mr. Dudley Kidd, "could make such excellent bird traps at the age of three." In parts of the same country the youngsters caught fish in the river, diving in to scare their prey into hand-nets; and as long as big game was still abundant they helped their elders as beaters on the hunt. In the meantime the little girls are at home, learning to cook, to daub the huts with mud, to balance water jars on the head, and other tricks of domestic life. With all this the children of both sexes are never overworked and may freely mingle jollity with labor. Discipline as a rule comes incidentally with the tasks, as when a boy has to herd cattle on a cold wet day.

This sort of system turns up again in northern Siberia. When a Chukchi boy is large enough to grip a knife handle, he gets a specimen tool and gradually learns to wield it in carving and as a weapon. At ten a child of either sex may have to tend herds of reindeer and get his first experience with restless animals. He sleeps more than older herders but has to take his share of hard labor. A few years later he is treated as a full-fledged herder. He has to give a detailed report when he gets home—telling all about the reindeer, the pastures, the mosquitoes and flies.

Our own pedagogues have had much to unlearn and relearn in recent years. They may not go quite so far as the Vedda or Akamba in barring corporal punishment, but nowadays they certainly feel more kinship with primitive methods than with the brutal punishments that flourished even in nineteenth century schools. They must surely approve of the large place given by savages to training for the tasks of real life. Even for the quaint schooling of the Maori noble some excuse can be found if you accept the aboriginal premises. *If* you firmly believe in magic, then learning incantations is surely a matter of great and general utility. Above all, the natural way of letting play and imitation largely take the place of deliberate and formal precept is quite up-to-date. As a Swiss scholar, Dr. Knabenhans, rightly notes, "The very tribes poorest in material culture have achieved a whole set of our most modern educational postulates." Well may we ask, What is Progress?

CHAPTER XVIII

WRITING

PUNS are a sorry form of humor; nevertheless they lie at the basis of higher civilization. A people is "civilized" when it is literate, and true writing developed out of mere pictures by way of punning.

Many primitive tribes draw objects so that they can be recognized; indeed, the French and Spanish artists of 20,000 years ago made such faithful pictures of bison and wild horses that a naturalist has no trouble in identifying the species and sex. Art of this type may, however, be used to convey a definite message and thus serve the purpose of writing. When a Plains Indian painted on his tent a man striking an enemy with a lance or driving off a herd of horses, any one familiar with the customs of the area knew that this was an autobiographical record. In other words, the owner was announcing to the world that *he* had performed the exploits in question. Again, on his travels in northern Siberia Dr. Jochelson once came upon a drawing scratched on birchbark as a letter to his Yukaghir guides. There was a river with its tributary, a few lines above the mouth representing a fish-dam. The artist's route was indicated by a line in the middle of the stream. Some distance from the mouth a grave with a double cross stood for a death and burial. Farther on there were three conical tents to denote a settlement—a temporary one, because of a string of two boats and four canoes ahead to show movement. One of the two migrating households reappears on the tributary with two boats and two canoes. "This means that the people of the tent consisted of two families, although they had only one tent. A boat is distinguished by its steering-oar and paddles while the canoe has only a double paddle." (Fig. 27.)

Such messages can be read *if* you know the system and the local conditions. But pictures cannot express such proposi-

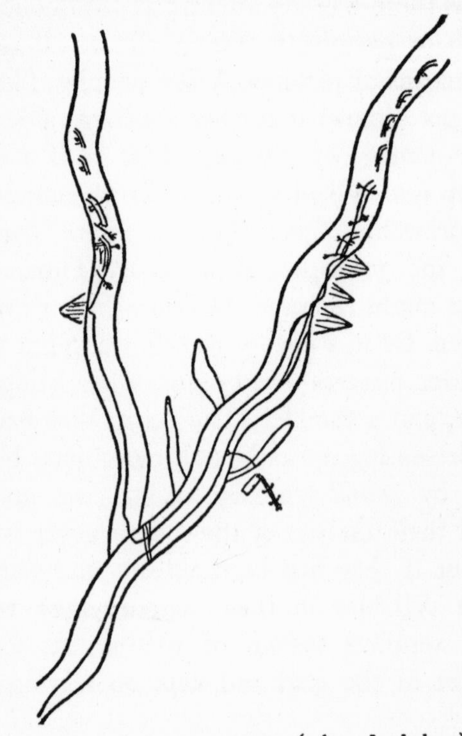

FIG. 27. YUKAGHIR LETTER (*after Jochelson*)

tions as "God is love" or "Honesty is the best policy." They cannot readily and clearly show the order of events. How, for instance, is a reader to know that the Yukaghir wanderers settled on the main stream first and later on the tributary? Further, even the most material things often cannot be clearly denoted by drawing. A circle might equally well represent the sun, the moon, a camp of tents, a hoop, a shield, or a coin. If one draws the crescent for the moon, the question arises whether or not the moon in general is intended, or only in the phases defined. Again, how could a Welsh rabbit or mince-pie be unmistakably portrayed?

Nevertheless, it is a sad commentary on the human mind that so far as there was any attempt at communication, apart from speech or gesture, it was in almost all cases by the inadequate means of pictures. A few peoples, like the Aztec of Mexico, got somewhat further and were able to write at least proper names—*by punning*. That is, if a name could be broken up into syllables each of which sounded more or less like a drawable object, then the entire word could be figured on the principle of a rebus. Thus, playing at charades, we might represent "Carmen" by a toy car and a group of men. Or in a picture puzzle we might write "isinglass" by three pictures—an eye, a human being with wide open mouth, and a tumbler. The Aztec thus had the principle of representing not only concrete objects but any idea whatsoever by *sound*-symbols. It was not an alphabetic method, for their analysis of the sounds never went beyond syllables. But if they had been able to find standard signs for all the syllables in their tongue, they would have achieved a complete system of writing. As it was, they stopped short of the goal and kept on relying mainly on pictures.

Babylonia, Egypt, and China went further and succeeded in reducing to writing the whole of their respective vocabularies. But in each case punning played a dominant part! Truly, a humble origin for literature and all it means to us. Moreover, to those three regions every complete system of writing may be traced. It was not as though all the peoples naturally took to the art—not even those now in the vanguard of progress (in their own judgment). Instead, with characteristic human laziness one society borrowed from another, making such adaptations as were absolutely necessary and almost morbidly avoiding them whenever possible. Even the three ancient nations mentioned may have stimulated one another in a general way, though the details of their systems are distinct. Egyptian and Babylonian writing both developed between 4000 and 3000 B.C., and we know that features of culture passed from one to the other. The Chinese once lived farther west, in contact with the outposts of Babylonian civilization. Though this remains unproved, a vague impulse toward writing might have been conveyed to them. It would be somewhat as if a person nowadays began to work out a new system of shorthand. He might be wholly ignorant of the systems in vogue. But he would know that there were such, also that speed was attained by leaving out vowels and combining distinct words into one; and this knowledge would inevitably color his invention. So the Chinese of 2500 B.C. might have picked up from western neighbors the notion of having many pictures with a standard meaning, even though their drawings would be different. Similarly, they might borrow the jolly idea of punning, which strikes such a responsive chord in simple minds.

What we do know beyond a doubt is that all writing in the Old World *was* borrowed from the three systems mentioned. In Babylonia, the Sumerians began first to chisel and later to press symbols into a substitute for paper. From early times on they used reed pencils on soft clay. At first they made true outlines of objects such as a fish, or at least indicated an ox by a horned head. Later the marks became wedge-shaped and ceased to resemble anything in nature. In short, a set of conventional symbols arose. However, as in Mexico, punning made it possible to represent words by their sounds—with the same limitation that syllables, not simpler sounds, were the unit. But that was sufficient for the phonetic symbols to be taken over by the Akkadians about 2800 B.C. Though they spoke a Semitic language not at all related to Sumerian, they were able to write it with the Sumerian syllabary as we can crudely write other languages with our English letters. Whenever a Sumerian reading resembled an Akkadian word, the old sign was now given this new meaning. Much the same sort of thing happened as when the medieval Londoners heard the King's road called "Route du Roi" and transmuted the name into "Rotten Row," which meant *something* to them, though something very different. The Assyrians followed the Akkadians of the ninth century, while the Persians of the sixth leaned heavily on a late form of the Babylonian system.

Whether Egypt developed her script independently or even earlier than Babylonia or not, she made greater advances and thus came to start the methods that have turned out to be most significant in later civilization. Like the Aztec and the Sumerian, the Egyptian scribe began with pictures, and like them he fell to punning and thus hit on the principle of *phonetic* writing. Like the Sumerian, he applied it in the form of syllabic symbols to all his speech. But he carried his sound analysis from syllables to true letters, of which he came to have twenty-four. There were symbols for all the consonants, the vowels being left to the imagination.

Had the Egyptians been bold innovators, they would now have thrown pictures and syllable marks into the discard. But progress is not that fast; so they kept the old-fashioned pictorial idea along with the consonant alphabet. They never had full faith in the new-fangled scheme, so after spelling a word they added a picture sign—just as if we wrote "man" and drew a human figure after it so there would be no mistake.

However, the essential achievement had been made, and when, about 1000 B.C., the less conservative Phoenicians learnt to write from the Egyptians, they took over only the consonants, not the pictures or syllabic marks, and wrote everything by means of twenty-two letters. The vowels were still omitted. Finally, the Greeks met the Phoenicians and borrowed their alphabet. In this they discovered marks for sounds that did not exist in Greek. Instead of cutting them out, they put them to work as the missing vowels, and thus the first *complete* alphabet sprang into being. Slightly modified by the Romans, it became the basis of ours.

Chinese writing has some features of its own. It is adequate for the writing of the entire vocabulary; yet it is not at all alphabetic nor even entirely phonetic. Like other advanced systems, it is rooted in picture-drawing, the characters later being conventionalized. The Chinese were no better fitted than other folk to make a realistic representation of words like "hay-fever" or "transubstantiation." Partly they got round the difficulty by using objects as symbols of abstraction: a tower might represent "height," and a man with crossed legs "entangle" or "connection." But of course they, too, fell to punning! How, for instance, could one write "come" so that it would not be read as "go"? Well, "come" was called *lai,* which also meant "wheat"; so the picture of the plant could stand for either word. In ancient Chinese, however, this method was inadequate because it led to ambiguity and because at that time there were not yet enough words of similar sound to go round. So the scribes turned to another makeshift: they combined two or more simple pictures to represent associated ideas. For example, a woman with a child expressed the Chinese concept of happiness. Similarly "friendship" was denoted by two hands together.

But, again, there was a difficulty: it was not easy to invent appropriate combinations by the thousand. Once more, the Chinese resorted to punning, but this time in a more refined manner. The older picture puzzle technique had the disadvantage of not being perfectly clear. If you wrote "village" and "thumb" by one and the same symbol, how was a reader to be sure which was meant? In order to remedy this, the Chinese now wrote *two* characters—one a picture of the thumb to give the sound as a whole, the other the sign for "tree," that is, "building material," to show that it was not the thumb itself that was indicated. Thus, a whole series of words sounding more or less alike can be neatly discriminated: *fang*, e.g., might mean "square," "district," "spin," "ask," "kettle," "board." The last five of these words all contain the old picture for a square, and this is a key to the pronunciation. But for "district" the symbol for "earth" is added; for "spin," the sign that means "silk"; and so forth. This combination method was a simple means of solving all difficulties, and, indeed, it holds for 90 per cent. of Chinese writing.

Thus the Chinese developed a partly phonetic scheme. They were not strict phoneticians, allowing *kung*, *kiang*, and *kang* to be treated as one and the same sound. Further, the characters have remained fixed as they were centuries ago, while pronunciation has changed. Hence, what was once a fair index to the sound often fails to give a proper clew to the sound values of today.

The history of writing is a grimly sardonic commentary on man's stupidity. How much of what we prize highest is bound up with the invention! Yet from first to last—and our sketch leaves out half of the story—there is muddling along, mulish clinging to unpractical devices, lazy borrowing of what others have accomplished. Even the Greeks got the essentials from their forerunners and more or less stumbled upon their contribution as a blind chicken will upon a grain of corn. And the great source of progress from picture- to *sound*-writing is man's silly inclination to play upon words!

CHAPTER XIX

ART

Stark-naked savages tattoo or scar their bodies, pierce lips and ears to stick a plug into them, or weigh down their necks, arms, and ankles with brass rings. Why? In order to look handsomer. They spend hours on pretty mosaics of colored stones, on designs to decorate their pottery, on embroidering their footgear. Triangles and squares are painted on rawhide bags for holding dried meat. Baskets are ornamented, and a canoe prow or stern will display a fine spiral in openwork (Fig. 17). Here and there not only objects of use are decorated, but art is created for art's sake, as in the miniature ivory and wood carvings of sea-lions, sledges, wrestlers, and drummers by the Koryak of Siberia (Figs. 31, 32).

The love of beauty, then, is universal. It is also very ancient. From the Bronze Age of Europe curious seven-foot trombones come down to us that suggest some sense of music. From this period there are also huge bronze safety-pins worked into elaborate and useless spirals. Earlier still, in the Stone Age, man wasted hours polishing stone axes all over when the only thing that counted practically was the edge. But even before pottery there were beautifully chipped flint leaf-blades (Fig. 23), and at an amazingly early period uncouth fist-hatchets gave way to finer symmetrical ones (Fig. 3). True painting, too, goes back at least to the reindeer-hunters of southern France and Spain—say, 20,000 years ago; and some of its specimens on the walls of caves are acknowledged masterpieces of realism.

In short, the love of art is one of the most deep-rooted, ancient, and elemental things in human nature.

Gradgrinds cannot understand this. Beauty, they insist, must have been the handmaid of practical utility. The capital paintings of the Spanish caves had an ulterior motive: the artist was practicing "imitative magic." A modern Pueblo Indian who wants rain draws a picture of clouds with falling drops and whirls a little stick about to mimic the booming of thunder. So the cave-painter wanted food, and in order to catch his quarry, naïvely drew the animals he wished to hunt.

This sounds plausible, but explains nothing as to the origin of *art,* whether the prehistoric painter had or had not a magical aim in view. For a magician does not need a permanent record. A medieval sorcerer made an effigy of his victim and stabbed or burnt it. Savages do likewise. To draw a bison in the sand and pierce its heart would have been enough for the ancient hunter. It is enough for the modern Australian to trace such sand pictures of the chrysalis of an insect that he wants to develop and multiply. But it was *not* enough for the cave artists of old. They were not content with something ephemeral to be blotted out at will. Instead they developed an amazingly realistic style (Figs. 28, 29, 30) and with experience elaborated their technique. In the earlier stages only one color was used; later red, brown, yellow, and black were combined in the same picture. *This* is the sort of thing we should like to have explained, and precisely here the magical theory fails. Why such meticulous correctness of anatomy when a sorcerer can shift with vague resemblance? Why color instead of mere outlines? Why more pigments at one stage than another?

The plain fact is that the prehistoric artist was guided by his technical knowledge and by what seemed esthetically fit. He could of course combine his art with magical ends, but *as* art it was something distinct, not reducible to magic or anything else. In Europe legions of Madonnas have been

FIG. 28. ANCIENT SPANISH PAINTING OF DEER HUNT, PROVINCE OF CASTELLÓN, LOWEST FIGURE LEFT INCOMPLETE BY ARTIST (*after Obermaier and Wernert*)

FIG. 29. GALLOPING BOAR; ALTAMIRA, SPAIN (*after Cartailhac-Breuil*)

painted in oil, but oil-painting did not grow out of a belief in the Virgin Birth.

Tough-minded folk have also tried to give a matter-of-fact account of music. Doesn't a brass band keep a regiment in step? Well, so would music in any joint labor. It is easier to stamp, pound, lift, and row in unison when there are rhythmic beats to guide the workers. That is how and why singing and drumming arose. This, too, sounds plausible so long as one does not think seriously about it. As soon as one does, the argument fades away. Rhythm is not the whole of music. Why would not regular *noises* turn the trick as well

FIG. 30. BISON; ALTAMIRA, SPAIN (*after Cartailhac-Breuil*)

as agreeable sounds? How would rhythm by itself foster any instrument except the drum? And what about songs that have nothing to do with any useful occupation—say, the numberless gambling-songs of the American Indian?

Art, then, must be taken as an ultimate fact in man's life; and, like all of culture, it occurs on no level below the human. Even chimpanzees do not carve, paint, or compose poetry, and their howling is not music. But what about birds? Do not larks and nightingales produce beautiful tones? Yes, but theirs is not music in a human sense. They are charming warblers, but man alone grasps the *relationship* of sounds to one another, and that is the crucial point. A parrot can learn a tune but in years of captivity never, except by chance, varies its absolute pitch. There is the rub. *All* human beings have the power of abstract thought to hear notes as members of a series with set intervals. A melody is felt to be the same whether sung by a tenor or a bass. When South Sea Islanders or American Indians sing into a phonograph, they readily take their cue from a pitch-pipe; in short, *they are able to transpose a set of sounds as a unit*, and that is what no animal can do. Music, then, like the other arts, is a distinctively human thing.

But are all races equally gifted? Offhand this seems an absurd assumption. Not to go outside of Europe, where are the great British composers? Is it possible to doubt that the Germans—with Bach, Mozart, Beethoven, Wagner, Brahms to their credit—are more musical than the British? It is not only possible to doubt but to disprove it utterly by two separate and mutually corroboratory arguments. First of all, this preëminence of Germany is very recent. A few centuries ago she was rather backward—definitely behind Holland, Italy, and even England. Mozart, in the eighteenth century, was still under the sway of Italian traditions. But for the development of racial traits 200 or 500 years mean absolutely nothing. Hence, if the Germans are musical now and were not in 1400, then their achievement in this line has nothing to do with their heredity.

Secondly, who are the Germans and the British racially anyhow? Both contain a Nordic element, mixed with a Mediterranean stock in Britain and with Alpines in Germany. Hence any difference must be due to this difference in heredity. But the more one ponders this logical conclusion, the more grotesque it becomes. The English are held less artistic because they share the same strain as the ancient

Greeks! On the other hand, if Alpine heredity turns the balance in favor of the Germans, why do not the people of central France and northern Italy show the peculiar traits of German music? For both countries are at least as Alpine as South Germany.

These riddles remain insoluble only because the questions are wrongly put from the start. Admit frankly that musical ability, while inborn in individuals and hereditary in families, is not inborn in *races*, and the whole difficulty disappears. For some time past German society has systematically fostered musical training, while British society has not. In one country natural ability had free range for development, in the other it found scant sympathy. That is the simple explanation—the only one that fits in with the facts.

What about Greek art, then? The same arguments hold. Early Greek drawing or sculpture was a stiff and crude thing. Vases of the eighth century B.C. bear human figures no better than those on Spanish rocks of 20,000 years ago. The animals are worse: horses are drawn in profile with all their legs shown. A century later the torso of a human body might still appear in front view while the legs were in profile. Not before about 500 B.C. did the Greeks learn to draw a human figure correctly from all points of view. And even then they were not always able to solve the problem in marble: it was still hard to carve the distorted body of a fallen brave. What *could* have happened within the brief span of a century to produce the golden age? It has been loudly alleged that the sex cells of the Athenians were different between 530 and 430 B.C. from what they were before or after.[1] They doubtless were in *individuals*, though why there were more geniuses then no one can tell. But to assume that the Athenians as a whole changed and rechanged

[1] See page 285.

is arrant twaddle. Did the English produce Shakespeare and the Elizabethans in one period and Pope in another because some factors dropped in and out of the sex cells of copulating Britons? And did other factors have to change in the *race* before Tennyson and Wordsworth could be born? We do not know why culture changes this way, but we do know that races are constant by comparison; and to explain the variation by what remains the same is shallow humbug.

Let us turn back to another art. European music rests on harmony; everywhere else there is nothing but melody. Is this due to racial abilities and disabilities? No; for harmony developed only between 1300 and 1600, and even the ancient Greeks had nothing of the sort. But if we cannot explain this most fundamental difference in terms of sex cells, we might as well give up the racial explanation. Thus, the American Indians have a meager outfit of instruments, such as drums, flutes, panpipes, rattles, and notched sticks rasped with a scraper. African Negroes enjoy a much richer outfit. They have horns, harps, lyres, xylophones, soundboards with keys that are twanged with the thumb. Have Negro sex cells, then, a "string" factor that accounts for the harps the Indians lack? Again, the Vedda of Ceylon have no instruments at all. Do they lack a factor in their sex cells that enables the Redskin to beat a tambourine? To understand what the racial theory means concretely is to recognize its imbecility. We do not know why Beethoven appeared in Germany as an individual phenomenon. It cannot be explained from Nordic heredity, for then he would have been more probable in Sweden and at least as probable in England. He cannot be explained from Alpine heredity, or he would have been more probable in central France. His achievements, then, were rooted in his inborn gifts as an *individual*. But if he got beyond his forerunners it was not only because he was greater in ability. "Beethoven enjoyed the advantage, over Haydn and Mozart, that the actual powers and technical efficiency of performers on orchestral instruments had greatly improved." There we have as close an approach to an explanation as we can get. The prodigy of genius had a setting that others of his race had not. His *individual* powers and the technique of contemporary *culture* were the things that made Beethoven possible.

Did primitive man achieve anything worth while in art—anything beautiful by *our* standards? He did, and in many different fields. But as in craftsmanship,[1] there was generally narrow specialism, so that artists in one branch were bunglers in another. Skillful as the ancient painters of France were in doing animals, they have next to no composition or human figures. Their contemporaries in eastern Spain, on the other hand, went in for scenes of daily life and left us pictures of an archer shooting a dart from his bow, a hunter in hot pursuit of a deer (Fig. 28), or women dancing around a naked man. But while these artists attacked new themes, they were wholly without conscience as to realism. Human figures abound, but they are anatomical atrocities—eyeless and noseless silhouettes with grotesquely long or thick legs. Nevertheless, there is a spirited impression of movement. It is a difference between two prehistoric schools with diverse ideals. Each cultivated its own principles in blissful ignorance of the other.

If, now, modern canons are applied, the French cave art is superb, bearing comparison with modern animal studies for realism. Even game running at top speed was correctly drawn, while until snapshot photography came into vogue all Western art misrepresented the horse's flying gallop ac-

[1] See page 105.

cording to an effete convention. These early realists had not yet learnt to farm or to shape earthenware. But in one phase of art they excelled otherwise advanced peoples. The Egyptians of 5000 B.C. were far ahead of them in general mode of life, but their attempts to paint a lion hunt are pitiable alongside of the old cave-paintings. In her excellent book on *Art Through the Ages*, Miss Gardner correctly says: "We can draw because the Greek first taught us how." The prehistoric cave-painter learnt to draw without the Greeks.

And as the ancient people of France learnt to draw, so the Koryak of Siberia, illiterate, non-agricultural, until a few centuries ago even without reindeer, learnt to carve. The early Greek sculptors took over the Egyptian conventions and made human beings in stiff frontal position, with both arms pressed to the sides and the left foot forward. Myron's well-known Discus-thrower in action is rightly treated as a revolutionary conception. Well, the untutored Siberians solved the problem that baffled the ancients for centuries. The bent and twisted bodies of their drummers (Figs. 31, 32) and wrestlers, the gleam of ecstasy on a medicine-man's face, are marvels of skill. "The plastic curves of the back and the tense muscles of back and sides are rendered with anatomical accuracy and realistic vividness," writes Dr. Jochelson with justifiable enthusiasm.

Even in music the primitives have more to show than appears at first blush. Today, of course, the gap between them and us is vast. But let us go back a few centuries, and what do we find? Our forefathers of the early eighteenth century had a moderate enough orchestra of strings and wind instruments. In quantity, at least, they were not so much ahead of East African Negroes, with their trumpets, horns, drums, xylophones (Fig. 33), harps, mandolins, and fifes! On the Uganda mandolin, now obsolete, the Negroes played songs to the glory of the King, while the harp was

FIG. 31. KORYAK CARVINGS, SIBERIA (*after Jochelson*). MEN BEATING TAMBOURINES

FIG. 32. KORYAK CARVINGS, SIBERIA. DRUMMER; MEN USING BOW-DRILL (*after Jochelson*)

used with love- and drinking-songs. Kings and chiefs had fife-players who marched fifteen miles while playing in accompaniment to the drums. Drums signaled birth and death, war and victory; and a king had as many as ninety-three—each with its individual name! There were fife and xylophone duets, and the chiefs kept bands with eight or ten horns, blown to make different sounds. Among the Africans generally a solo singer alternates with a chorus, and out of this grows a kind of polyphonic music. It is the sort of thing Europe had in the Middle Ages before her people had a

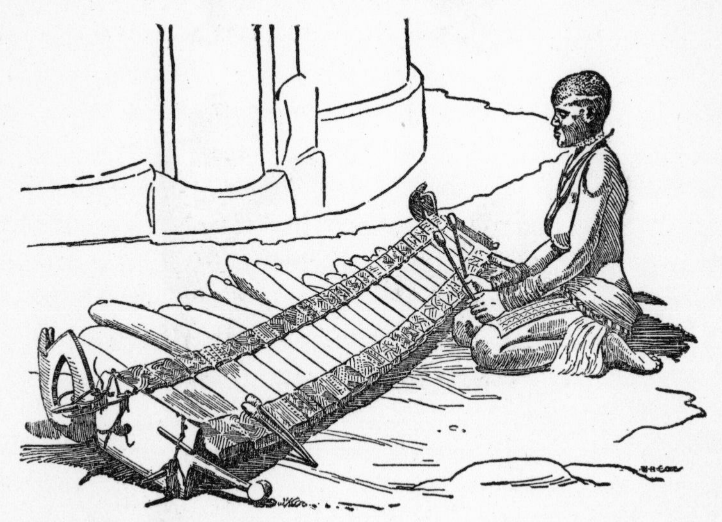

FIG. 33. NEGRO PLAYING XYLOPHONE (*after Lestrade*)

notion of harmony. In principle the native is only a few centuries behind. But in one respect the savage world has the advantage in complexity. Try to beat a drum with a group of Indians while they are singing to a rhythm different from that of the drumming. In West Africa, too, trained white musicians are baffled by a tune accompanied by a set of drums, each with a separate rhythm, while hands are clapped to still another.

In painting, sculpture, and music, the primitive has made a good beginning, even though he is handicapped by his tools, materials, and lack of scientific knowledge. In literature he has an even start. Every primitive language has a vocabulary large enough to express the whole of its speakers' experience. So even crude tribes have a chance to do nobly in poetry and prose.

To speak of the "literature" of illiterates sounds like an Irish bull. But Homer's poems were no better when written down than when they were sung. So the stories South Sea Islanders, Negroes, and Redskins hand down by word of mouth may be as true novelettes as any appearing in *The Saturday Evening Post.* In plot and episode they recall our fairy tales. Giants or cannibals are shown infesting the country of long ago until some bold or crafty hero conquered them. Haughty beauties spurn their suitors and are properly punished for their pride. Spirits befriend poor but worthy boys, who thus climb to the top of the social ladder. The weak but cunning hare triumphs over the stupid hippopotamus. Tricksters overreach themselves and are treated to a dose of their own medicine.

Sometimes one gets a poor idea of savage originality from these stories. Not only has any particular tribe its favorite themes, but they occur over and over again in the most distant regions. Even details are borrowed. From Wisconsin Indians comes a deluge myth in which the hero bids the beaver dive for earth. It obeys, but dies before reaching bottom. Then the muskrat goes down and brings up a little dirt in his paws, from which the earth is re-created. This tale is told from the Atlantic to the Pacific, and with little variation. In one place it is the turtle that succeeds, in another the hell-diver or toad. But almost everywhere there are several trials, with failures at the start, the successful one brings only a little bit of mud, and so forth. Variations are trifling.

This sort of thing becomes monotonous. But do not the novels of civilized men bristle with ever-recurring motives? What about the eternal triangle? Or the conflict between duty and desire? Or lovers laughing at an irate father? Cut the basic facts of human life to the bone and they are few enough; that is why realistic tales *must* deal with them. If fortune or a god favors the humble, they may rise, and their fate lulls the despair and disappointment of actual experience. Powerful fools *are* hoodwinked by weak but clever adversaries. Gluttons and lechers do become the butts of ridicule. Children disobey their parents. Wives run away with their lovers. How can such themes fail to appear over and over again when they belong to the daily incidents of any well-regulated human society?

As a matter of fact, the savage's tales not only mirror real life but allow free rein to fancy. Further, while it is true enough that any striking episode may travel to the four corners of the globe, it is equally true that there is hardly a body of folklore without wholly original features—such as cannot be duplicated from anywhere else. Some of the ideas are grotesquely funny, others splendidly imaginative. In a North American tale a hunter whittles his legs into points with which to stab his comrade. In another a faithless wife is decapitated by her husband, but her skull is able to tan hides and rolls in pursuit of her children. Among some tribes the trickster when cornered regularly asks his feces for advice. In Arizona gods wrap themselves in clouds tied with sunbeams, and Polynesian lovers travel moonward on a rainbow.

What primitive man can do in the way of long narrative is shown in the Hawaiian romance of Laieikawai. It is not much shorter than some of our novels. There are forty named characters, and as with Dostoyevsky, a wise reader will card-index them. The structure is certainly loose. There is free and easy shifting from one scene to another, and important personages have a way of dropping off by the wayside. But let us take a glance at European literatures. Fielding, the realist, makes a passenger tell in detail the sad experiences of a lady as the stage-coach whirls by her house; even the love letters are quoted verbatim! Thackeray's apostrophes to the reader are as notorious as George Eliot's ethical reflections. Germans and Scandinavians let lyrical moods take the place of incident. In short, a close-knit plot is a recent thing and rare at that. Altogether the problem is puzzling and reminds one of man's efforts at government: [1] he can be safe *or* free, but hardly both at the same time. So narrators, savage and cultivated, can spin simple yarns well enough, but as soon as they try something more pretentious the web turns into a strangely tangled fabric. So we had better not be too hard on the Hawaiian romancers.

Savage prose merges into poetry. Here is a ceremonial speech made by a Crow warrior during the Tobacco ceremony:

"They went on a raid, among them went I. They charged the enemy, they killed some, I snatched a gun. Then I went homeward. As I was coming, the Tobacco you had planted was extremely plentiful, round about the chokecherries were extremely plentiful. I came on. When I reached the camp, sick people there were none. Peacefully you were harvesting the Tobacco."

So when a Crow makes an offering of an albino bison skin to the Sun, he falls into a more or less set rhythmic speech:

"Hail, father's kinsman, I have just made a robe for you, I give it to you. Here it is. Do you give me a good way of living. May my kin and I safely reach the next year. May

[1] See page 155.

my children increase. When my sons go on the warpath, may they bring horses. When my son is on the warpath, may he return with blackened face [the sign of victory]. When I am on the hunt, may the wind be in my face, so buffalo gather towards me. This summer may my plants thrive and cherries be plentiful. May the winter be good, and illness not reach me. May I see the new grass of the summer, may I see the full-sized leaves when they come. May I see the leaves faded, may I see the very first snowfall. May I see the spring, may I and all my folk safely get there."

Again, here is how a visionary from the Lake Superior country describes his experience:

"Concerning all sorts of things did I dream—about what was everywhere on earth did I dream; and about the sea, the suns, and the stars; and about all things in the circle of the heavens from whence blew the winds, did I dream. And about the spirit that was above did I dream; by him was I spoken to, by him was I given the knowledge of what would happen to me. And by all the people of the stars was I blessed. . . . By a great throng of the sky-people was I blessed; everywhere over the earth and on high was I conveyed by them, how it all looked I was shown, how it was everywhere in the circle of the heavens that I had dreamed about."

True primitive poetry is sung, and we cannot fully appreciate it without the music. What is more, even the intrinsic merit of the words eludes us. The languages are so different from ours that even a careful rendering falls very short of the original. Yet through literal translations, checked by the native text, we catch glimpses of the very same emotion and beauty we prize in our own poetry.

A Yukaghir lad will improvise such love-songs as the following:

She is white as snow,
Her eyebrows are black as ink,
Her hair is soft as silk,
She shines like the sun,
I am hurrying to her
Never to part with her.

And a maiden thus gives vent to her feelings:

When our camps separated
I looked after him.
He is tall like a mountain ash,
His hair covered his shoulders
Like black squirrels' tails.
When he disappeared
I lay down in the tent.
Oh, how long is a spring day?
But the evening came
And through a hole in the tent cover
I saw my love coming;
When he came in
And looked at me
My heart melted
Like snow in the sun.

A different note is struck by a Greenland Eskimo woman while picking berries:

Great grief came over me,
While on the fell above us I was picking berries.
Great grief came over me.
My sun quickly rose over it.
Great grief came over me.
The sea out there off our settlement
Was beautifully quiet—
And the great dear paddlers
Were leaving out there—
Great grief came over me
While I was picking berries on the fell.

The Polynesians had a more complex society than the Greenlanders, and it affected their poetry. Each blue-blood prized his family tree and had his minstrel learn it by heart. "A long recitation of the genealogies of chiefs provides immense emotional satisfaction." The Hawaiians, accordingly, took to the genealogical tables of the Scriptures like fish to the water and repeated them as the choicest passages of the Bible. A bard had to know his patron's pedigree letter-perfect, for a single error might cost him his life. No wonder Polynesians achieved prodigies of memory. When a certain chant was taken down in Hawaii and Oahu, there was not one line out of the 618 that varied in the versions from the two islands.

The long pedigrees set a pattern, and other itemized reports became popular. In one Hawaiian tale the bulk of the "story" consists in the list of places seen by a young traveler. In chants such geographical rosters are even more prominent. We do not find them beautiful, but the natives do.

The professionalism of Polynesia meant complexity. Stylistic tricks multiplied, language became ornate, figures of speech abounded. Fighting nobles are compared with cocks: the feather brushes waved over them and the red paddles of their fleet are likened to the motion of a cock's feathers. Are not all three red, and do they not all move up and down?

Hawaii is a cockpit; the trained cocks fight on the ground.
The chief fights—the dark-red cock awakes at night for battle;
The youth fights valiantly—Loeau, son of Keoua.
He whets his spurs, he pecks as if eating;
He scratches in the arena—this Hilo—the sand of Waiolamo.
He is a well-fed cock. The chief is complete,
Warmed in the smoke-house till the dried feathers rattle,

With changing colors, like many-colored paddles, like piles of
polished *Kahili*,
The feathers rise and fall at the striking of the spurs.

Another sample of approved elegance appears in the plaint of the deserted sisters inserted into the romance of Laieikawai:

Our brother and lord,
Divine brother,
Highest and closest!
Where are you, oh! where?
You and we, here and there,
You, the voyager,
We, the followers,
Along the cliffs, swimming 'round the steeps,
Bathing at Waihalau,
Waihalau at Wailua;
No longer are we beloved,
Do you no longer love us,
The comrades who followed you over the ocean,
Over the great waves, the little waves,
Over the long waves, the short waves,
Over the long-backed waves of the ocean,
Comrades who followed you inland,
Far through the jungle,
Through the night, sacred and dreadful,
Oh, turn back!
Oh, turn back and have pity,
Listen to my pleading,
Me the littlest of your sisters.
Why will you abandon,
Abandon us
In this desolation?
You have opened the highway before us,
After you we followed,
We are known as your little sisters,
Then forsake your anger,
The wrath, the loveless heart,

> Give a kiss to your little ones,
> Fare you well!

This is certainly more elaborate than anything from the Eskimo. But is it better poetry? There are many devices unknown to the simpler people. Repetition is subtler, the studied antitheses are not without esthetic flavor. But much of the sophistication is a bit crude, and in many other samples one not bred to the style might resent the rosters of proper names and the involved puns that thrill the Polynesian. Such a one may prefer the noble baldness of the Greenlanders. But as with the prehistoric French and Spanish painters, it is a matter of taste and of ideals. We are again facing two schools of art with distinct aims, and their products cannot be measured by the same yardstick.

The East Africans in and near Somaliland also have professional poets—itinerant minstrels and merry-fellows. So here as in the South Seas craftsmanship has been elaborated, perhaps under Arabic influence. Pithier lines can hardly be found than such as these:

> When thou art pepper, I am mustard.
> When thou art a needle, I am a knife.
>
> A javelin without blood is not a javelin!
> Love without kisses is not love!
>
> God has created the python; justly he has created the antidote.
> He has created love; justly he has created patience.

Here is real craftsmanship, and with it comes its usual fosterling, technical inanity. These Galla are not content to use rhyme and assonance, they have become drunk with love of verbal jugglery and relish meaningless jingle just for the love of the sound.

Perhaps this trait is due to the Arabs, whose poets set

great store by stunts. Their verse has fixed rules of meter and sound, and a virtuoso will try to rhyme ninety words in a single poem. Their professionals also created a stereotyped form, the *qaside.* It began with a lover's plaint, made a sudden transition to the singer's camel, then to the landscape, often introduced a combat, and wound up with a eulogy of the patron or his tribe. This was terribly artificial—just like the sonnet cycles of our Elizabethans. An English poet of the period had his theme traced in advance. He would praise the superlative beauty of his lady, pass on to the transitoriness of all beauty, contrast the immortality of verse, dwell on the pangs of absence, and so forth.

Art is enriched in the same casual way as invention, as food-stuffs, or any other phase of culture. Ornamental designs spring up without being willed; the craftsman later becomes aware of them and consciously reproduces them. For example, Plains Indian women often marked off an oblong stripe on the margin of a rawhide case, inscribed a long isosceles triangle, and filled it with pigment. This act inevitably made the blank space into a K-shaped figure. This would stand out quite as clearly as the triangle made on purpose, and was actually painted as a separate pattern. Further, as soon as two such inscribed strips are put together symmetrically, an hourglass figure results, and that also is treated as an independent unit. Thus, two new designs appear, quite incidentally, to be added to the tribal stock (Fig. 37).

Plaiting, too, may yield forms not planned by the worker. If one warp element regularly crosses one weft element in a basket (Fig. 34), such interlacing not only holds the fabric together but creates a checker pattern. A difference of shade in the warp and weft throws it into relief, and then it may later be painted on pottery or otherwise produced at will. If the basket is twilled, that is, if more than one element is regularly crossed, diagonals appear, and they may be com-

FIG. 34. TWINING TECHNIQUE, YIELDING GUILLOCHE; GUIANA BASKET IN CHECKER (*after Roth*)

bined into diamonds and other figures (Fig. 35). Some baskets are held together by twining (Fig. 34), and this leads to the familiar guilloche design.

FIG. 35. TWILLING, YIELDING DIAGONAL LINES AND DIAMONDS (*after Roth*)

Features of poetry like rhyme and assonance may appear in the same incidental way. Take a language like the Polynesian, with very few sounds and full of vowels. What is more likely than that lines should end in similar vocalic combinations? For instance:

> Taki taha ngaohi haane mea
> Ka tau folau ki he puko lea.
>
> (Let each person prepare his own things
> For us to voyage to the talking puko tree.)

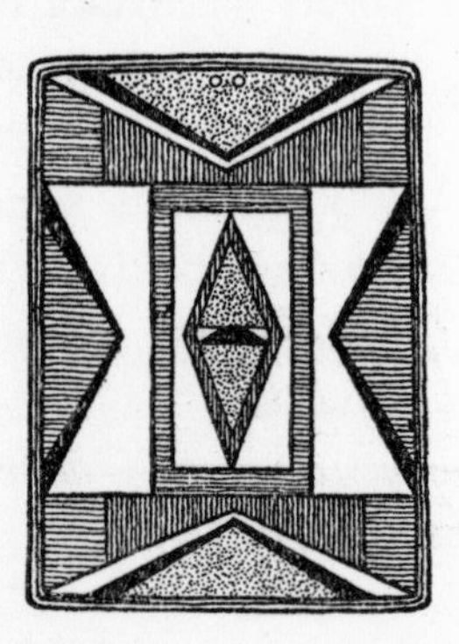

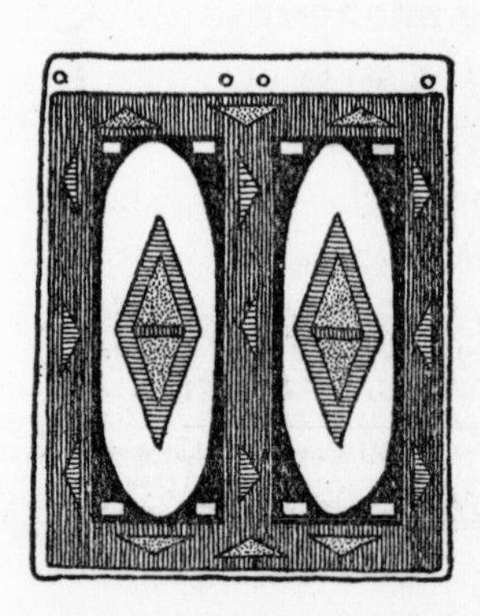

FIG. 36. CROW RAWHIDE DECORATION IN SHOSHONE STYLE; HIDATSA RAWHIDE DECORATION (*after Lowie*)

Let the minstrels once become aware of the jingle, and they will begin to use it as a conscious trick.

To take modern instances, let us look at the nonchalant way in which oil-painting slinks in, nobody can say just when. Velazquez (1599-1660) is credited with first using oil as his sole medium, but the Van Eycks had developed the technique in Flanders before 1440. They, too, however, were not the inventors. Long before them painters used oil to give luster to pictures in pigments mixed with the white of eggs. Gradually oil-colors were promoted from a superficial gloss to the body of the painting. So our orchestras started as a musical by-product and finally got to lord it over song. Early eighteenth century composers used instruments as they would have used voices. Symphonies started as overtures to operas. They were at first written only for strings, occasionally reënforced by trumpet solos. Gradually other instruments were added, but for the longest time composers treated this part of their task in scurvy fashion. Why should they exert themselves for the opening while the audience, interested only in arias, were bandying polite greetings or rustling into their seats? So the composers mechanically followed the style of violin sonatas, without trying to use the several instruments for their distinctive effects. They did not divine the individual quality of horns: they stumbled upon it because no one could play violin parts on them. Slowly they developed a feeling for the timbre of each instrument and "a totally new and extremely subtle branch of art" emerged "from the chaotic products of indifference and carelessness."

Primitive art has its masterpieces. The Koryak sculptor is ahead of the archaic Greek, an Eskimo lyric is as true a mood picture as any on record, Pre-Ceramic animal studies are as lifelike as modern ones. It is not because of its quality that savage art makes such a sorry showing beside our own, but because of its lesser scope and quantity. And the handicaps are exactly the same as in primitive man's cuisine, invention, science, and everything else. To him that hath shall be given. Basketry was the one craft that might yield esthetic motifs to a Californian Indian. Where there are dozens of crafts, spontaneous novelties are bound to occur oftener. Each by itself may not be of superior worth, but there are more of them.

But the whole of a culture acts on the pursuit of art, and so again the savage artist cuts a sorry figure beside his civilized brother. The Pre-Ceramic painters of Spain did not know human anatomy; Michelangelo did. Where would our composers be without the knowledge of physics that makes our modern instruments a possibility?

Nor is it merely a matter of scientific knowledge. It is a question of knowing what art has already achieved. The French cave-painters did not profit from what those of Spain accomplished in composition. The Greeks were still limited in range of interest. We have inherited their ideals of flawlessness and added to them. The innovations in technique and theme may be worth little or much, but they show new possibilities. No one thinks that the Dutch genre painters of the seventeenth century are the peers of the earlier Italian masters, but they did strike a distinctive note that had been lacking. We have in our writing and our museums a technique for preserving literature and the fine arts for posterity. The savage has nothing of the sort. He does not know what can be and has been done. He has not had the chance of borrowing from all ages and all climes. Our artists get inspiration from the Greeks and the Egyptians, the Chinese and the Hindus, even from the primitive himself. They find techniques and ideas ready-made. The savage picks up stray bits from a few of his neighbors. No wonder that his artistry is narrowly cribbed. It is really not he that is pitted against our artists. It is a tiny fraction of humanity that is pitted against the whole.

How much of any modern poet, painter, sculptor, musician, is intelligible without wholesale borrowing from the past and present? And what would English literature be without that of Greece, Rome, Italy, and France? Take Shakespeare. His is a star case, precisely because of his mediocre education. Yet if he could not read much of the classics in the original himself, there were translators and friends who could. He could borrow plots from Plautus as well as revamp the old chronicles—many of them already overhauled by earlier playwrights. Even in his sonnets he was not warbling native wood-notes wild. When he wrote his cycle, he stuck faithfully to the quite conventional scheme of ideas made popular in his day.

The sonnet itself had come in under Henry VIII. But did the British invent it? Not they. The Italians used it before 1300, and Wyatt and Surrey merely introduced it into England. Then some writers clung to the foreign pattern. Others were like the Siberians who copied riding from equestrian tribes but found that their breeds had to be straddled over the forelegs.[1] This school, and Shakespeare among them, whipped the Italian rhyme scheme into harmony with more congenial native patterns. But the stimulus came from abroad. Without it Shakespeare would not have written sonnets, and British poetry would have been poorer by an important verse type.

But there is still another factor—population. During the sonnet mania, between 1590 and 1600, over 2,000 sonnets were printed in England. No Polynesian or North American Indian tribe could possibly be so productive. And here quantity does mean quality. Where a hundred cultured amateurs and professional poets devoted themselves to verse, some were bound to rise above the common herd, to improve technique and display a sprightlier fancy.

So in the painting of the Renaissance. There were dozens of artists nurtured in similar traditions, working over the same themes. Not all of them were content to be slavish followers. When Leonardo da Vinci painted the *Last Supper*, he ranged all his figures along a table parallel to the frame. He thus stressed the horizontal line. Others

[1] See page 118.

tried different effects. Tintoretto put the table obliquely. Tiepolo kept it straight, but put some disciples on one side and Christ on the other. Thus he forced the eye in a slanting line from the foreground toward Christ and gave an effect of depth.

Such experimentation, unconscious as a rule, is found among primitives too. All the Plains Indian tribes have the same general style of painting rawhide cases with triangles and rectangles. There is no question that the style developed

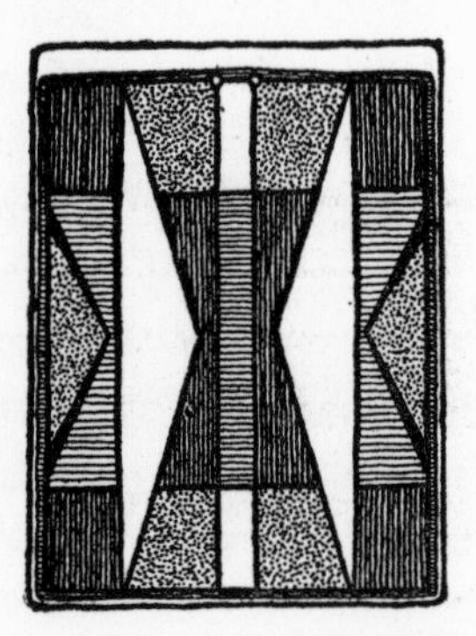
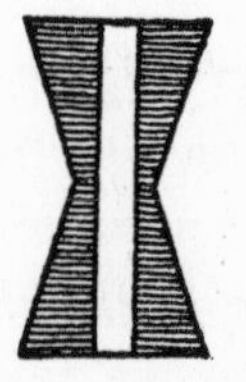

FIG. 37. DECORATION ON FLAP OF CROW RAWHIDE BAG; ORIGIN OF K AND HOUR-GLASS DESIGNS (*after Lowrie*)

only once within the area and spread to its margins. Yet there is a good deal of tribal individuality (Figs. 36, 37). The Arapaho of Wyoming arrange their designs in narrow panels, the Crow of Montana in wider ones. The Shoshone fancy a framed square in the center, such as most other tribes disdain. The Hidatsa of the upper Missouri and the Dakota Indians favor a two-panel arrangement with the same design in each (Fig. 36). There was evidently at one time individual originality that fixed these several tribal styles. But, apart from any other difference, there were a dozen artists plying a brush in Italy for every rawhide decorator of the Plains; hence there were not so few novel conceptions and more original ones.

Art—the esthetic impulse—goes well back into the Stone Age. But notwithstanding its great age it remains perennially young. The Gradgrinds try to put it to work for all kinds of worthy causes. Tolstoy in his moralistic moods disapproved of Turgenieff—all except *The Sportsman's Sketches,* which passed muster because they helped free the serfs. How antediluvian the question of Russian serfdom appears at the present day! So with Ibsen. Was not *The Doll's House* hailed by every radical in Europe as a social gospel? Today women have rights no one dreamt of in Ibsen's time, and so the play fails to thrill the most rabid feminist. But the psychological plays like *John Gabriel Borkman,* the poetical plays like *Peer Gynt* and *Brand,* the lyrics that bear no message but to the spirit of beauty, still hold us spellbound. We always have worthy causes with us. Some are won and become boresome like feminism. Others are lost because they are boresome from the start. Art goes on and survives them all.

CHAPTER XX

RELIGION

Chimpanzees are without religion; all primitive groups have it. But what a religion! Imagine East African Negroes revering the tip of an antelope horn crammed with clay and herbs; or our American aborigines worshiping wrapped-up bird- and weasel-skins, plumage, and the like. A Plains Indian once offered to show me "the greatest thing on earth." He produced a bundle, untied it, solemnly pulled back one covering after another, and at last displayed—a bunch of feathers.

Yet the anticlimax was not so great as it seemed. In themselves the feathers meant nothing. But their owner had once seen them in a vision that became the event of his life. The mysterious apparition that then came to him wore such feathers and told him to wear them in battle: if he obeyed, he would escape death and wounds. He followed instructions and remained unharmed. No wonder he prizes the symbol of his experience. He cannot summon his divine helper at will, but at least he can always keep the bundle about as a souvenir of the occasion. So with the Negro. He is not worshiping the horn as such. If it can ward off danger, heal wounds, and bring good fortune, it is because of an indwelling god. There lies the source of its awe-inspiring quality. What the savage prizes as sacred is the *supernatural power* linked with the inanimate object. The power may belong to a god or spirit, or it may be an impersonal force. But it is the power and not the dead thing that is worshiped. Even when a Negro carves an image, it has to be made holy by putting power into it. Without that it may be a work of art, but not a religious object.

Life is one big puzzle. You bend every effort on the hunt and fail while a lazy good-for-nothing brings home plenty of food. Your comrades on a war-party are killed, but *you* escape. Neighbor X looked hale and hearty when he suddenly fell dead. Why does cousin Y always win at button, button, who's got the button? Why did his wife bear twins? What's the meaning of that owl hooting about the lodge night after night? All this is strange, some of it uncanny. There is supernatural power floating about; the universe teems with it. By hook or by crook you had better get some if you want to live safely, gain social position, win at gambling, or prevent *your* wife from bearing twins. You have to solve an equation with an infinite number of unknown quantities, and unfortunately your happiness, your life and death, depend on finding the right answers. So tread softly in the universe. If you follow the trails charted by the wise men of old, they will lead to happiness—provided Force Number 1,678,872 does not upset their calculations. *What* roads to pursue, depends on what society you are born into. Let us look at a few of them.

The Jagga of East Africa has a clear-cut pattern of piety. When he falls ill, starts on an important journey, or finds himself in a quandary, he turns to the ghost of an ancestor. The dead are not the only reservoir of supernatural power for him, but they are the most important one. You can tap it by feeding them. For while the soul is less fleshly than the body it is not *pure* spirit and is not immortal as a matter of course. It must eat to live, and if neglected it kicks up a row. Did you hear the lions roaring near camp the other night? So-and-so has not been tending the grave of his grandfather; so the spirit sent the beast of prey as a gentle reminder. He had better slaughter a bull and put the ghost at rest.

To a Crow Indian it would never occur that coddling his ancestors was a way to fortune. Of course ghosts sometimes make a nuisance of themselves, but the divine power that counts lies elsewhere. It is well to pray to the Sun and make him an occasional offering. But above all there are innumerable shadowy beings that come in visions. If you wish to steal horses from the enemy, recover health, or become a chief, the thing to do is to go to a lonely spot, fast, pray, and (by way of showing how serious you are) chop off a finger joint. Then perhaps some supernatural person will pity you, adopt you as his child, and grant your wish. That is the standard way in which men accomplish anything unusual. Whenever a man outshines his fellows in honor or happiness, obviously he must have once met the friendly supernatural face to face. Not every one can gain the prizes of life, of course, but every Crow may at least try for them in the approved fashion. Fast, pray, and cut off your flesh and bone, and then perhaps some mysterious being will bless you.

Not so in Siberia. There such wooing of the divine would seem presumptuous. One does not *seek* a vision, one gets a call, and then simply *must* accept the post of "shaman"—of prophet, priest, and doctor rolled into one, with a tambourine as foremost badge of office. When the spirits first summon their protégé he suddenly begins to grow languid and to tremble. He starts yawning violently, utters incoherent cries, and is seized with sudden chills. He rolls his eyes wildly, leaps about in a circle as if insane, totters to the ground, and lies twitching like an epileptic. He has lost all sensation, grasps red-hot iron, and swallows pins without taking harm. At last he takes up the tambourine and begins to beat it.

Henceforth the spirits will inspire him as their mouthpiece.

Plainly enough one has to be predisposed to get such a call. By all accounts the Siberian shamans are psychologically abnormal. Says Dr. Bogoras: "The shamans among the Chukchi . . . were as a rule extremely excitable, almost hysterical, and not a few of them were half crazy." One of them flew into a hysterical rage at the slightest provocation, another could not sit still, some had a constant nervous twitching of the face, others were homosexual. In 1901 Dr. Jochelson witnessed a performance among the Yukaghir. The shaman called forth his supernatural patrons with such "screams, whistling, grinding of teeth and terrible facial contortions, that the Yukaghir would be terrified. In general his performance was like an attack of madness or delirium tremens." The first sounds of his drum were enough to put him into a frenzy. His wife held out a piece of burning birchbark toward his mouth and he swallowed it. "Indescribable screams, cramps all over the body, jumps, big and small, kept on for two or three hours. I, as a spectator, was so exhausted, and my nerves were so unstrung, that I could not do any more work that evening." Through these psychopathological go-betweens the average Siberian gets into touch with the divine forces that surround him.

But much of the supernatural power is impersonal and has to be approached by a different path. A South African Negro does not need a shaman in a trance to pump the spirits about his future. He casts his bone dice and interprets the throw. Elsewhere the savage imitates what he wants to happen in a ceremonial way, and it happens. When you want rain in New Guinea you do not pray to the ghosts. You take a cup, fill it with water, and throw in pebbles till it overflows. If there is too violent a shower, you merely dry the cup over a fire. In the same spirit our Arizona Indians swing a little stick about to make a booming noise like thunder; rub a notched stick to mimic a croaking frog—since the frog is connected with water; and paint clouds with raindrops on the walls of their underground chapels. All this is no mere play. The acts are performed seriously and even reverently. Even the dice thrown by the diviner are sacred. He calls them his Bible and will not sell the set to a missionary. They are a part of what he holds divine in the universe.

Words are magical as well as acts. Set forms of them may be stronger than the gods themselves. In New Zealand a nobleman's education, as explained above,[1] consisted largely in learning the proper spells for every possible occasion in life. If he chanted the right formula at sowing-time, his crops would prosper. By another set of words he could make a truant sweetheart return, or kill his enemies. But woe to him if he committed the slightest slip! Even a mythical demigod had to die because at his birth his father forgot part of the baptismal service. There is no tampering with the mysterious forces of the universe. It is like pouring out concentrated sulphuric acid instead of water; worse—for the acid does not make you feel like a miserable sinner.

Numbers also have to be reckoned with. No Crow procession would simply walk out of a tent to the ceremonial lodge. The leader has to make three feigned attempts and to pass out at the fourth trial. The performers make four halts on the way and sing four songs at each. It is the same way with the East African Jagga. When they pray to the sun or moon, they spit four times toward them, and in making an offering to the dead, they count up to four. A ceremonial goblet has to be raised four times before drinking; and the fourth month of the year is held particularly lucky. Ten is another lucky number; so the Jagga sow or start

[1] See page 174.

house-building on the tenth day after a full moon. Seven, on the other hand, forebodes evil. So does any odd number, and also the left side of the body. No left-handed man is taken on a war-party, and if you stub your left toe on a journey it is a warning that you had better turn back.

There are also material things that somehow harbor a mysterious force for good or evil. For the Jagga, saliva is a sort of panacea and general disinfectant against threatening calamities. He spits on a newborn baby by way of blessing it,[1] he spits on a dead snake in his path or on spilt milk, he spits on the hide of a sacrificial goat. The Ekoi of West Africa smear chalk over an infant for good luck and credit a certain black substance with reviving the dead. On the other hand, menstrual blood frightens the boldest savages into fits. A Louisiana Indian once unwittingly ate of food cooked by his wife during her illness. As soon as he learnt the truth he vomited what he had eaten. In Wisconsin the Winnebago even nowadays "refuse to eat in Christian houses for fear of losing their powers through partaking of food prepared by a woman undergoing her monthly terms." Holy objects lose their power by coming into contact with menstrual blood—"even the spirits die of its effects." With a similar idea a Crow will not let a menstruating woman stay in a tent where there are sacred bundles: they have to be taken out until she recovers. Formerly she would never have been allowed near a wounded man or with warriors setting out on a war-party. Again, in northwestern Canada it is a foregone conclusion that a hunter loses his luck if a woman crosses his track during her illness.

With ghosts, guardian spirits, divination dice, mystic spells, sacred numbers and objects, there is a power to the right and left, smiling or scowling. Each acts in a universe

[1] See page 3.

of its own, often separately from all others. Now and then a savage philosopher brings all of them into a coherent scheme, but at best he catches a fleeting glimpse of unity. What boots it if a kind creator orders all spirits to help the Winnebago who offer them tobacco? Menstrual blood has a sinister effect even on the spirits. The Sun is great, and a Crow will pray to him. But he gets his war-charm from a mysterious buffalo that comes in a vision and may mean more to him than the Sun; he prays for long life to an oddly shaped rock, and is careful to perform sacred rites four times. A Jagga has an intermittent belief in a great god, but he turns more regularly to the dead. However, life is too puzzling to be solved by a single ghost-worshiping recipe. There is the evil eye; there are sorcerers who practice imitative magic; [1] there are curses and amulets against them. There is nothing simple about primitive religion.

In well-organized savage states the elaboration comes to pass all bounds. The Baganda of East Africa, for example, worshiped the ghosts of their dead, but in addition there were the gods of each clan and the national deities who protected the state and the King. Each had his temple, his priests, his ritual offerings, and a medium whom the god would suddenly possess. But all this was not enough. With sinister powers lurking everywhere, there had to be literally hundreds of talismans to ward them off. "Every home had its supply, and no person would have thought himself or his family safe if he had not had a number of them about him." A peasant wore a charm to conciliate his chief; a wayfarer had charms against wild beasts and disease; a woman put one about her waist to prevent barrenness; a warrior carried some along to ward off weapons, others to strike terror into his foeman's heart. The King would send six special antelope

[1] See page 188.

horns with his army—each guarded by a medium of its own to advise the general, each identified with an indwelling god. Such objects were made by a class of religious performers distinct from mediums and priests, to wit, the medicine-men. They diagnosed illness, treated the sick, exorcised ghosts, and sold drugs or charms. They also threw leather dice to foretell the outcome of a disease or proposed journey. But that was only one of several quite distinct ways. Some diviners threw nine sticks into a pot of water; if they formed groups of even numbers, it was a bad omen, otherwise all was well. Still others killed a fowl and watched how many times the blood spurted out or examined the way the fat lay between the entrails. The Baganda had bloody sacrifices of beasts and men in honor of their gods, festivals that were strung out over days when a temple was rebuilt, and poison ordeals to decide guilt. Every event of note was linked with some ritual act. A man jumped over his wife when he set out on a trip and when he got home, when she had given birth to a child, when the child was named, before dividing up a catch of fish, and so forth.

This medley of faith and observance is really more complex than civilized religion. Why, then, does it remain on a lower level? The answer seems plain. It revolts us philosophically *because* it is a medley, not a coherent system—ethically, because the supernatural powers act without regard to moral principle; scientifically, because it flouts our ideas of cause and effect. But the difference is not so great as it seems. When an earthquake destroys hundreds of lives, we do not blame demons but declare that the ways of Providence are inscrutable. Our terminology is different, but in effect we are avowing that the supernatural forces of the universe are amoral according to our understanding. When scientists fail to understand a phenomenon in Nature they speak of chance. That may sound better but explains no more than does the action of spirits. As for unification, does every thought and deed about supernatural powers among ourselves flow logically and inevitably from a belief in a supremely good and powerful creator?

Of course the believer in revealed religion can never treat primitive religion as on a par with his own. The reason is obvious: in any such comparison the savage starts with a handicap, for he is pitted not against civilization, but against civilization plus Providence. Compare his faith with that of the ancients, and the odds are no longer distressingly against him. When Whirlwind, the Cheyenne warrior, goes to battle, it is true that any great divine Spirit he believes in may recede while the hawk who gave him a war talisman stands foremost in his consciousness. Did not Whirlwind come unscathed out of the last skirmish, though every feather of his bonnet was shot to pieces? Only the hawkskin on it was untouched: *there* was the source of vital power in an emergency. But let us glance at Homer's Odysseus swimming towards the mouth of a stream. He prays not to Zeus, but to the god of that particular stream. At that moment the minor deity counts for more than all the gods on Olympus. In critical situations Greek and Cheyenne alike cast philosophy to the winds.

As for ethical ideals, the gods of the ancients were notoriously no better than they should be. But did not at least their thinkers and moralists develop more refined ideals of deity? Yes, but Redskins and Negroes also have their philosophers. American myths shock us when their outstanding hero plays the part of a lewd, greedy, and unscrupulous buffoon who steals his comrade's food and in a disguise courts his own daughters. But there is another side to his character. As the patron saint of a secret society, as the inventor of handicrafts, as the being addressed in prayer, he looms as a pure, if somewhat shadowy, personality. It is as though two separate characters had become merged not so much in the Indian's consciousness as in his terminology. He *calls* two beings by one name, but they are not the same to him. When he tells funny stories, he means the trickster; when he prays, he is thinking of a god. He may of course confuse the two, but some conception of a nobler type of being exists.

This notion of the deity is found in Africa also. The Ewe of the West coast practice magic and do homage to the earth gods who cause drought, disease, and death. But they likewise believe in a god living far off in the sky. He retired thither in disgust at men's sinfulness and has since played a minor part in their worship. Nevertheless, he gets an occasional offering of white sheep. One division of this people, the Ho, go further. Every morning they pour out water on the ground and pray as follows: "O Mawu Sodza, owner of palm wine, owner of meat, give me today my food and grant that today I may remain alive." Here there is no trace of any traits defiling the divine character. Mawu sends nothing but help and blessings, and he is so strong that no one can overpower him.

On the other side of the continent the Jagga have a similar concept. Iruva, the Sun and Heaven god, is neglected in their cult, while the ghosts govern daily life. Yet he is considered creator of the first human beings, and all their tales stress his benevolence. They bless in his name, pray to him in an extremity, and even sacrifice beasts to him if the usual offerings to the spirits fail to help.

So in Siberia, the Yukaghir, with all their spiritistic séances, prayers to the gods of mountains and forests, rivers and the fire, also have a vague notion of a Supreme Deity called Pon, and their Sun is more definitely "a beneficent being, the protector of the oppressed, the guardian of justice and of morality." He is angered by bloodshed and he punishes incest.

But what does all this signify if such a faith is overshadowed in everyday life by belief in ghosts, evil magic, and a thousand weird supernatural forces? It would mean little if civilized man generally and actually held the faith he is supposed to hold. But theory is one thing and practice another among modern Caucasians. As a Canadian Indian once remarked to me, "White people will do anything." Let us turn to examples.

In 1927 the Rev. John R. Crosby reported witchcraft thriving "within sixty miles of materialistic Pittsburgh, side by side with the most aggressive forms of evangelical Christianity." In Indiana County, Pennsylvania, he found a colony of the South Russian sect of Thondrakians, who combine Christian doctrine with an unshakable faith in magic. Epileptics, they say, are possessed by the devil; women in confinement, by both good and evil spirits struggling for mastery. Hunchbacks, Negroes, and childless widows have the evil eye. Albino cattle and poultry bring good luck; a lump of beeswax melted in the sun removes a swelling; diseased eyes are bathed in the broth from a hawk's head; a barren woman takes milk with honey and eggs prepared by the mother of a family of seven living children in the presence of a witch. "I have seen a father send his son suffering from hemorrhage of the nose to bleed over the corn patch in order to fertilize the crops." Sorcery is common. An incensed Thondrakian steals his victim's shoe or sock to make him lame, fills it with hot coals or dips it in scalding water at night, and at the same time removes his own footgear. On the seventh day he takes the purloined object to the witch, who keeps it as long as necessary. The technique can be varied for all parts of the body. "This custom seems to be extremely popular, and is presumably efficacious, as the enchantress's hut resembles a clothing store. . . ." Death can be caused by manipulating the victim's hair, nails, or skin.

The professional sorceress of this community, one Marie Kountzik, inhabits a hut filled with herbs and charms. Black cats, a raven, and a flock of goats keep her company. Her fellows are convinced that "her father and the father of her own children was the devil himself, or, if not, at least one of his subordinates." They avoid her shack during the hours of darkness, and when a regular meeting of the initiates into the black ritual is reported, "it is a brave Thondrakian who leaves his home." The witches take on the shapes of black animals and resume their usual form at sunrise. They use a candle made of human fat, "which renders the celebration invisible to all except initiates." Dr. Crosby discovered a defective child of seven pining away because Marie Kountzik had bewitched it to revenge herself for not being invited to the naming ceremony. She appeared unbidden, removed the baby's cap, and announced that the infant would wither away. "The parents naturally did not consider that any medical attention or parental care could avail against the spells of the enchantress and allowed the child to grow up at its own sweet will in a room that was practically sealed in order to avoid the entrance of wandering evil spirits."

South Russians are of course ignorant and immoral foreigners. But along the bayous of Louisiana, in Iberia Parish, there is a mixed population of Negro, French, English, and Scotch descent. Well, it is not only the Negroes who shiver with fright at the screech of an owl and protect themselves against the bird by turning a shoe over on the window sill or tying a knot in the sheet. When a certain white child was troubled with shingles in recent years, its parents hunted up a black cat—at great inconvenience—docked the tip of its tail, and with the blood made a cross on the patient's chest. In another case, "the child nearly dead with diphtheria had the still warm body of a cat, killed and cut open for that purpose, placed on its throat and left there for several hours." Colored folk in the region resort to an old hoodoo doctor for toothache or asthma. A white neighbor is quite as likely to go to the Negro *traiteur* for these ailments—sometimes while being treated by a physician of his own race.

Even in so respectable a state as Illinois, villagers of eminently respectable (British) ancestry believe that carrying a potato in your pocket will cure rheumatism, that seeing the new moon over your left shoulder is very unlucky, and that persons married on a cloudy day will have a cloudy life. In Ontario the same fashionable ancestry seems to go well with similar notions. Eighty years ago cows were still bewitched so they would yield no milk unless a cross were marked on their horns and foreheads. Until recently bread was thrown into the water to find the corpse of a drowned person, for it would eddy about or sink at the right spot. These worthy Anglo-Canadians believed that the seventh son of a seventh son could tell fortunes and perform marvelous cures. They treated an inflammation of the eye with saliva or cow dung; and Mr. F. W. Waugh, writing in 1918, tells of a witch-doctor whom his grandfather consulted for an attack of dyspepsia.

Are these the superstitions of the illiterate? But only two centuries ago the best people had a firm faith in the royal touch. Young Samuel Johnson was taken to Queen Anne to be cured of the scrofula, and about the same time the learned anatomist Dionis, surgeon to the Queen of France, wrote as follows: "Many of those touched by the King declare that they have been cured; hence I advise all afflicted with this complaint to try so easy a spiritual remedy before submitting to the surgeon's hands." After the coronation and before certain holidays the King's physician and other doctors, surgeons, and barbers scrutinized a throng of candidates and sent off all except those seriously afflicted. These were made to kneel in two files, with hands clasped. The King appeared with his retinue, approached each patient, traced the sign of the cross on his face, and said to each one, "The King is touching thee, God heals thee" (*Le roi te touche, Dieu te guérit*). After his coronation Louis XIII thus treated 800 scrofulous persons, while on one Good Friday Louis XIV had as many as 1,800 patients. After the coronation ritual he and his successor touched, respectively, 2,000 and 2,400 people.

These were odd but harmless practices. Not so those which grew out of the belief in sorcery. Three or four hundred years ago, when Western Europe, not yet overrun by hordes of Southeastern barbarians, had a purer Nordic population than today, witchcraft was the prevalent belief of the duly constituted authorities—then as ever of course the purest Nordics in their respective countries. When a West African chief charges his own daughter with closing his eye by evil magic, we stand aghast. King James I of England was convinced that Dr. Fian, a Scotch schoolmaster, had thrown cats into the sea and thereby raised a storm against his sovereign returning from Scandinavia. The King examined him in person and ordered him to be tortured: "His finger nails were pulled off with a pair of pincers, and under what was left of them needles were inserted 'up to the heads.' "

The same monarch was not content with the law against witchcraft that held under Queen Elizabeth. The death penalty had hitherto been imposed only on those sorcerers accused of killing their victims. Under James's influence the statute was changed so that whoever used evil spirits for any intent or purpose should die as a felon. It was hard to prove murder. It was easy to convict on the testimony of village gossips that So-and-so kept a familiar spirit. Of thirty-seven witches executed in this monarch's reign, seventeen would have escaped under his predecessor. So strong is man's inherent and inevitable tendency to progress.

We are not here dealing with the prejudices of an illiterate mob. King James was a scholar. Before his accession to the throne he had investigated the matter of demons in a special treatise and laid down fundamental points of evidence for detecting witches. They bore on their bodies marks left by the devil, and they would float on the water, for the pure element would refuse to receive those who had renounced their baptism. James became morally indignant against the "damnable opinions" of Johann Weyer, a German physician who in 1563 had declared that the "witches" were pitiable mad women without power to hurt their fellow men. By this, wrote the King, "he plainly bewrayes himself to have been one of that profession." Educated opinion largely supported this conclusion. The learned Professor Thomas Erastus of Heidelberg also had denounced his tolerant colleague Weyer as himself a sorcerer. In 1653 a Cambridge philosopher, Henry More, published *An Antidote to Atheisme*. He used the stories of witchcraft as a telling argument for the reality of the spirit-world. He believed in nightly assemblies of the witches and repeated the tale of a sorcerer who "was carried over Shelford Steeple upon a black Hogge and tore his breeches upon the weathercock." This scholar wrote in the century of the scientific renaissance. Why not? As late as 1717 the last defendants in a British witch trial were put through the swimming ordeal by the enraged populace—only thirty years after Newton's *Principia.* To be sure, they were acquitted in court.

On the Continent magistrates were not so progressive. Let us take a glance at the witch trial of Zug, Switzerland.

On August 9, 1737, a seventeen-year-old girl, Katharina Kalbacher, came before the tribunal of Zug and made the following declaration. At the age of three she had been put into the custody of one Joseph Pfand. One day while this goodman was at church, his wife made the little girl cut herself and follow her. When the blood had been placed in a tumbler, the devil appeared, black and horned, and compelled her to abjure God and all his saints. Then they all rode stark-naked on sticks to the witches' gathering-place. These assemblies occurred frequently, by day and by night. The witches were invisible and had each her familiar devil, who counseled her as to the harm she might inflict on man and beast. Katharina had been made adult from her fourth year on. Henceforth she would take the form of a dog, cat, owl, mouse, or black pigeon, and in this guise she damaged some fifty head of cattle, fish, and fowl belonging to a convent. She had also filched two hundred florins from the nuns by passing through the keyhole of their well-locked strong-box. Katharina further confessed that the devil had made her and others cause a conflagration in the town of Sursee; that he had likewise given them hair, poison, pebbles, and human bones to throw into the air, thereby causing a shower of hail in Lucerne, Münster, Sursee, and Zug. She informed against some half dozen accessories by name—all of them poor women who were eking out a livelihood as itinerant peddlers. West African justice would have made them drink poison; in progressive Central Europe they were tortured. Some of them admitted their guilt under torture, some recanted after confessing.

Kathri Gilli refused to confess and was subjected to treatment not yet reported from Africa. On August 23, 1737, her prosecutors urged her to avow the truth and save her soul. Did she recognize these sticks (those supposedly used by her to ride on)? She did not, and was tortured. Did she confess having made a contract with the devil? She declared her innocence and was pulled into the air with a spiked iron collar around her neck. Even this argument failed; so hot water was poured over her. The defendant wailed terribly but still affirmed her innocence. After a long while she was let down. On the twenty-sixth she was urged again to confess and avoid torture. Declaring her innocence in God's name, she was promptly blindfolded and, with hands tied, was stretched in the rack. How long had she been holding commerce with the devil? Wailing, she implored all the saints to help her, for she had no knowledge of these matters. She was accordingly hooked to a rope attached to the ceiling, weighted with a rock, and raised by means of a pulley. The judge bade her declare the truth and forestall further suffering. She said she was being made a martyr and knew of nothing. The second degree was then applied in the form of a heavier weight. She called upon Jesus, Mary, and the Saints, affirming that "the most wise authorities" (*die hochweise Obrigkeit*) were wrongly informed. Pulled up with the heaviest stone—two-hundredweight—the stubborn wench still disclaimed all knowledge of witchcraft, and was excused after an hour and a half of this performance. On August 29 the defendant was whipped with three switches—in the name of the Holy Trinity; two days later she was treated to the iron collar and the third degree; on September 3 she received over three hundred lashes.

There followed an intermission: for about a month Kathri enjoyed peace—in a kennel-like prison cell not big enough to allow the inmate to stand erect or stretch out at full length. In the meantime a new complication developed. The peddler's pack used by Kathri was found to harbor a bag with white powder and a box with some salve. According to the accuser, the powder was poison used for destroying cattle and making hail, while the salve was smeared over the sticks ridden to the witches' meeting. In her simplicity the defendant expected the magistrates to believe that the powder was oatmeal and the salve nothing but butter! How could so improbable an interpretation find credence? Nevertheless, the judges decreed a physiological experiment. They made the executioner feed his dog a handful of the suspected substances. He reported that it had neither helped nor harmed the beast. Thereupon Katharina Kalbacher, the informer, explained that the powder was truly poisonous, but God would not allow an innocent dog to suffer from it. The counsel of this madwoman prevailed, while Kathri's offer to be herself tested with the supposed poison was spurned. To relieve the monotony of the proceedings she was once more tortured. On January 23, 1738, came the last cross-examination. Kathri still asserted her innocence, but her physical strength was gone, and while questioned she tumbled to the ground. Several days later she was found dead in her cell. Of her co-defendants several were pinched with red-hot tongs and burnt at the stake. By order of the court the ashes were buried under the gallows "lest any one take harm therefrom." The informer was treated more kindly: "By special charity, because despite her great misdeeds she had laid an accusation against herself before the most wise authorities, she shall be taken to the place of judgment in a tumbrel and there executed with the sword."

The judges were acting in good faith. They had nothing to gain by condemning a few indigent peddler women. They were not fiends who delighted in brutality for its own end, for again and again they begged their victim to confess and avoid torture. They were doubtless above the average of their contemporaries in learning. But their notion of the deity did not prevent a belief in the influence of Satan, and they saw nothing improbable in the idea of witches straddling sticks for a midnight ride, destroying beasts or men, and producing hailstorms. Some forty years later, in 1782, a maid—the contemporary of Kant, Hume, Goethe, and the Encyclopaedists—was beheaded in Glarus, Switzerland, for bewitching her master's child.

As the Jagga believe in a moral Creator *and* in food-craving ghosts; as the Siberian combines his faith in Pon and the Sun with an equally firm belief in dozens of spirits active for good and evil; so sixteenth, seventeenth, and eighteenth century Europeans were Christian monotheists *and* believers in devils and evil magic. The great De Haen (1704-1776), a Dutchman by birth and for some twenty years professor of medicine in Vienna, still persecuted witches. Neither Christianity nor science had been able to blot out savage ideas of the supernatural.

Are we beyond that sort of thing today? It is true that witch *trials* are a thing of the past. But are they gone forever? It is not well to be over-confident. Whenever popular excitement reaches a climax, legal forms and ideals go by the board. It was so in the Haymarket riots, in the Dreyfus case, in the recent war. So long as the *belief* in evil magic persists, favorable conditions might again give legal sanction to the prosecution of witches. Was not a French priest lynched less than five years ago for bewitching a peasant in his village? We may press electric buttons to switch on lights and drive automobiles, but the supernatural that baffled the reindeer-hunters of France 20,000 years ago is still floating about. Who wants a hotel room numbered 13? Is there not an office building in New York with the "fourteenth" story directly above the twelfth? Are there not rainmakers in the United States today? Do not many of our friends knock on wood to preserve their boasted good luck?

But must we not reckon with the advance of science? Must not all faith in the supernatural, whether as "superstition" or as "religion," wane as science gains ground? The idea is intriguing but naïve. Science has made spectacular changes, but it has not altered the basic facts of life. It has not "conquered Nature," as we like to boast; it has submitted to Nature, adapted itself better to the conditions of reality, and avoided some avoidable difficulties. It has not abolished the problem of evil. Sometimes it has merely removed some of our troubles and substituted others. Agriculture improves, population increases, but we are worrying over the food supply of the future. Life lengthens with better sanitation, and it means that there are more men who undergo prostate operations, more women who develop cancers. Our engineers achieve their impressive stunts, but the levees of the Mississippi break asunder. Earthquakes, typhoons, and similar disturbances remind us that we are not yet in control of the universe. If we were gods, the supernatural would cease to interest us. As it is, science is constantly leaving us in the lurch where we most want its aid.

Man turned to the supernatural as he came to feel his impotence in the universe at large. The poor fellow does not want to be God; he wants to survive in the struggle for existence with some minimum wage of happiness for his pains. He could not help being religious 20,000 years ago; he will be religious 20,000 years hence.

In the meantime anthropologists are eagerly studying the phenomenon of religion. They are making rapid progress: they already see that the African Negro is not worshiping a mere stick of wood but some power behind it. In another 10,000 years they will see that the Bavarian peasant, too, is not a mere idol-worshiper. Perhaps by 20,000 A.D. their view will be generally shared by the educated public.

CHAPTER XXI

HYGIENE AND MEDICINE

As RATS leave a sinking ship, so vermin will leave a dying man according to Greenland theory. Hence a louseless Eskimo is ill at ease. How pleasant and congenial is it for bosom friends to while away the hours catching the lice from each other's heads, "then gravely placing them between the teeth of the owner"! This mutual service is an absorbing pastime throughout the savage world. The people of the Amur River know of no better way to show conjugal devotion or true friendship. In the Altai Mountains or southern Siberia the Turks are no less addicted to the sport. Their furs teem with lice; the nimble-fingered natives are forever scouring them in search of game and devour them with a smack of their lips. Dr. Radloff personally counted eighty-nine specimens caught by his guide within the space of a minute. No wonder primitive folk-tales are full of references to this widespread and edifying custom.

It is not the only one of its kind. On the upper Nile, vessels are cleaned with cow's urine, and in the Altai with the filthiest rags of hide. The Siberian Turks never rinse out their pails because that would kill off the calves and keep cows from yielding the regular supply of milk. An Altaian woman thinks nothing of scratching her back with a ladle that has just been used to stir her food. I myself have seen a Hopi woman brush her hair one minute and the next sweep in her corn flour with the same little broom. Eskimo women wash their hair every day, and their bodies often enough, but not with water—with urine. The Altaians, on the other hand, never wash at all. A thick crust of filth settles on their skins, and their shirts turn into grease-soaked rags rotting away on their bodies before they are taken off. Greenlanders ease themselves outside their houses, and the loose dogs act as scavengers, but the dogs' excrements litter the floor. Disgusting, is it not?

But other primitive tribes make a better impression. Day in and day out the Cheyenne of our Western Plains took their plunge, even when they had to break the ice in the wintertime. Among the Baganda of East Africa the veriest peasant has a reed fence setting off his and his wife's bathroom. In the South American Chaco the Chiriguano start the day with a bath and repeat the performance several times before nightfall. Some of them live in arid country, and when the dry season balks them they will at least take a thorough wash every morning. As for the Polynesians, their cleanliness is proverbial. "Independently of their washing their mouths and hands before and after meals," wrote Captain Cook of the Tahitians in 1769, "both sexes never omit to wash with water three times a day—when they rise, at noon, and before they go to rest. They also keep their clothes extremely clean, so that in the largest communities no disagreeable effluvia ever arises, nor is there any other inconvenience than heat." These Polynesians were without question incomparably superior to all their civilized Caucasian contemporaries. European cleanliness had had its ups and downs, and by the eighteenth century was very far from the crest of the wave.

To begin with the beginning, the Greeks of course were gentlemen. In Homer wayfarers are always treated to ablutions when they get to a hospitable dwelling; an archaic vase shows us women enjoying a shower in two separate stalls; and the Spartans sweated themselves. The public baths had tubs or pools and were connected with the gymnasia. There was no soap, but lye, sodium carbonate, and pumice took its place, and the body was anointed with oil and liniments. Soap, incidentally, has an interesting history. Various weeds yield an excellent lather. They are still put to use in the Orient for cleaning shawls and served the same purpose among the ancient Greeks and Romans. When our Hopi Indians ceremonially adopt a woman, they still lather her head with the local soap-weed. But neither here nor among the ancients was soap linked with daily ablutions. Pliny credits the Gauls with preparing soap from goat's fat and potash, but for them and the Romans also it was a hair cosmetic. Galen in the second century of our era is the first to mention soap for washing either the body or clothing.

The early Romans started as rustic boors, but at least they swam about in the Tiber or washed their arms and feet every day in a dark and narrow space alongside of the kitchen. Every nine days a real bath was the rule. As the city grew, the river got filthy, but the Romans engineered aqueducts and put up pools beyond the gates. Greek notions set the standard, and so soon there were gigantic public baths. These "thermae" had separate sections for lukewarm and hot water, swimming-pools and steam heat, gymnasia, libraries, and art exhibits. Under the Emperors a bath a day was no more than proper for a self-respecting citizen, and gentlemen of leisure indulged themselves four or five times. Even at night the thermae were kept open, lit by countless lamps.

Not so in the early Middle Ages. To be sure, Christianity did not oppose baths per se—so long as they were intended to serve cleanliness or health and not sheer pleasure. But the ascetically-minded naturally set up lofty standards. One saint was for letting the sick bathe as often as they pleased, but others—especially the young—were to do so rarely, and monks were to be allowed ablutions at Christmas and at Easter. The Benedictines washed their heads every Saturday.

But the crusaders got into touch with Oriental customs and were stimulated into more frequent indulgence. Hence sprang the great public establishments of the Middle Ages, which became truly popular and indispensable institutions. Where a millionaire nowadays would endow a college, the same charitable impulse then made him give money for baths. In earlier centuries Scandinavians and Germans who nowadays give tips under the name of "drink-money" called them "bath-money." "Soul-baths" were founded on behalf of the salvation of deceased relatives. Even a creditor had to provide an imprisoned debtor with one bath a month.

Before the crusades Europeans had preferred tubs; now sweating came into vogue. As soon as the room was heated, the keeper blew a signal horn or had his attendants bawl the glad tidings through the streets. Sometimes a parade was organized on Saturdays to lure journeymen into the bath. The arrangements for bathing were essentially the same as among the Finns, the Russians, and many North American Indians: rocks were heated red-hot and, with water receiving them or poured over them, produced vapor. Each patron received a switch to whip his skin, and when he had sweated sufficiently, cold water was poured over his body. With the same idea Scandinavian peasants and Plains Indians would dash into the nearest creek or wallow in the snow. However, sweating did not wholly supersede other forms. In Paris, for instance, some customers were content to sweat, but others paid an extra fee and wound up their visit with a warm bath.

As in ancient Rome, so in medieval Europe the public baths became an institution with very wide functions indeed.

First of all, they were kept by barbers, and so nothing was more natural than to have a shave and haircut follow the sweating. But the barbers of that day were also surgeons and had an eye to business. As their descendants still lure a heedless customer into extravagant shampoos and facial massages, so the medieval barbers took pains to persuade their clients that nothing would add more to their happiness than being cupped and bled. But by an easy transition the bath where men of leisure whiled away hours of the day became a rallying-place, something like the coffee houses of a later date. Why bathe at home when one could so much more agreeably meet pleasant company at the sweat-house? There one might swap the news of the day, throw dice, and drink a jug of beer with boon companions. So the bath turned into a club in which bathing was a quite incidental affair. When a Danish wrecking-crew had done their work and got a barrel of beer in payment, they would naturally take it to the public bath to befuddle themselves there. About the close of the sixteenth century King Christian IV of Denmark, accompanied by his retinue, once proceeded to the bath house at Bergen. First he beguiled the time by shooting at a target; then he played a game of chess, and at last he went back to his palace. In Germany the Meistersinger turned the bath into a studio for the practice of minstrelsy.

Quite naturally the institution turned into a night club and a house of assignation. The barbers hired pretty girls to rub down their customers; men and women were often separated by the thinnest of partitions, and often they sat in joint tubs. Preachers began to wonder whether the sweat-house was more of a bath or a brothel.

Its downfall was imminent. The devout denounced it as a hotbed of vice. Then there was fear of infection. When syphilis began to sweep over Europe about the end of the fifteenth century physicians naturally warned against the use of public baths, which were sometimes closed by law. There was in addition an economic reason. The firewood indispensable for producing the required heat got scarcer; hence the price of a bath rose until the bulk of the people could no longer afford it.

By the Thirty Years' War bathing had thus ceased to be a German practice, and it was not taken up again until more than a century later. In 1832 a German writer still speaks of finding human beings who could not recall having taken a single bath in all their lives. The French were not superior to their neighbors. When Parisians no longer went to the sweat-house, they stopped bathing altogether. About 1640 a manual of etiquette advised its readers to take an occasional bath, to wash the hands every day, and to have their faces washed *almost* as often (*il faut aussi se faire laver le visage presque aussi souvent*). As late as 1782 a similar handbook solemnly lays down the following rule: "For cleanliness wipe your face every morning with a white linen. . . . It is not so good to wash it with water, for that makes the face more sensitive to cold in the winter and to sunburn in the summer."

It was thus very natural for Captain Cook to admire the Polynesians of 1769 for their sanitary habits. They were far ahead of Louis XIV, whose valet would pour a little perfumed alcohol on his hands by way of washing them. They were ahead of that elegant queen, Marguerite of Navarre, who finds it proper to write in an amorous dialogue with a lover: "Behold these beautiful hands; though I have not cleaned them for a week, I wager they eclipse yours."

But even the humble Eskimo do not cut so sorry a figure alongside of Europeans of modern times. About the close of the Middle Ages the children of gentlefolk were warned not to blow their noses with the hand that in those forkless days[1] held the meat. To use the *left* hand was quite proper. In 1530 Erasmus advises the use of a handkerchief, but considers it permissible to use two fingers instead, provided the foot is immediately set on what falls to the ground. A century later a single finger was still held allowable. There is no evidence that polite Europeans swallowed their parasites, but otherwise there was little to choose between them and the primitives. A French author in 1393 teaches his fair readers six ways of freeing their husbands from fleas, and a treatise in 1539 provides infallible recipes against fleas, lice, nits, and bedbugs. On a gala night at the Louvre we must picture the grand seigneurs of the period and their ladies arriving perfumed and bedizened with diamonds but with dirt-veneered skins. They ate with their fingers and knives and smeared the grease over their napkins, which had to be changed with every course. Henry IV was said to stink like a carrion (*il puoit comme une charogne*). From Erasmus we gather that in 1530 many West Europeans cleaned their teeth with their urine. Vermin were bred wholesale in the coiffures of eighteenth century ladies. The pathetic struggles of Nordic, Alpine, and Mediterranean humanity with sewerage have been set forth in an earlier chapter.

In the most brilliant capital of Europe the standards for nursing the sick between 1750 and 1800 would be incredible if they were not vouched for by unexceptionable authority. During his visit to Paris Emperor Joseph II inspected the largest hospital there. He was shocked to find in one and the same bed a sick man, a corpse, and a patient breathing his last. About a dozen years later Louis XVI suggested an investigation by the Academy of Sciences, and a committee including Lavoisier, Laplace, and Coulomb was ap-

[1] See page 48 f.

pointed. Their restrained report more than confirmed the Austrian monarch's observations. Patients and corpses were found lying together, and sometimes six men were jostling one another in a single bed. There was no special operating-room. In those days before anaesthetics were in vogue the nerves of the sick were racked by the sight of preparations for the ordeal and by the cries of the victims. Virtually no attempt was made to separate even contagious diseases. Women smitten with the smallpox were in the same room with fever patients. Linen was taken off one inmate's body and put on another. The itch naturally passed from patient to patient and even infected the nurses and the surgeons. "The Hotel Dieu," the Commission declared, "is an inexhaustible source whence this sickness spreads over Paris."

The Charité was better managed than the Hotel Dieu, but even there the sick rooms were not heated until 1786, and before that it was the commonest phenomenon for a patient to get a frozen nose or ear. The offending part was simply lopped off, and that was the end of it.

We are once more facing the story of urban life and its difficulties. The idea of founding public infirmaries was in itself progressive and noble. But man developed no new organ to cope with the problems of overcrowding. As the Siberian Chukchi who became a reindeer nomad invented a tent that was the negation of what a tent should be, so the metropolitan European was wholly nonplussed by urban life. He built and managed hospitals that defeated the purpose of their existence, so that the most pretentious specimen in France had a mortality of 22 per cent. and became a center of infection. Our great-grandfathers were savages, and hygiene is a nursling of the last fifty years.

Savages know that a whack over the head is likely to do harm, but as a rule they do not regard sickness or death as a natural phenomenon. A man falls sick because he has broken the taboo against eating bison tongue, or because an ancestor's grave stands neglected, or because some demon has entered his body. Possibly an enemy has got hold of his nail parings, hair, or discarded rags and tossed them into a pond with a curse. Quite likely he is "germ"-ridden: bits of charcoal, hairs, pebbles, snails, worms, have got inside his body and misbehave. Or his soul has been kidnaped. Professor Karl von den Steinen once innocently told a Brazilian Indian that all men were mortal. It struck the native as a wholly new and unbelievable proposition. It seemed like saying, "Sooner or later all men are murdered or bound to find a violent end."

Like theory, like practice. Hence curing is a part of religion rather than of science. There are household remedies for simpler ailments, but any serious case belongs to the diviner, the priest, the god-inspired medicine-man. Take the Jagga as a typical East African Negro. Whenever he is sick, the first thing is to call a soothsayer. Is the sickness caused by a sorcerer or a ghost? In the latter case, is it one of the recently deceased or of an older generation? Does he belong to the paternal or the maternal side of the family? After the diagnosis, a goat is slaughtered as an offering to appease the ancestor. Also the butcher alternately strokes the patient and the beast, for that is the way to transfer the disease to the animal.

In Siberia the spirits have snatched away the sick man's soul; so the doctor's task is to bring it back. Dare he attempt such a job? Well, he has patron saints to guide him to the Kingdom of Shadows. When he treats a patient, he first beats a tambourine and conjures his familiar spirits into it. Or perhaps he will call his forefathers and inhale their souls by the simple device of taking a few deep breaths. He wears a special coat to represent a bird's skin so that he can fly at will, and metal discs on it are his sun, moon, and stars to light his path when he travels to the underworld. With this outfit he is ready to defy the demons. He beats his drum and works himself into a trance till he falls down in a dead faint. When he comes to, he has marvelous tales to tell. His soul went to the Kingdom of Shadows, tracking the soul of his patient. He found it surrounded by its deceased kin and challenged them in bold words: "The soul that with you finds itself I come to take." They would not give it up; so he came to blows and, thanks to his helpers, took it by force. By way of safe storage he inhaled it and stuffed up his ears so it could not escape. All that remains is to put it back into the sick man's body and to ask his familiars to guard it.

The Salish Indians on Puget Sound have similar notions, which their doctors put into dramatic form. The ghosts have carried the sick man's spirit to the land of the dead, which lies in the west. A single physician would not be strong enough; so a college of eight are hired. They assemble in a house with their sacred boards and poles, and face westward. Each sings his sacred song. They are following the path of the ghosts till they reach a swift stream. At this point in the play each must walk a bee-line on a narrow pole. Woe to any one who slips, for he will come to grief. After a while they get to a second river and cross in imaginary canoes. At last the land of the dead is in sight. But the ghosts refuse to yield their victim peacefully, and a terrific battle ensues. Boys here take the part of the enemy and shoot burning cedar splints at the ceiling. The doctors triumph and bring back the purloined spirit, fighting rear-guard actions with the dead. They now face eastward, singing the song of the recovered spirit. As soon as the patient hears it, he gets up to dance. Then all that remains is for the doctors to pocket their fees. But if the sick man fails to rise, they have not recovered the right spirit and get nothing.

The Cochiti of New Mexico also stage a sacred play on such occasions. Disease is a matter of witchcraft. Sorcerers have made an image of the sick person and stuck cactus spines into his ears and stomach. They have cast pebbles or snakes into his body and, to be on the safe side, have also snatched away his heart. The poor man has heard them hooting about his house as owls or prowling near by as coyotes, for they can take what shape they will. Against these evil-doers a whole fraternity of physicians are drafted. With eagle feathers they try to brush away the objects shot into their client. Then they defy the sorcerers, and some of them go outside for a pitched battle with them. It is a dangerous enterprise, for their enemies are of gigantic strength, hurl them to the ground, and bespatter them with dirt. There are cries of combat, and at last the doctors rush back, panting and disheveled, with mud and ashes coating their heads. Their leader is carrying in the victim's effigy and tears it up till he discovers a grain of white corn. That is the kidnaped heart, and he returns it to its rightful owner. When he has sucked out the alien objects from the patient's body and vomited them out in the form of pebbles, thistles, ants, snakes, or what not, all is well. The evil magicians are of course impersonated by some of the doctors themselves, who change their voices, pad themselves with rags, and wear a corn-husk disguise on the head.

Similar ideas turn up in Wisconsin. A Menomini medicine-man builds a lodge, prays, sings, and shakes a rattle by way of inviting his spirit helpers. The patient and his friends outside hear him greeting and questioning them. Thus he finds out what is wrong. Sometimes they promise to help him. He then blows a wooden whistle. This coaxes the departed "shade" into the whistle, which is promptly stopped at both ends so the truant cannot escape. The tube is then fastened over the patient's breast, and in four days he is well: his soul has come back to where it belongs. But there may be another cause of illness. Possibly a sorcerer has been at work, shooting strange objects into his victim. Then the physician stoops over the patient, swallows some bone tubes from his outfit, blows on the sore spot, taps it woodpecker-fashion with a bone tube, and with this sucks out the trouble-makers. They may be so strong as to bowl him over, but undaunted he swallows the tube and at once vomits all the bones and all the objects cast into the sick man by his enemy. He shows the onlookers the quill, fly, worm, frog, finger nail, or what not that has been torturing him, and the cure is perfect. This is the favorite method of curing a man in most of America, in Australia, and other regions. Some foreign body has got into the sick person. The doctor removes it and exhibits it as a tangible proof of his skill.

How is it possible for savages to put up with such humbug? Are they not fools to fall prey to such transparent fraud? The answer is simple. Often enough the patient *is* cured. Either he enjoys a sturdy constitution, or his illness, while real enough, is of the psychic order. He has been frightened into illness by the thought of being bewitched. As soon as the physician shows him the bit of charcoal or pebble shot into him, the sick man takes courage and recovers. If he dies, it is because the hostile supernatural power is too strong for the physicians. *Our* doctors also lose patients. Their excuse is that science has not yet advanced far enough: *Nature* is too strong for them. Their theoretical explanation differs, but to the patient and his family it makes little difference *why* he dies. In either case medical technique is inadequate and fails to perform the task set.

However, the savage is not without sensible methods of treatment based on observation. In North America, in Hawaii, in South and East Africa, patients are made to take a vapor bath. This is often a religious rite, but it is more. Incidentally, at least, it makes the sick man sweat and often helps him recover. Massage is another common technique. The Crow use it for stomach trouble. I have seen an old man "kneading" a youth's abdomen with a stick that widened out at the bottom like a darning-last. Again, savages apply many herbs for swellings, diarrhoea, constipation, and other ailments. Most of these domestic remedies have never been tested scientifically, but some are undoubtedly of genuine value. How, pray, did we get quinine? From the South American Indians. In 1638 a vicereine of Peru suffered from an intermittent fever. Her Spanish physicians were unable to cope with it; then some one recommended the aboriginal remedy. She tried it and got well. Her physician brought quinine to Spain, and after bitter opposition it was established as the first great specific. Incidentally it upset all current theories of disease.[1] In the same century the ipecacuanha root was brought to Europe from Brazil. Our local anesthetics go back to the Peruvian's coca.[2]

Even primitive surgery is not to be sneezed at. Everywhere the butchering of game or the slaughter of domestic beasts as offerings taught the rudiments of animal anatomy. The Havasupai Indians of Arizona set and bandaged a fractured arm, bound it between thin splints, and tied it close to the body. Other people were masters at trepanning; we do not know why the ancient Peruvians and prehistoric Europeans cut out parts of the skull, but they often made a neat job of it. So did recent Melanesians, who according

[1] See page 260.
[2] See page 65.

to Professor Von Luschan succeeded nine-tenths of the time. In 1786, on the other hand, the Commission appointed by Louis XVI to investigate the Hotel Dieu hospital [1] reported that the same operation was invariably fatal there.

But surely the medical science of Western civilization towers immeasurably above that of savages? It does today. But even at present there is not so much to brag about, and the story of the past is not a pretty one. If the wits of all ages have leveled their shafts at doctors, if Petrarch, Molière, and Shaw have at different periods turned vitriolic about them, there has been ample provocation. Let us look at a few facts.

Western science starts with the Greeks, and Hippocrates (460-377 B.C.) marks the peak of ancient medicine. He was certainly a sensible man, for he recommended few medicaments, relied on observation and experience, surveyed a maze of facts and blazed trails. Nevertheless, in his anatomy, physiology, and pathology the greatest of Greek doctors in the golden age of Greek culture was only a few steps from the primitives. He did not know that there were such things as ovaries and did not connect the testicles with semen. Following older philosophers, he pictured the womb as two-winged: boys developed on the right side, girls on the left. The human organism, he believed, is made up of four juices —blood, phlegm, yellow bile, and black bile. If these fluids are properly mixed, all is well. But let one or the other predominate—especially phlegm or the yellow bile—and at once there is illness. The brain is a gland that secretes the phlegm, and the heart is the seat of the "pneuma," which regulates the four prime juices.

A hundred years later Aristotle (384-322 B.C.) had not advanced a jot in his notion of the brain. Its main function,

[1] See page 241.

he averred, was to cool off the heat generated by the heart! The semen contained the germ of the human body, and the female organism did nothing but provide material for its development. Four centuries later Galen (129-200? A.D.) held saner views of the nervous system and had some glimmerings as to the circulation of the blood. But his overample pharmacopoeia contained such definitely primitive medicines as human and dog excrements, and his general physiology and pathology do not differ advantageously from those of a speculative Sioux Indian or Hawaiian priest or Yukaghir medicine-man. A Siberian recognizes one soul in the head, another in the heart, a third pervading the entire body. Galen's life-principle, the "pneuma," is also threefold; it resides in the brain, in the heart, and in the liver. For the Yukaghir disease is soul-loss; most commonly, the head-soul flees from an evil spirit that has entered the body. Galen does not bring in such demons, but elaborates infinite nonsense of his own. He defines medicine as the science of health, of disease, and of a neutral something in between. He declares that every human being is predisposed to illness, for invariably one of the four humors or juices is overdeveloped. He traces sickness to a change in the solid and fluid parts of the organism. He believes that every remedy acts according to its predominant temperament. It may be warm, cold, moist, or dry; each of these qualities may be weak or strong; and two of them may be jointly predominant. This mythology is more intricate than the Yukaghir beliefs, but not a whit nearer the truth. Nevertheless it reigned supreme in the Roman Empire and dominated the Middle Ages.

Of course skillful physicians and effective cures were not lacking even at the lowest ebb of science. A man does not lose his common sense and his manual deftness by practicing medicine. In individual cases intuition, observation, and logic will do wonders. But so they will in the practice of Christian Scientists and of savages. Trustworthy European witnesses who are still living report amazing cures by Tiurai, a native doctor in Tahiti. Turn the matter as one will, as a *science* medieval medicine was inconceivably backward. Here and there germs of progress can be noted. The Arabs treasured what the Greeks had left to posterity and made it accessible. In some respects they even made contributions of their own. They surpassed the ancients in the treatment of eye diseases, and Rhazes of Bagdad (850-923) wrote a creditable monograph on smallpox and measles. But they also flavored medicine with astrology, and the great encyclopedia or Canon of Arabic medicine by Avicenna (980-1037) clung slavishly to Galen's juices and qualities, doing no end of mischief. The physicians, as Petrarch said, spun syllogisms, but failed to cure. Hoary scholastic nonsense went hand in hand with astrology and a belief in witches. There was even plain humbuggery. Arnaldus de Villanova (1234?-1311) is lauded as the most impressive figure in medieval medical history. This is the counsel he gives to his disciples: "If you wholly fail to understand your patient's case, tell him confidently that he has an obstruction of the liver. If he answers that his pain is in the head or some other part of the body, assert boldly that it comes from the liver. Be careful to use the word 'obstruction' (*opilatio*), for the sick do not know what it means, and it is important that they should not." Altogether we can simply stand aghast at the state of the profession in, say, 1500 A.D. and later.

The Crow Indians believe that all things in the universe go by fours. One of the celebrated European doctors of only four centuries ago, Kornelius Agrippa (1486-1535), makes a plea on behalf of the number seven. Was not the world created in seven days? Did not Adam and Eve stay seven hours in paradise? Are there not seven beatitudes? Small wonder, then, that human life as a whole is pivoted on the same mystic number. The newborn infant's life depends on its seventh hour, teeth appear in the seventh month, at twenty-one months the child begins to speak, at seven years the milk teeth are shed, at fourteen comes puberty, at twenty-one maturity, at thirty-five growth ceases, at forty-nine the perfect age is reached, and seventy years mark the close.

The same writer—a pensioner of Francis I of France and physician-in-ordinary to his mother, Louise of Savoy—instructs us concerning the influence of the heavenly bodies. The sun governs the brain and heart, the thighs and the right ear; the tongue, the hands, the legs, and nerves are Mercury's wards; Saturn presides over the blood, the veins, the back, and the nostrils; Venus claims the mouth, the kidneys, and the genitalia; and the moon is in charge of the body generally, and of the brain, stomach, and lungs in particular. Another writer of the period enlarges on the signs of the zodiac: the Twins govern the arms and shoulders; the Lion, the heart, liver, and back; the Virgin, the intestines; the Scorpion, the internal genitalia; Sagittarius, the external sex organs; and so forth. A practicing physician was supposed to pay proper attention to the heavens. A wounded arm, for instance, was dangerous if the injury occurred while the moon was in the sign of the Twins; and in this celestial condition no one would advise bleeding. Expert medical opinion uniformly explained the plague in astrological terms. In 1623 Gui de la Brosse, physician-in-ordinary to Louis XIII and founder of the Botanical Garden in Paris, did so at great length in a special treatise. Richelieu's doctor, the equally distinguished Citoys, was quite as explicit: "The pest is caused by the malign aspects of the planets, above all by the conjunction of Saturn and Mars in human signs such as the Twins and the Virgin. Solar and lunar eclipses are of the same order."

Such were the men who prided themselves on not being mere apothecaries or surgeons, let alone peddlers of nostrums. It cannot be denied that the latter fell below standards of professional etiquette. In 1676 the council of Leipzig forbade them to appear with jesters, whose ribald jokes and antics unbecoming to Christians (*grobe Zoten und denen Christen nicht geziemende Narrentheidungen*) were deemed offensive. But over a century later a German writer recalled having seen an itinerant quack giving a vaudeville entertainment with his clown while dispensing medicines. The Herr Doktor mounted a stage—a magnificent figure, booted and spurred, clad in a scarlet uniform and wearing a cocked hat topped with plumes. Beside him stood his servant in harlequin's garb, armed with a lath, purposely misunderstanding his master's orders so as to amuse the rabble. The doctor opened a huge medicine chest, explained the virtues and price of each remedy, and lashed the clown for his ridiculous glosses. Whoever wanted a particular medicine tied the coins in his handkerchief, and thus threw them on the stage. Harlequin opened the container, put in the nostrum, and flung it back with some jocular remark. When enough of the stock-in-trade had been sold, the doctor walked a tight-rope and finished with a few sleight-of-hand tricks.

But undignified as the spectacle was, in essence the quack was no worse than duly trained members of the profession. He did prescribe the wearing of a finger ring against the gout. But why not? The great Johann Baptista Van Helmont (1577-1644), steeped in the knowledge of his day at the

University of Louvain, thought a metal ring was excellent for hemorrhoids; believed that the dropsy would give way to a girdle of live toads; and had *seen* a peasant cured of this disease by a bellyband from the slough of a snake (*vidi rusticum hydropicum sanatum, alligata anguium senecta per ventrem et renes*). As a remedy for pleurisy he recommended a powder from the penis of a stag or bull, but the blood of a he-goat would do—provided it was got by castrating the animal as it hung from its horns, with its hind legs tied to them.

It is true that the famous Fleming was a mere theorist in medicine. Not so Moise Charas, a distinguished practitioner in Paris, Holland, and Spain, a member of the French Academy of Sciences, and professor at the Jardin des Plantes. His *Pharmacopoeia* (1691) was hailed with enthusiasm by the physicians-in-ordinary of the French royal family. The Dean and Faculty of Medicine at Paris vaunted it as a treatise containing the best of the ancients' legacy together with the latest acquisitions of science. Well, according to this standard work, the salt of the woodlouse and the earthworm were effective against the gout, the dung of a peacock against epilepsy, and the oil of ants against deafness. Charas had a worthy successor in Nicolas Lémery, who received equally weighty testimonials from the highest authorities and whose main treatises ran into anywhere from five to more than twenty editions. In his *Pharmacopoeia* he provides the following recipe for an oil against sciatica, paralysis, and nervous disorders: "Take two little newborn dogs. Cut them in pieces, put them in a varnished pot with a pound of living earthworms, boil for twelve hours until the little dogs and the worms are well cooked." The *Dictionary of Drugs* by the same author furnishes many details as to the virtues of stones. Thus we learn that the little stones in the head of a pike are good for stones in the bladder and for cleansing the blood; those from the head of a perch were to be crushed and taken internally as an aperient. With fine discrimination Lémery refused to believe that a sapphire could strengthen the heart and counteract poison, but accepted it, when pounded up fine, as a remedy for diarrhoea and a hemorrhage.

The problems discussed by medical students of the period were worthy of their masters. Here are some of the choice thesis subjects investigated by candidates for a degree at Paris, with their respective dates:

1589. Is the air more necessary than food and drink?
1622. Is water more wholesome than wine?
1639. Should a girl mad with love be bled?
1643. Is it of advantage to get drunk once a month? (*An singulis mensibus repetita semel ebrietas salubris?*)
1648. Are pretty women more prolific than others?
1669. Is woman lewder than man? (*Est ne femina viro salacior?*)
1720. Is a woman the more prolific the lewder she is? (*An quo salacior mulier eo fecundior?*)

No wonder enlightened wags like Molière showed scant respect for a guild that encouraged such trivialities.

During the Middle Ages, and even later, doctors of medicine were indeed essentially organized into trade unions of ignorant pedants pledged to a holy war against all quacks not educated in the official brand of charlatanism. The Church never pursued heretics with more zeal than the Parisian Faculty of Medicine displayed against the herbalists and greengrocers who supplied the rabble with nostrums. At a time when doctors prescribed bleeding for the smallpox, for measles, and as a general preventive of disease—in 1659—Dr. Gui Patin boasted of how a distinguished lawyer had been saved from a bad case of pneumonia by being bled seventeen times! "If he had been treated by some charlatan, . . . he would be dead." But the physicians' chief competitors, the real objects of their hatred, were the surgeons and the barbers. No sooner did these under-dogs impudently raise their heads than the doctors smote them hip and thigh. For the doctors were graduates of the University, gentlemen who wrote Latin and *scorned every form of manual labor.* Until the eighteenth century they would not stoop to treat venereal diseases; they would not touch a woman in childbed; and they would literally sooner have a patient die than lose caste by personally bleeding him. Such tasks belonged to the surgeon. In the seventeenth century at least two human bodies a year were supposed to be cut up under the auspices of the Faculty. But that did not mean that the learned professors themselves so much as dirtied their finger tips by touching a corpse. *They* sat in their chairs while those lowly mechanics, the barbers or surgeons present, made the dissection under the guidance of their superiors. Yet with a despicable dog-in-the-manger attitude the Faculty clung to their monopoly in corpses and fought tooth and nail whenever the surgeons had got hold of a body for closer study.

From these logic-chopping fools intent only on preserving their vested interests no progress could be expected. That came from the fold of the menial barbers. In 1532 there arrived in Paris a poor lad named Ambroise Paré. As an apprentice he learnt to shave, comb, and dress wounds like his fellows. Then came several years' experience in a hospital, and at last he became a master surgeon-barber, opened a shop, and hung out the usual three basins as a sign of his trade like other members of his union. When war broke out he served as an army surgeon and had the amazing temerity to use his eyes and his head in the field. At that time wounds from firearms were considered poisoned and were burnt out with boiling oil. After one battle there happened to be a dearth of oil, so many patients were treated without it. Paré could not sleep from worrying over their fate, when, lo and behold! they were found uniformly in better condition than the rest. Once more a great discovery had been made quite casually.

Paré (1510-1590) is hailed as "one of the greatest surgical geniuses of all times." He operated with rare skill and influenced every phase of his science. Unlike most reformers he was a model of modesty and virtue. But all this was no security against being hounded by the learned medical professors. How dare he write in French when the scholar's tongue was kitchen Latin? How dare he discuss the treatment of fever? That was crossing the bounds which divide surgery from medicine. The Faculty was outraged and brought legal action against him. Fortunately Paré had proved his caliber in the highest circles and as court surgeon enjoyed royal favor. But it took the authority of the King himself to quash the indictment.

As Paré looms in the history of surgery, so the Belgian Andreas Vesalius (1514-1564?) towers in that of anatomy. He was the first to prove by dissection that the great Galen had depended on his knowledge of lower animals and was hopelessly wrong in his notions of human anatomy. Vesalius was of course bitterly assailed by the medical guild, and his former teacher Dubois, a shining light of the University of Paris, denounced him as not Vesalius but "Vesanus" (mad). In England William Harvey (1578-1657), who overthrew Galen in physiology, was not more fortunate. It took him seventeen years to develop his theory of the circulation of the blood (1628). Another pun promptly branded him as a charlatan (*Circulator*); the Parisian Faculty of Medicine, ever true to its traditions, rejected his teachings; and he lost most of his professional practice.

Medical opinion was no more tolerant in German-speaking countries. In 1529 Paracelsus attempted to print important papers on syphilis. The town council of Nuremberg gave its imprimatur, but the medical faculty of Leipzig circumvented publication. The profession did not undergo a spiritual rebirth in the eighteenth century. That Jenner (1749-1823) should meet with obstinate opposition when he introduced vaccination might have been expected. But he was denied even a hearing: his essay on the causes and effects of the *variola vaccina* was rejected by the editor of the *Philosophical Transactions.*

But certainly the wonderful nineteenth century, when science was a word to conjure with, must have brought a change. It did not. There is the pathetic fate of the great Hungarian reformer of midwifery, Ignaz Philipp Semmelweis (1818-1865). When a young assistant at the Obstetric Clinic of Vienna, he was shocked by the frightful mortality from childbed fever. In 1846 there were 460 deaths in the first clinic and 105 in the second. The foremost authorities of the world then held quaint notions as to the causes of the disease. Some connected it with erysipelas; others treated it as milk-fever. Mere changes in the weather were made to account for the greater prevalence of childbed sickness. Women in confinement were said to be peculiarly sensitive to obscure cosmic influences that sometimes swept over whole districts.

At that time all physicians in Austria had to make as many autopsies as possible, from which they would hurry to their patients. Semmelweis hit upon the brilliant idea that the doctor's hands might carry infection from the corpses to the women in confinement and *thus were themselves the cause of the fever.* He made every obstetrician under him disinfect his hands before approaching a pregnant woman. The effects were striking and uniform. The mortality at once decreased from 8 to 1.28 per cent.

Semmelweis provided long series of statistics. He showed conclusively that the clinic which followed his method had an incomparably lower number of deaths than the one that did not. He riddled the explanations that women died from poor ventilation, premature getting up, overcrowding, and atmospheric influences. He proved that women overtaken with labor on the way to the hospital were immune to the fever in spite of the unfavorable conditions they were exposed to. He pointed out that in schools for midwives the fatal cases were far fewer than in institutions for the training of medical students. The midwives of course did not have to make post-mortem examinations! But neither logic nor statistics prevailed. Committees were appointed to look into the facts, but the medical grand moguls prevented them from meeting. Semmelweis was ousted from his assistantship, assailed by eminent professors at home and abroad, and finally driven into an insane asylum.

It is a favorite pastime of some historians to paint a lurid picture of the Church arresting progress. But it was not the Church that hounded Semmelweis or put obstacles in his path. It was the illustrious Virchow who remained skeptical until it was too late to encourage the bold innovator. It was the celebrated Professor Scanzoni in Würzburg, the eminent Von Siebold in Göttingen, and their peers, who misunderstood, lied, and slandered.

Are doctors, then, sheer frauds and callous fiends? By no means. For the most part they are honest and kindly enough. But when hundreds of people flock into any calling, we cannot expect the average member to be an intellectual giant or a moral hero, whether he is a physician, an artist, or a hodcarrier. Semmelweis had the courage to proclaim that before his discovery he must have caused the death of an indefinite number of women. But such frankness cannot be expected from the everyday practitioner who feels that he must live and support his family, and above all save his face. On the intellectual side it is much easier to mumble outworn formulae about unknown cosmic influences on pregnant women than to find out what specifically causes the fever. And when some one else does point out the true cause, how is the poor practitioner to know that it is not a freak idea—"clever, but not sound"? After all, psychologically he is much in the same situation as a critic who faces a new work of art. How could you tell forthwith that Wagner's music was not pure claptrap? There is only one practical difference. If you pronounce *The Ring of the Nibelungen* to be empty noise there is little harm done. But on the other hand, if you thumb your nose at Semmelweis and keep on gayly dissecting corpses and delivering women with unwashed hands you are a carrier of disease and death. But how can this difference be fairly blamed on the physician? Nature unfortunately does not give men insight in proportion to the seriousness of their tasks.

Even at their worst, doctors as a class are not below the moral par of the man in the street or the savage medicine-man. A Crow leech expects to be cured by the very technique he employs on his patients. A civilized physician also practices what he preaches. Dr. Patin cured a colleague in 1661 by dint of twenty-two bleedings, but when smitten with a bad cold allowed his own veins to be opened seven times.

"My profession right or wrong" expresses a keen and touching sense of group loyalty, no less sincere than the patriot's. How dare a mere psychoanalyst treat mental disorders which the regular practitioners neglect? How dare a mere chemist like Pasteur poach on the sacred preserves? This sort of attitude even nurtures a martyrdom of its own. When quinine came into vogue, Stahl of Berlin (1660-1734) would not give up his theory of fever. *That* was one of Nature's peculiar means of curing, he contended, and must not be interfered with. He declared that he would rather perish than use the new remedy, and he doubtless meant it. Men get intoxicated with their theories and are willing to die for them. It is a pity, though, that they want others, too, to die for them.

In short, medicine developed like all other branches of culture. The desert swaths are wide, the oases few and far between. In some periods official medicine is a farrago of utter nonsense; sometimes the greatest doctors mingle sound judgment with savage imbecility. De Haen of Vienna (1704-1776) was the first to use the thermometer in the sick room, but defended the belief in magic and prosecuted witches.

True progress in medicine, as everywhere else, has often come as unplanned as Paré's repudiation of boiling oil.[1] It has come through borrowing on the grandest scale. Doctors have not only borrowed cocaine and quinine from the Peruvian Indians; they have taken over more and more of the results of pure science. Where would modern medicine be without X-rays, microscopes, photography, serum therapy, and chemical analysis? But let us remember that most of these fine things do not date back a hundred years. Imagine the treatment of eye diseases before Helmholtz devised his mirror for looking at a living retina! Yet that happened as

[1] See page 256.

late as 1851. Characteristically, a famous contemporary surgeon told Helmholtz he would never use the instrument since the dazzling light was dangerous for diseased eyes. Another colleague was willing to concede that physicians with defective vision might find the ophthalmoscope helpful, but since his own sight was excellent, he would not need it.

Let us remember that we are still a good way from the goal. It is not only diseases like cancer that baffle our practitioners. The Spanish proverb still holds good: "If you have a cold untreated, it will last a month; call a doctor, and it will take thirty days."

CHAPTER XXII

SCIENCE

Is THERE such a thing as primitive science? To recall some of the beliefs set forth in earlier chapters is enough to make any one doubt it. How can any rational being suppose that it makes any difference whether one sings a song once or four times, that rain will fall if you make a cup overflow, that your hunting luck is improved by chanting a magical formula and spoiled by crossing the path of a menstruating woman? If this sort of thing seems pitiable, savage speculation about the origin of the world and man is worse. What a notion to have the Creator send birds and beasts to the bottom of the sea to fish up a bit of mud so he can fashion it into our earth! As for primitive ideas of the heavens, the Crow Indians tell how a sister and her six brothers escape from an ogre and then decide to turn into something everlasting. After a debate they rise to the sky and form the Great Bear. Eskimo astronomy is of the same order. The Moon was once living in a house with his sister, the Sun. Night after night he lay with her in the dark. At last she wanted to find out who was her lover, smeared her hands with soot before lying down, and rubbed her hands over her sweetheart's shoulders. When the lamps were lit in the morning, she discovered her brother's incest. Indignantly she cut off one of her breasts and tossed it to her brother, saying, "As you seem to be so fond of me, eat me then!" Then she dipped a stick with moss at its end into train-oil, ignited it, and dashed out, rising into the air. The Moon pursued her with a similar stick, but his lamp moss went out, leaving only some glowing embers. That is why the moon does not shine so brightly as the sun.

The rest of Greenland science is on the same plane. Two hags bickering over a seal-hide up in the air cause thunder by rubbing the skin. Snow is nothing but the blood of the dead; rain, the water overflowing a basin in the sky. The first earth created was quite flat and without water, but the deity was displeased with the human beings on it, so he split up the earth. The water poured forth and men were hurled into the cracks and turned into the spirits of the underworld—broad, noseless folk. The earth was re-created and at first completely covered with ice, which gradually melted away. Then two mortals fell down from the sky, and their descendants peopled the earth.

These are indeed childish ideas. But the Eskimo can do better. They not only recognize more constellations than the average city-dweller in the United States, but divide the year according to the new moons. They note the first time the star Alpha Aquilae (Atair) is seen in the morning twilight. Both from this star and from the position of the sun they can tell when the shortest day has arrived. Above all, their geographical sense would pass belief if it were not confirmed by every white visitor. After traveling in a district once in his life, an Eskimo can give an accurate account of it years later. He will state in what spot narwhals abound, where there are bears or seals or gulls. In 1883-85 Captain Holm drew a sketch-map of the East Greenland coast between 66° and 68½° Northern latitude. He had never had an opportunity personally to explore this region, but used the natives' descriptions and drawings. In 1899-1900 Captain Amdrup went there, and according to Holm it was "amazing to see in how many points the sketch-map in question corresponds with the reality. . . . The position of several places and islands is given so exactly that they lie either at the latitude given in the sketch-map or very close to it." The Greenlanders themselves carve out maps in wood, indicating not only the contours of the country but also its relief (Fig. 38). In recent times they have learnt to draw maps on paper. "In these the Eskimo display an accuracy which has been put to the proof by many of the earlier and more recent travelers. . . ." Captain Hall has published

FIG. 38. ESKIMO MAPS (*after Thalbitzer*)

the facsimile of a chart drawn by a wholly uneducated Eskimo based on his travels over a distance of 1,100 English miles. On comparing it with the Admiralty chart of this region, Francis Galton wrote down this verdict: "I have seen many MS. route maps made by travelers a few years since, when the scientific exploration of the world was much less advanced than it is now, and I can confidently say that I have never known of any traveler, white or brown, civilized or uncivilized, in Africa, Asia, or Australia, who, being unprovided with surveying instruments, and trusting to his memory alone, has produced a chart comparable in extent and accuracy to that of this barbarous Eskimo."

Professor Speck tells us that the Indians of northeastern Canada display a similar geographical genius. In an extraordinary way they remember and visualize the configuration of the land, so that Government surveyors make use of their ability. "By the Indians sheets of birch bark are inscribed with the point of a knife, sometimes with a burnt stick or pencil, with the utmost freedom and confidence to show the relative positions of lakes, rivers, and portages." Other phenomena are ignored for the simple reason that they are of no practical value to hunters and travelers who use only waterways.

In this connection the Micronesians may also be mentioned. Waves, winds, or currents often carry them far out of their way, so that men from the Caroline Islands have been known to drift to Formosa. The Marshall Islanders, however, have tried to aid navigation by charts—simple frames of leaf-stalks tied together, with curved sticks to represent swells, and shells here and there to indicate the atolls.

The savage everywhere has the sort of knowledge that lies at the basis of science. He knows the plants, animals, and rocks of his area as no one but a naturalist among us knows his. Take any field that interests a native, and you will be astonished at the wealth of his vocabulary. The distinctions he draws in his speech prove how accurately he has observed the facts. A Kirghiz nomad in Central Asia calls a horse *kysyl* if it is pure white; *kök*, if the hairless spots about the mouth and flanks are black; *kysyl kök*, if the head, the rear of the thighs, the mane and tail show a brownish tinge; *kara kök*, if these regions have a darker grayish shade. A brown horse with white chest is *schabdir;* if mane and tail are white, it is called *ker*. White piebalds with large dark spots are classed as *ala;* with small speckles they are *schybar*. We might expect special terms for stallion, gelding, mare, colt. But the Kirghiz goes far beyond such a crude classification. A newborn colt is *kulun*, a two-year-old *tai*, a three-year-old *kunan*, a four-year-old *dönön*. A mare is *baital* before, *biä* after, having offspring; if she fails to give birth by summer, she is *kyssyr biä*, if altogether barren *tu biä*. These are only a few relevant samples; add the words for horsegear, those connected with the butchering, milking, riding, and pasturing of horses, and the grand total is impressive. So is the corn vocabulary of the maize-growing Hopi or the bison vocabulary of the Plains Indians. These people have severally adjusted themselves to Nature in definite ways and made close observations of what was essential to them. They are using the same sort of mental operations as ourselves: they observe, they classify, they draw inferences and make practical applications. The very same people who at one moment think the most arrant nonsense turn at another into past masters of logic. In this they resemble not only the civilized man in the street but even great scientists.

But do they ever rise beyond purely practical matters without at once becoming absurd? Well, here and there alien races exhibit a quite academic intellectual curiosity. Let us listen to a Lutheran missionary, the Rev. Hr. Gutmann, among the Jagga of East Africa: "It was late in the evening, the mountain wind was rattling the tin roof, and I heard the merry laughter and squabbling of my young wards. Suddenly there is a gentle rap at the door. I cry out, 'Come in!' My servant enters and looks at me with a smile of embarrassment. When I ask him what he wants, he replies, 'Sir, we have laid a wager, and you are to settle it.' Well, that was nothing extraordinary, for they bet with passionate eagerness: about the meaning of this or that foreign word or Scriptural proper name, whether Zanzibar is British or German, whether it is possible to sleep in the water for a night, whether this or that trick is feasible, whether a man would dare to walk through a ghosts' grave at night, and so forth. Nevertheless I was astonished when he added: 'We are discussing whether there is an end to numbers, or whether if we go on counting we finally get to a number from which one must turn back.' That was a first flight from the narrow circle of their arithmetical experience into infinity."

This may be no more than a glimmering of abstract thought. But the Maya Indians of Yucatan had more: they actually invented a zero symbol and a position system of notation. To grasp what this meant we have to realize the history of these fine things in Western civilization. The Greeks had nothing of the sort. Accordingly, they worked the simplest examples by methods complicated beyond anything we can conceive. As Whitehead has said, "Probably nothing in the modern world would have more astonished a Greek mathematician than to learn that, under the influence of compulsory education, the whole population of Western Europe, from the highest to the lowest, could perform the operation of division for the largest numbers." The Romans made some steps in advance, but it was the Hindus who developed our system of numerals and the Arabs who brought it into Europe during the Middle Ages. Where the Greeks and the still relatively pure Nordics of a thousand years ago miserably failed, a Central American people achieved one of the greatest triumphs of abstract thought. Europe caught up with the benighted Redskin by borrowing from India ultimately and from the Arab world directly.

In science as in every part of civilization there has been

no one chosen people. We owe much to the Greeks, but the Greeks freely picked up what they could in Egypt and Babylonia. Egyptian geometry was a crude rule-of-thumb affair, but it formed the groundwork of Greek mathematics. Thales (about 600 B.C.) was glad to profit by contact with the priests of the Nile country, and when Democritus (about 420 B.C.) bragged about his skill he said, "In constructing lines according to given conditions no one has ever surpassed me, not even the so-called rope-stretchers of the Egyptians." In astronomy the Babylonians were preëminent. Even before 700 B.C. they measured time through the shadow cast by a vertical rod, and this device was introduced from Babylon into Greece by Anaximander (547 B.C.). From the same source came the Greek zodiac. Indeed, most of the classical names of stars are translated from Babylonian originals. By 800 B.C., long before Greek learning had scored its triumphs, the royal astronomers of Babylonia were able to predict eclipses of the moon.

Further, remarkable as Greek science certainly was, it had its weak sides. An aristocratic bias among the ancients made them look down on any one who *applied* science as a mere mechanic. Besides there were plenty of slaves to do the menial tasks of life; hence there was little stimulus for the invention of machinery. To be sure, Archimedes (287-212 B.C.) not only calculated the circumference of a circle and helped to found theoretical mechanics, but also constructed engines of war to defend Syracuse against the Romans. However, according to Plutarch, he himself scorned such practical applications and "would not deign to leave behind him any commentary or writing on such subjects," his heart being "in those purer speculations where there can be no reference to the vulgar needs of life."

This attitude must have been harmful even to the progress

of *pure* science. Helmholtz, perhaps the greatest German scientist of the nineteenth century, has told us emphatically that every physicist must be something of an amateur mechanic. He himself would try to construct instruments he needed in order to learn what were the practical difficulties met. What seems a slight error in the instrument may have very vital effects on our knowledge of Nature. Here the physicist may be helpless: only the craftsman who knows what the materials permit can solve the practical problem. If he succeeds the scientific result will be accurate; if *he* fails, it may be worthless. "What," asks Helmholtz, "would physics and astronomy be like, what our notions of the cosmos and our atmosphere, where would be our telescopes, electrical telegraphs, electric illumination, what would have been the course of navigation and surveying, without the constant and intelligent aid of practical mechanics?"

In this respect the Romans made up for what the Greeks lacked. Their practical building and engineering filled a real gap in human accomplishment. For many centuries their work in these fields was not even approached. The medieval Moors and Spaniards were only too glad to march over the roads laid out by Imperial Rome. The industrial side of our present civilization certainly owes something to that source.

Even on the theoretical side, the Greeks had their foibles. Their abominable notation kept arithmetic and algebra halting behind geometry. Here we have seen the Hindus enter the scene.[1] But they did much more than give us our numerals. The campaigns of Alexander the Great (330 B.C.) brought India into touch with the Mediterranean world. The Hindus profited from the vistas opened to them and made contributions of their own, for example, the notion of negative numbers. While the Arabs were probably less

[1] See page 267.

original, they did put together the heritage from the ancients with what they learnt from the Hindus. Thus they achieved a civilization in Spain that was definitely higher than anything known elsewhere in the tenth century. Their works on algebra remained standard textbooks in most of Europe until the end of the Middle Ages. The very term we use for this branch of mathematics is Arabic. So are various words in our astronomical vocabulary, such as zenith and nadir.

Clearly enough, our modern science is a coat of many colors, a patchwork of Egyptian, Babylonian, Greek, Roman, Hindu, and Arabic shreds.

Science is a part of culture. It is not something apart floating in an ether of pure reason. Those who foster it have the Jekyll-Hyde character of the craftsmen and herders, tillers and leaders of men, whose psychology has been described in previous chapters. Hence the history of science is shot though with the same sort of irrationality, and its devotees produce sense and nonsense in fairly equal profusion.

Sometimes the irrational features may not matter much one way or the other in the long run. Thus science has fashions that change like the styles of skirt and hair-dressing. Sixty years ago the watchword was evolution. The concept was applied indiscriminately to everything under the sun—astronomy, history, and sociology as well as biology. In botany and zoölogy, more particularly, it was *à la mode* to work out the probable pedigrees of species from the lowest to man. Suddenly there was a change and attention came to be fixed on heredity. Are there still here and there biologists who want to trace the genealogy of some animal form? The more respectable members of the guild shrug their shoulders. Why bother about dotards and their depraved tastes? Yet the new workers are as firm believers in evolution as the older generation. But if evolution has taken place, why not let some one work out its steps? One might as well ask why our ladies no longer wear hoop-skirts or plaster their faces with patches. It simply isn't done, you know. Is there any reason to suppose that biologists will forever go on working on heredity to the neglect of other things? Not the slightest. Unless the parents of our future biologists develop some wholly new factor in their sex cells to make their offspring different from all past and contemporary human beings, we may predict with great certainty that within another hundred years students of life will be devoting themselves to entirely new problems and will bestow only a glance of pity on their predecessors of today.

If the scientists of a period irrationally resemble one another in their interests, they irrationally differ in their outlook for another reason. They are not built the same way. Some are prophets, others doubters, still others artists. Again, some undoubtedly missed their true calling in not becoming draymen or shyster lawyers. Some of them have flashes of marvelous insight but spend most of their time in futile speculation. Others are never absurd and never rise above a high level of common sense. Still others are at once brilliant and sane. Again, there are scientists who cannot communicate their thought till their last doubts are lifted. Newton came very near never publishing his great work at all. After years of labor Darwin was pushed into publishing his *Origin of Species* by a purely external occurrence. Pasteur kept an "Olympian silence with which he loved to surround himself until the day in which his work seemed to him ripe for publicity. He said not a word about it, even in the laboratory, where his assistants saw only the exterior and the skeleton of his experiments, without any of the life which animated them."

At the opposite pole from such as these stand scientists like the late anatomist and anthropologist Hermann Klaatsch (1863-1916). Ideas were constantly buzzing about in his brain, and he printed them slapdash, often without the slightest attempt to test their worth. Thus he traveled about in Australia and took a liking to the natives; so he tried to prove that they were a sort of poor cousin to the Caucasian—"nearer to us than Malays or Mongols are," and more deserving of our sympathy than the Negroes. He even convinced himself that their speech was akin to ours. The native word for "liver" in Queensland is *jepar*, which promptly reminded Klaatsch of the ancient Greek *hepar*. A handful of such resemblances was enough to clinch the argument. With men of this type personal relations are all-important. So Klaatsch promoted his friend Otto Hauser, a dealer in antiquities now thoroughly discredited as to scholarship, to the post of the highest authority on Pre-Ceramic culture. Again, from the Reindeer Age of France enormous quantities of horses' bones have come down to us, lying at the foot of cliffs along with many finely flaked flint blades. The obvious interpretation is that these men of, say 20,000 years ago, drove wild horses down the steep heights as the Plains Indians are known to have chased bison. But Klaatsch finds that this is "not very imaginative"; so he converts the hunters into horsemen brandishing spears. It is true that even in Babylonia the domesticated horse was unknown before about 2300 B.C., but why worry about a trifling difference of 15,000 years or more? Even in comparative anatomy, his special field, Klaatsch was predestined to see one side of the question and to neglect everything else.

He favored the Australian aborigines because he had happened to meet them face to face. Similarly in the study of evolution he stressed the evidence from limbs because he had happened to make researches in that direction. Thus he came to derive man not from the apes but from an infinitely lower form of primate. The general evidence from blood-tests and comparative anatomy counted for naught.

Does it follow, then, that such scientific romanticists are a dead loss to intellectual progress? By no means. Had Newton and Darwin carried their caution just a wee bit further, they would never have published at all—to the great detriment of physics and biology. Again, there is the case of the Neanderthal skull.[1] In 1856 there was unearthed in Germany a strangely flat skull-cap with receding forehead and very pronounced bony ridges in the region of the eye-brows. It was obviously human but not like the skull of any modern man. Did it, then, represent a hitherto unknown type, a new race or species of *Homo?* Rudolf Virchow, the skeptic among German scientists, declared that it did not—it was merely a skull deformed by disease. With many students the weight of his authority carried the day. Still there were hothead propagandists of evolution like Ernst Haeckel, who insisted that the skull belonged to a new and more primitive form of humanity. Indeed, within the next fifty years one specimen after another of the Neanderthal shape was brought to light. Accordingly, today hardly any one doubts that parts of Europe were once inhabited by a genuine race or species of man different from ours. One could hardly suppose that every one of a dozen samples found by chance in different sections of Europe was pathologically disfigured. The enthusiasts have thus triumphed. So there is no guarantee that science will benefit from pure playing safe. It is

[1] See page 9.

well to be cautious about believing, but also about disbelieving. If you are too open-minded to suggestions, you may indeed be constantly setting out on a wild-goose chase. But, on the other hand, if you close your mind to new arguments, you are bound to miss the zest of discovery and may arrest progress for decades. Life has no haven of security for the timid, and science advances by the quite unreasonable clash of conflicting temperaments.

Science is a by-product of life. In wrestling with the daily tasks of life, in hunting and root-gathering, in chipping stone and firing pots, the savage amassed the sort of knowledge that lies at the basis of our biology, mineralogy, physics, chemistry, and technology. Astronomy, like so many features of higher culture, came in by the back door. What stimulus was there for the Babylonian priests to gaze at the sky? They were interested in learning the effect of the stars on human life. Their astronomy was rooted in astrology: they inferred the future from the position of the constellations. More particularly, they considered the aspect of the heavens at the moment of a person's birth and thence foretold the whole of his career. It was this phase of Babylonian science that was especially prized by the ancient Greeks!

And, as in other departments of culture, so in science not a little depends on lucky flukes. Towards the end of the sixteenth century the telescope was invented in Holland by sheer accident; how, precisely, does not seem to be certain. According to one tale, a spectacle-maker's children were playing with two lenses and found that looking through them brought a far-away church spire nearer. Their father sold the combination *as a toy*. In 1609 Galileo happened to hear of the device while in Venice. On his return to Padua he improvised a telescope and later improved it. Without the report from the Netherlands the idea would probably never have occurred to him. He was able to reinvent it by his knowledge of optics. *If* there was such an instrument as described, it must consist of a convex lens *with* a concave one, for by itself the one would give a blurred image, and the other alone would not magnify. But in Galileo's hands the telescope did not remain a toy; it became a tool for exploring the heavens and ushered in a new era of astronomy.

To take a more recent case, few inventions have revolutionized the treatment of eye diseases more than Helmholtz's ophthalmoscope. We have the great scientist's own account of how he conceived an instrument for examining a living retina. He calls it a discovery rather than an invention: a lucky chance presented itself to a trained worker who knew enough to use it. The facts were as follows: Helmholtz longed to study physics, but lacked the means. Much against his will he had to turn to medicine. This unpromising start, however, proved most fortunate, for as a medical student he learnt of the crying need for the instrument he afterwards devised. That evidently was not enough; at least one physiologist before him had hovered on the brink of the discovery but had fallen short. Why? Because he had not mastered the *physical* side of the question. Helmholtz, with his natural aptitude for the subject, had the principles of optics at his finger tips. He saw the physician's problem, he controlled the physicist's technique, and *solved* the problem. It was a lucky chance that Helmholtz should ever have gone into medicine at all, that any one in 1851 should be familiar with both medicine and physics, and that some one should have Helmholtz's insight in joining the two fields. In principle the occurrence was not unique. By the same sort of luck some alert-minded Siberian must have hit upon the plan of riding a reindeer. There was the reindeer already broken in with a sledge, and there were those bold foreigners mounted on horses. Why not use the reindeer as they did the horse? Without seeing the strangers, however, the idea might never have come into any one's head.

Like charwomen, bond salesmen, and doctors, scientists live in Main Street. No Rotarian pilloried by advanced thinkers is more eager "to be on the band-wagon" than the average devotee of Truth. The lore that has come down to him from his masters and is accepted by the respectable members of his congregation is sacred. Any doubt, any new idea, is suspect. What would Mr. Grundy say if you asserted that atoms were not so real as the warts on his face, that disease is caused by germs, that immigrants' children differ from their parents in the shape of their heads? Shudders run down one's spine at the thought of being blacklisted by one's trade union.

Today it is a commonplace of physics that energy cannot be destroyed. All that ever happens is that a given quantity of one form, say electricity, may be changed into a definite quantity of another form, such as heat. But this is an incredibly recent bit of knowledge, and when it was first given to the world scientists by no means fell all over themselves with joy. J. R. Mayer offered a paper on the subject to Poggendorf, the editor of the foremost physical journal in Germany, and Poggendorf would not publish it. It was subsequently (1842) printed by Liebig in his *Annals of Chemistry and Pharmacy*. Still there was some excuse for Poggendorf: Mayer was a medical man, was not conversant with all the concepts and terminology of physics, and thus perpetrated some rather shocking blunders. But the excuse does not hold in the case of Helmholtz. His essay "On the Conservation of Force" (1847) is rated as a classic of technical virtuosity; yet it met at first exactly the same fate as Mayer's.

When Galileo made his momentous discoveries in the heavens, the principal professor of philosophy at Padua refused to look at the moon and planets through the telescope and went so far as to prove that the newly discovered bodies could not possibly exist. His argument ran as follows: "There are seven windows given to animals in the domicile of the head, through which the air is admitted to the tabernacle of the body, to enlighten, to warm, and to nourish it. What are these parts of the microcosmos? Two nostrils, two eyes, two ears, and a mouth. So in the heavens, as in a macrocosmos, there are two favorable stars, two unpropitious, two luminaries, and Mercury undecided and indifferent. From this and many other similarities in Nature, such as the seven metals, etc., which it were tedious to enumerate, we gather that the number of planets is necessarily seven. Moreover, these satellites of Jupiter are invisible to the naked eye, and therefore can exercise no influence on the earth, and therefore would be useless, and therefore do not exist. Besides, the Jews and other ancient nations, as well as modern Europeans, have adopted the division of the week into seven days, and have named them after the seven planets. Now, if we increase the number of the planets, this whole and beautiful system falls to the ground."

Why should not learned men of the seventeenth century argue like Crow Indians when Swiss judges of the eighteenth century listened to evidence on witchcraft like a West African Negro tribunal? [1] That master mathematician Pythagoras had blazed a trail in numerical mysticism and declared ten to be the perfect number. There were only nine visible bodies in the universe; so his school had in-

[1] See page 229.

vented a tenth, the "counter-earth," to eke out the tale. The trifling space of 2,000 years was not enough to bring Galileo's opponent to a more rational point of view. He was indeed in excellent company. There was the famous doctor Agrippa; [1] there were towering figures of contemporary science. Kepler (1571-1630) did not indeed reject Galileo's findings. But he did wonder how there could be more than six planets; he found in the sphere an image of the Holy Trinity; and he died as astrologer-in-ordinary to the Duke of Wallenstein. Yet the greatest of all scientific generalizations, Newton's theory of gravitation, rests on Kepler's laws.

At that time astrology was not an outcast but a full-fledged part of the academic curriculum. Melanchthon lectured on it at Wittenberg; there were university chairs for the subject in Bologna and Padua. The great Danish astronomer Tycho Brahe (1546-1601), whose accurate and extensive observations made Kepler's generalizations possible, was a firm believer in horoscopes. He deplored the charlatanism of those who *lightly* undertook to foretell the future from the position of the stars at a person's birth. Such conduct was indeed reprehensible. But there was a *true* astrology based on painstaking study. Tycho wrote fervently in its defense, and he honestly applied its principles in foretelling the careers of his royal patron's sons.

Indeed, the evidence on behalf of astrology was satisfactory and at times overwhelming. Count Pico della Mirandola had been skeptical; yet in accordance with three separate predictions he died in his thirty-second year. Is not a physicist content when three distinct lines of experiment yield the same result? Then there was the case of Emperor Frederick III. He had been born in an hour when Mars was frowning. He also knew that good fortune was smiling on

[1] See page 250.

the King of Hungary. Hence, he avoided war with this monarch and gained his ends by diplomacy. There, boasted Melanchthon, was a fine sample of applied astrology! Again, when Magellan started on his voyage, he asked his friend Ruy Faleiro to accompany him. But Faleiro declined: he had read in the stars that the astronomer of the expedition was a doomed man. As a matter of fact, his substitute was murdered on one of the islands visited.

Tycho Brahe himself scored unbelievable triumphs. He foretold the fate of two of the Danish King's sons with uncanny accuracy. At the birth of Christian IV he announced the following horoscope: "Prone to warfare, amorous, with a lively sense of justice and an interest in spiritual matters that, however, will plunge him into great danger [the Thirty Years' War], humorous, appreciative of art, a lover of pomp, musical, lucky in mining operations, but subject to great matrimonial difficulties." According to Troels-Lund, it would be difficult to characterize the monarch more adequately after his career than Tycho Brahe thus pictured him at his birth. He was even more spectacularly successful in prophesying the fate of Prince Hans, who was to be exposed to the greatest danger in his eighteenth or nineteenth year and could escape only by the direct intervention of God. "It was quite natural," writes Troels-Lund, "that the initiated were in suspense when eighteen-year-old Duke Hans left his country to take part in the Spanish siege of Ostende. Recalled, he went by fleet to Russia, for Christian IV had arranged a marriage between him and the Czar's daughter. The brothers parted with tears. . . . When he had reached Moscow, where the Czar gave him a friendly welcome, much time was spent in lengthy formalities. The Duke fell sick, while the Czar by messengers harried him with questions about preliminaries. On October 28, 1602, he breathed his last, without having seen his bride, far from home, from his kin and friends. Saturn had triumphed. When the news of his death rather than of the marriage celebration finally got to Denmark, no sane man could be in doubt. Tycho de Brahe had read the stars aright."

But this is the very sort of demonstration that confirms the savage's beliefs. Patients do get well when their kidnaped souls are put back where they belong. In August, 1928, the Zuñi Indians of New Mexico performed a ceremony to make rain, and after every dance, Dr. Forrest Clements tells me, there were heavy showers. On the other hand, I have personally seen a shaman in Arizona stop threatening rain by shooing away the clouds. What doubting Thomas would defy such plain testimony of his senses?

Like savages, scientists are at once irrationally credulous and irrationally skeptical. They are ready enough to believe in astrology, but they will not accept the conservation of energy. The reason is clear. Astrology had the stamp of age-long approval; it was part of the sacred lore handed down by the past. Aside from that it made a strong direct appeal to man's interest in his future. It was thus doubly buttressed. Poor Mayer and Helmholtz had no such support. Pusillanimous thinkers followed the path of least resistance. They applied the excellent principle that a new idea is more likely to be wrong than right. Unfortunately they applied it to an exceptional case.

Scientists are led astray by tradition, which imposes fixed ideas upon them, by timidity, which even apart from tradition makes them afraid to use their eyes and see the truth naïvely; and by the unchecked play of fancy and emotion. These stumbling-blocks are infinitely more important than any coercion from without. For many authors the Church is the chief scape-goat in the history of science. But the

Church did not invent Babylonian astrology nor the numerical mysticism of Pythagoras. She neither set Tycho de Brahe to set horoscopes nor did she explain childbed fever by the influence of the atmosphere. When science stagnates, it is mainly because scientists are not equal to their tasks—because they are hide-bound worshipers of the past, because they are weaving webs of phantasy like Polynesian priests; in short, because they have never risen above the savage level.

Scientists need not be afraid of the Church half so much as of their own sectarianism. By grim fatality masters must have disciples. The great scientist is great in flinging down his gauntlet to tradition. His pupils learn from him everything but his spirit, swallow his least happy thoughts along with his flashes of insight, form mutual admiration societies, and excommunicate the outsider until a new master comes along and sweeps their dogmas into the waste-basket.

But surely all this belongs to the past. Independence of thought has become a byword in our rationalistic age. Received opinions are flouted. We have become so sane that never again can learning and nonsense be coupled as they were in Tycho Brahe. Such optimism is touching. How many contemporary scientists are the peers of Kepler and Tycho Brahe? Why suppose them immune to the folly of yester-century?

To glance at eugenics is enough to shatter such smugness. Ignoring the quacks for the present, let us summon the shade of Sir Francis Galton, the founder of the movement, a genius and a British gentleman whom we need not blush to put alongside of the great astronomers.

To Galton we owe the brilliant idea that men are not all alike in their mental traits. They differ from birth. One excels in memory, another in imagination, a third in power of visualizing. Put two individuals in the same situation, and the results of their work will not be the same. If there is an inborn deficiency, no amount of training can fully or even largely make up for it.

This was a bold stroke, for it flew directly in the face of a fixed dogma. Before Sir Francis the idea reigned that "doggedness," "infinite pains," could achieve anything, that education could perfect any human gift. Galton thus upset psychological theory and educational practice. It was evidently not advisable to fritter away a boy's time on painting or mathematics if he was predestined to lag behind his mates in these studies.

Galton further insisted that inborn differences are not distributed in random fashion. Able persons are of able stock; dullards are bred of fools. Heredity counts and is infinitely more important than environment. Horse-breeders achieve wonderful results by mating horses of good stock. Why not apply selection to *human* breeding? Evolution has been so painfully slow; can it not be speeded up? Let us check the birth-rate of the unfit and promote the union of the fit. Then within a short space of time the average of mankind will be brought to the level of a Newton, Beethoven, Michelangelo; the peaks will be supermen such as we can hardly conceive.

These are indeed lofty aims. In an age of waning faith they were naturally proclaimed by their founder as a new religion. But even within the few years since Galton's death the creed has become debased. In the United States, at least, eugenics is a cloak for Know-Nothingism. For Galton the greatest geniuses produced to date were not sufficient; his American disciples are content with the estimable commonplace old New England families. Galton declared it "far more important" that the best stock should increase than that the worst should be repressed. Our Know-Nothings clamor about the "degenerates" in our public institutions and caterwaul about the "low" racial strains of our immigrants. At best these propagandists are devoid of humor; at their worst they are unscrupulous forgers. The most thorough study of race mixture ever undertaken is Professor Eugen Fischer's among the Rehoboth "Bastards" of Southwest Africa.[1] They turned out to be tall like the Nordics, kinky-haired like the Hottentots, rather light-skinned like Europeans than otherwise, but dark-eyed like the African, and so forth. There was thus no suggestion of *racial* prepotency in either direction. But this conclusion was not grist for the Know-Nothing mill. For propagandists it is important to shout from the housetops that race mixture is a thing of evil. Hence one of our most prominent eugenists boldly announces that the cross between a white man and an Indian is an Indian; between a white man and a Negro, a Negro; between a white man and a Hindu, a Hindu; between a European and a Jew, a Jew. "The children of mixed marriages between contrasted races belong to the lower type."

This statement, to be sure, was not written by a professional scientist, but it comes from a man sponsored and shielded by biologists of high repute. For them the end justifies the means. It is a venial fault to lie about heredity provided it is done on behalf of restricted immigration. Galton himself, we may be certain, would never have connived at such tactics. But he misread human nature; he did not realize that men of science turn shyster lawyers when their emotions are aroused. With touching naïveté he assumed that a community might be trusted to select desirable citizens according to their "civic worth." How can any so-

[1] See page 28.

ciety at large be trusted if even the high-priests of Truth cannot? Did not Socrates—whom Galton reckoned as the greatest of philosophers—die as a criminal in what Galton considered the most brilliant community that ever existed?

What is meant by "civic worth" anyway? Plato was for banishing poets, and Galton himself refers to artists as "a sensuous, erotic race, exceedingly irregular in their way of life." One step further, and we shall have them shut out from marriage. Has the scientist "civic worth"? Not if Galton rightly ascribes to him "fearlessness of inquiry and veracity." In many states that is the last thing rated desirable: they want conformity, unquestioning obedience. Some of our American eugenists are explicit on the point: criticism of existing conditions is to them in itself a sign of depravity.

It was thus no maudlin sentimentality but a healthy intuition that made Alfred Russel Wallace recoil from eugenics as "the meddlesome interference of an arrogant scientific priestcraft." In trusting either state officials or even scientists to perform the practical tasks of eugenics, Galton betrayed a childlike optimism not one whit nearer the facts than the older belief in the infinite perfectibility of human beings. Men can be trusted to act according to their supposed interests; they may be trusted to be ruthless in imposing their own ideals on others; but they cannot be trusted to control human beings for the ultimate benefit of the species.

Galton was optimistic, as the founder of a new religion must be. He delighted in meeting objections with ingenuity. If man was to be improved, would it be possible to combine physical, intellectual, and moral fitness? Galton confidently declared that *all* good qualities were correlated. To be sure, eminent British judges had a dearth of children, which boded ill for perpetuation of their eminent fitness. But

Galton would not have it so. Judges, of course, had to marry heiresses; an heiress is by definition an only child. Hence it is she, coming of infertile stock, that must bear the blame for the childless marriage. Again, physique and intellect *ought* to go together if eugenics is to work. Galton remains undismayed. Queen Elizabeth was right if, as the tale goes, she chose her bishops with an eye to the calves of their legs. "The youths who became judges, bishops, statesmen, and leaders of progress in England could have furnished formidable athletic teams in their times." But in England scholars and officials have always largely come from the upper classes, who play cricket and ride to hounds. How about taking a glance at a learned gathering in France or Italy?

Heredity hypnotized Galton as the portent of the stars had hypnotized Kepler. It lulled his critical faculty. The Age of Pericles was a period of marvelous achievement; hence it had to be explained in racial terms. By partly unconscious selection Athens "had built up a magnificent breed of human animals." That is how, between 530 and 430 B.C., she came to produce fourteen illustrious persons—more than has ever been achieved in ratio to the population by any other group; and two of her prodigies have never been equaled since. "We have no men to put by the side of Socrates and Phidias, because the millions of all Europe, breeding as they have done for the subsequent 2,000 years, have never produced their equals." However, the Athenians rashly intermarried with inferior strangers; so the quality of their offspring was lowered and the glory of their civilization passed away.

As scientific proof this is from beginning to end tommyrot. No one *knows* anything about any partly unconscious selection in Athens; no one *knows* anything about the effects of their marriages with strangers after 430 B.C. These pleasant enough figments, however, are not so bad as the childish attempt to grade great men as one grades prize hogs. Nothing is harder than to rank geniuses. They differ not merely quantitatively but qualitatively, and in every branch of endeavor the judge's taste is bound to enter. Galton glibly recites estimates picked up God knows where as if they were of absolute validity. Who says that Michelangelo is inferior to Phidias? Is it not a fact, by the way, that no work has survived which is definitely known to be by the ancient sculptor himself? And by what token, pray, must Socrates be rated above Kant, Newton, and Leibnitz? By what criterion, finally, does Galton put his Athenian statesmen and commanders into the "illustrious" class? What does any one know about Themistocles, Miltiades, Aristides, Cimon, and Pericles to warrant us in placing them beyond, or on a par with, Pitt, Disraeli, Roosevelt, Foch, Frederick the Great? Absolutely nothing. It might have occurred to Galton that ruling over a tiny city-state and leading her armies was a different thing from governing the giant commonwealths of modern times, and that it is not easy to find a common standard.

All this seems obvious. Why, then, did not Galton see it? He did—when the holy madness was not upon him. The European Renaissance was a brilliant period, like the Age of Pericles, and it, too, attracted Galton's attention. But for some reason it did not tempt him into absurd fictions. He explains it sanely—in terms of environment. Why, he asks, does it contrast so sharply with the era that preceded? Can it be because of a change in hereditary ability? Galton answers decidedly: it cannot. "These sudden eras of great intellectual progress cannot be due to any alteration in the natural faculties of the race, because there has not been time for that, but to their being directed in productive channels." Here there is no nonsense about unconscious selection, no puerile comparison of unknowable incommensurates, no retailing by rote of third-hand judgments. Without his blinkers Galton's vision is as clear as any one's. But it is not easy to keep one's sight undimmed in founding a new faith. The man who tries to *control* human destiny is as liable to error as he who reads it in the starry firmament.

The case of Galton might point a lesson, but it will fail to do so, for men never learn from history. Our scientists will continue amassing new facts and interpreting them anew. The body of knowledge will increase to gigantic bulk and our "conquest of Nature"—that is, our more and more intelligent submission to Nature—will progress. But the individual scientist will go on spinning his cobwebs of fancy, weaker-willed fellows and disciples will make them into a holy of holies, and for the greater glory of their sect they will excommunicate the infidel, gloss over the patent facts, and even condone deliberate fraud. Science has made advances; the scientist is still a primitive man in his psychology.

The intellectual caliber of scientists was put to a test by the European war. As a class they failed miserably. The same men who had prated fervently at international congresses about the cosmopolitanism of science turned jingoes with the declaration of war. Ostwald, the great chemist, had been working for years for a universal language and a better understanding of peoples. Now he suddenly announced that Germany as the supreme organizer was bound to impose her efficiency on the countries still dawdling along on an individualistic basis. Preëminent German scientists renounced honorary degrees and distinctions that had been conferred by English learned societies. Britons and Frenchmen were not slow to reply. The gist of their utterances was that German science had never amounted to much; its reputation was based largely on bluff. Before the war Pierre Duhem, the French historian of physics, had expressed himself none too favorably about some great *British* physicists. He regarded their lack of logical precision as a national trait and contrasted them with French and German thinkers. But in 1915 his views of Teutonic psychology suddenly changed. Now the Germans were merely uninspired plodders working along with the patience and docility of medieval monks. In England Sir William Ramsay and Sir Ray Lankester expressed themselves in much the same spirit. In 1916 a Canadian scientist broke loose in *Nature* and accused German scientists of a conspiracy of silence about the accomplishment of English-speaking savants. The Germans were to be made to confess their indebtedness to Newton, Faraday, and Clerk Maxwell. Apparently this wiseacre had never read what Helmholtz and Boltzmann have to say about these men; he did not know that Willard Gibbs, America's outstanding figure in the more abstruse aspects of exact science, was rescued from obscurity by Ostwald; and that almost every chapter in Mach's historical writings glows with admiration for the achievements of great Britons. But by 1916 scientists for the most part no longer cared what they wrote provided they could advertise that they were on the band-wagon of mob prejudice. This sentiment prevailed after the armistice and has by no means wholly disappeared. For several years at least scientists of the Allied countries declined to meet Germans socially. Some of them organized and held "international" congresses from which Germans and Austrians were excluded!

This is sad enough. But it is more humiliating to compare recent practice with that of the eighteenth and early nineteenth centuries. About 1748, while Spain and England were at war, Ulloa was returning from an expedition to measure the arc of a meridian. He was captured and sent to England, but British men of learning came to his rescue. He was released and *elected to the Royal Society.* Were the hostilities between the two countries of a minor character? Well, the Napoleonic wars were not. Having regard to the times, they were quite on the same level of magnitude with the late unpleasantness that began in 1914. Yet while Prussia was crushed and dismembered, Alexander von Humboldt peaceably climbed Vesuvius with his friend Gay-Lussac and remained one of the eight foreign members of the French Academy. With the consent of his king he made Paris his headquarters and published his principal monographs in French. In 1841 there was talk of war between France and Germany. Humboldt wrote to his old friend Arago, asking whether these political differences would have any effect on their personal relations. The astronomer is insulted by the very suggestion. "I must not," he writes on March 12, 1841, "I will not, believe that you have *seriously* asked me whether I should be glad to have you come to Paris. Could you doubt my unchanging affection? Know that I should regard any uncertainty on this point as the most cruel insult (*la plus cruelle injure*)." Compare this attitude with that of Professor E. Gaucher of the Parisian Faculty of Medicine, who was not ashamed to confess in 1916 that since 1870 he had not felt it possible to invite a German to his house.

Again, in 1806 Humphry Davy wrote a paper *On Some Chemical Agencies of Electricity.* French scientists awarded him a medal for the best experimental work on electricity. He accepted it notwithstanding the life-and-death struggle between England and Napoleon. Said he: "Some people say I ought not to accept this prize; and there have been foolish paragraphs in the papers to that effect; but if the two countries or governments are at war, the men of science are not. That would, indeed, be a civil war of the worst description; we should rather, through the instrumentality of men of science, soften the asperities of national hostility." In the fall of 1813 Davy, accompanied by Faraday, went to France and regardless of the war was welcomed by French scientists. He may have rasped their sensibilities by his personal idiosyncrasies, but they treated him as a distinguished colleague and they loved Faraday.

What a contrast in mental maturity between the scientists of 1813 and of 1918! Men of learning had not yet been debauched by chauvinism. They might be snobs like Davy, they might hobnob with kings like Humboldt, but intellectually they were freemen who guarded the interests of mankind as a whole.

The history of science from, say, 20,000 B.C. until the present may then be summarized as follows. In the accumulation of knowledge there has been great progress. In the psychology of the scientific observer there has been no fundamental change since the Reindeer Age. In point of scientific ethics the last hundred years mark a period of retrogression.

CHAPTER XXIII

PROGRESS

Is THE long-distance view of civilization depressing? Well, what could be expected? Life is grim. The savage who believes in sinister forces lowering on every side expresses everyday experience more accurately than the philosophers of optimism. Culture is a part of reality, and so the grimace of Life must glare at us from every page of its history. A German scientist aptly said that man developed when conditions were ripe for his being, but *before* the conditions for his *well*-being. There lies the key. Human societies can exist with a minimum of rational adaptation. The Tierra del Fuegian [1] is symbolical of human fate. He was not cold enough actually to freeze to death; he continued to live and reproduce in intense discomfort. So in eighteenth century Paris the unhygienic hospitals spared a sufficient number of Frenchmen for the Revolution and Napoleonic adventures. So the twentieth century war failed to kill off, even indirectly, half the combatants. The survivors may have suffered physical and spiritual agonies, but they got through it all and have been multiplying as before.

Naïve elementary students of evolution are puzzled by a strange phenomenon. Why are there today any simple forms of life like bacteria? Have not *they* had the same opportunity to rise to greater heights in millions of years as man? Why are not *they* human or, at least, mammalian by now? The simple-minded freshman is nonplussed because he assumes that progress is spontaneous. It is not. Only when

[1] See page 19.

some special—and, on the whole, improbable—cause enters the scene, does anything new happen—and then as likely the organism is destroyed as made fitter. The principle holds for culture. A change for the better—in any conceivable sense of that vague term—never occurs without due cause, and a change for the worse is quite as probable. Frequently an innovation may be desirable in itself—for example, reindeer nomadism or urban settlement—but it disturbs the nice balance attained in the simpler state. Then there is all the fearful travail of readjustment. For seven centuries Western civilization has been none too efficiently struggling with the problem of urban life. The equilibrium reached by peasant communities was upset when men and women began to flock to the towns. The results were overcrowding, squalor, disease, gangs, insecurity. These have not prevented survival, but survival is on a lower level of social harmony than in ruder conditions.

Among the Crow Indians a man who strikes his fellow citizen stands disgraced. Years after the event his neighbors still point at him the finger of scorn. When the Danish missionary Hans Egede learned to know the ways of the Greenlanders, he marveled at their peaceableness in the absence of magistrates and written laws. "Strife and dissension, hatred and persecution, very rarely occur among them. When they see our sailors quarreling and fighting, they say these seem to forget that they are human. Similarly they say that an officer who flogs his men treats them not like human beings but like dogs." Property is as safe as life and limb. In 1907 I camped with the Assiniboine in southern Alberta, some distance from the nearest whites. During the daytime I had to ride about, visiting sundry informants; yet I never missed a button's worth. Such security is a foregone conclusion for a settlement of Plains Indians in peace time, and modern civilization fails to give it.

It *is* harder to govern a million than a campful, a thousand equals than classes with warring interests. The point is that the savage solves his simple problem; we fall short of solving a more intricate one. Not that the savage as a savage is immune. As soon as he founds autocracies in Africa or castes of blue-bloods in Polynesia, human dignity becomes the prey of sadism as in any bureaucracy-ridden modern state. Man evolved in conditions that fitted him for membership in a small group. He has not changed biologically so as to fit into monster cities or commonwealths. Hence science, democracy, and religion jointly may palliate but cannot cure the ills of "the great society."

Man has the same biological task as the chimpanzee. Both must match their forces against powers of destruction, or go to the wall. Man has forged ahead of the ape by passing on his experience to the next generation. He has piled up one means after another not only for surviving, but for surviving in greater comfort. However, he mars his legacy of gold by binding it up inextricably with a heritage of dross. Posterity learns to chip a stone knife *and* to chop off a finger joint with it in mourning or prayer. Firearms shoot down game *and* human beings. Rulers elaborate law for large states *and* devise torture chambers. Biologists study heredity *and* try to tinker with human beings.

The result is largely to nullify the good achieved. As if Life were not an inexhaustible source of ills, man gratuitously adds to the load. The struggle is no longer merely one of adaptation to Nature, but largely with "the trolls that infest our hearts and brains." Is the game worth the candle? Our chimpanzee may inherit nothing in the way of tools, dress, or hut to aid and shield him; but neither is he summoned to trial for bewitching a fellow ape or sacrificed as a messenger to the ancestors of an anthropoid chief. If he falls short of the species Wise Man (*Homo sapiens*), he has escaped membership in the variety Dunce (*insipiens*) to which all known forms of *Homo* naturally belong.

However, on weathering the first shock of disillusionment, a more serene view may prevail. To be sure, we must forgo a shallow optimism. Man is not and never will be the master of Nature. Tom Thumb cannot juggle the giant spheres of Life and Death, or bear the weight of the universe upon his puny shoulders. However astronomy may advance, it will not help us cut up the moon into slices of green cheese. Nature, whom we so glibly boast of conquering, has set limits we cannot overstep. Yet as soon as we grasp our true place in the universe our disappointment lessens. *Man developed with the conditions for his being, but before the conditions of his well-being.* He is biologically what he was 20,000 years ago. His brain is not a whit better than the Pleistocene reindeer-hunter's. His science has been a by-product of adaptation to Nature. His social arrangements arose as a response to simpler conditions. Biologically there is no reason why he should act sanely except where insanity means extinction; or why, lacking new factors in his sex cells, he should rationally organize a *complex* society.

We are still savages. But the word loses its sting when we recall what savages have achieved. What a chasm, after all, yawns between the ape and the lowliest of men who made fire, chipped stone, and planned a game-drive! To say that we are savages is to say that we are human.

Compared with that earliest man, or even with the later reindeer-hunter, we have gone far. At least in material culture and in sheer knowledge there has been a steady gain. Only we must think in terms of thousands and tens of thousands of years rather than in terms of centuries. Imperial Rome towered above the Middle Ages in her sanitary and engineering arrangements. In some ways the Greece of 500 B.C. was ahead of Europe in 500 A.D. Hence it is quite possible that a thousand years from now humanity will be in many respects on a lower level than today. But it is improbable that man will have slid back to the hunting stage of 10,000 B.C. Single peoples have indeed dropped husbandry to fall back once more on the chase, but not once during a myriad years have men as a whole turned back in their economic processes. On the contrary, they have steadily, though slowly, pushed ahead—from root-digging to hoeing, from hoeing to plowing. So in their tools: particular peoples may have unlearned the art of smelting metals, but from 4000 B.C. to the present it has never been obsolete on the face of the globe. Again, in actual knowledge there has been no permanent loss. Eddies of retrogression play a minor part. The Dark Ages were not so dark as they are pictured; and with Kepler, Galileo, and Newton science went beyond the bounds of ancient learning.

The ethical outlook is less encouraging. Stone Age savages like the Eskimo and Crow are as altruistic as we are—within a limited group. We have indeed heard the gospel of humanity, but its practice is flagrantly subordinated to the principle of chosen peoples or castes. Retrogression has been frequent and periodic. Nationalism is held up as a natural step to internationalism, but where in any large commonwealth has even nationalism been achieved? Have we not our solid South? Does not Canada insist on a separate representative at Washington to safeguard her interests as distinct from the British Empire as a whole? Has not even tiny

Norway a clamorous minority that insists on recognition of a distinct dialect? The Middle Ages were in principle international, and so was the learning of a century ago. Since then there has been backsliding, with the intellectuals as the worst delinquents. Contrast Humphry Davy in 1806 with the German scientists of 1914 who spurned British honors! Contrast the spirit of Alexander von Humboldt, the Prussian baron and courtier, with the shameless Know-Nothingism of eminent biologists now living in a great Western republic!

But perhaps we are asking too much. The ancient reindeer-hunter was surely no cosmopolitan, and if, man to man, our scientists are not his betters, what can we expect? Perhaps in 5000 A.D. they will again be international like Humboldt and Davy. Perhaps by 20,000 A.D. Nature may alter the sex cells, so that naïve tribalism and the grosser forms of sadism will yield to self-criticism and a broader tolerance. It is not probable, but in 18,000 years much may happen.

Few of us will live that long. We must find solace in compensations. Well, it is something to have heard the glad tidings of a united humanity, something to hear the faith reaffirmed from time to time by solitary enthusiasts in the wilderness. That much we are ahead of chimpanzee and savage. It is something, too, to break a lance in the fight with smugness, with sadism, with Know-Nothing propaganda. Win or lose, the Miltonic phrase holds: "That strife was not inglorious, though the event was dire."

Yakut

A

Ifu

Aus

ARCTIC
Tungus
Lapps
EUROPE
A S I
Altai
Kirghiz
AFRICA
Ewe
Lango
Uganda
Masai
Galla
Somali
Jagga
Anda-man-is
Vedda
INDIAN OCEAN
Zulus
Map of the World showing
ATION of PRINCIPAL TRIBES

APPENDIX

HINTS FOR FURTHER READING

GENERAL BOOKS

A. L. Kroeber, *Anthropology*, 1923.

This book gives a sane, up-to-date and fairly untechnical account of human evolution, race classification, and prehistory. It discusses theoretical interpretations of culture with reference to selected topics, but gives no systematic account of the several departments of culture.

R. R. Marett, *Anthropology*, 1912.

A very brief but sound and well-written introduction surveying the whole field.

E. B. Tylor, *Anthropology*.

Though written long ago, the chapters from "Arts of Life" to the end of the book are still eminently worth reading and give the topical description eschewed by Kroeber.

PREHISTORY

NOTE. All the standard texts give so much detail and technical terminology as to confuse the general reader. The best thing he can do, accordingly, is to look at the *illustrations* of any of the following, with as little reference to the text as possible. This does not, of course, apply to readers already somewhat familiar with the subject.

W. J. Sollas, *Ancient Hunters*.
M. C. Burkitt, *Prehistory*.
M. C. Burkitt, *Our Early Ancestors*.
H. Obermaier, *Fossil Man in Spain*.
G. G. MacCurdy, *Human Origins*.
H. F. Osborn, *Men of the Old Stone Age*.

RACE

F. Boas, *The Mind of Primitive Man.*

This book explains why great caution is necessary in rating different races. Contrary to the interpretation by superficial readers, it does not argue that all races are equal.

F. Boas, *Anthropology and Modern Life.*

Similar points are set forth more briefly and popularly in a chapter of this volume.

PRIMITIVE LITERATURE AND ART

NOTE. In the absence of good general books, the only way to learn something about primitive literature is to read some of it in accurate translations. The following are good examples.

M. W. Beckwith, *The Hawaiian Romance of Laieikawai.* (Bureau of American Ethnology, 33d Annual Report, pp. 293-630).

A faithful rendering of this Polynesian classic, with the original text and excellent notes on the Polynesian style.

W. Thalbitzer, *The Ammassalik Eskimo.* II: *Language and Folklore.*

An invaluable collection of songs and narratives in Eskimo and English by one of the foremost students of the Eskimo language and culture.

Washington Matthews, *Navaho Legends.*

A collection of tales typical of our Southwestern Indians and containing many episodes widely distributed in North America.

F. Boas, *Primitive Art.*

While much of the text is too technical for the general reader, he will be able to profit from the ample illustrative material.

See also under Prehistory.

SEX AND SOCIAL ORGANIZATION

B. Malinowski, *Sex and Repression in Savage Society.*
This essay deals suggestively with relevant facts among the Trobriand Islanders.

B. Malinowski, *Crime and Custom in Savage Society.*
An important and readable treatise on the legal institutions of savages, with special emphasis on the Trobriand Islanders.

R. H. Lowie, *Primitive Society.*
A systematic but tough treatment of marriage, family life, clans, associations, government and law.

EDUCATION

Dudley Kidd, *Savage Childhood.*
Full of concrete material on the Bantu children of Southeast Africa. The author's general remarks and psychologizing can be ignored.

RELIGION

E. B. Tylor, *Primitive Culture.*
This classic gives abundant material on primitive culture and survivals in modern civilization.

R. R. Marett, *The Threshold of Religion.*

R. R. Marett, *Psychology and Folk-Lore.*
These volumes of essays suggestively deal with selected topics.

R. H. Lowie, *Primitive Religion.*
The book gives a description of four typical primitive religions, a critique of some outstanding theories in the field, and a discussion of selected topics.

SCIENCE

Note. For one interested in the *psychology* of scientific investigation and the place of science in the history of civilization, the ordinary histories are inadequate. The subject is too vast to be covered in its entirety by any one mind. The best thing is to take the survey of a limited field by one who is at once a specialist in the field and also an historian. I know of only one author who answers this description and accordingly cannot unqualifiedly recommend any other:

Ernst Mach, *The Science of Mechanics.*

Ernst Mach, *Popular Scientific Lectures.*

For a summary of dates and facts of the history of science, the reader may consult Sedgwick and Tyler's *Short History of Science.*

ACCOUNTS OF INDIVIDUAL TRIBES

E. C. Parsons, editor, *American Indian Life.*

A series of sketches by many of the best-known American anthropologists depicting for the most part the life of a typical individual from each of the tribes dealt with. The volume will convey to the reader some notion of the amazing diversity of primitive life on a single continent.

A. L. Kroeber, *Handbook of the Indians of California.* (Bureau of American Ethnology, Bulletin 78, 1925.)

While the book is not in its entirety adapted to the needs of the lay reader, every one can enjoy the accounts of the Yurok and the Mohave Indians (pp. 1-97, 726-780).

K. Rasmussen, *The People of the Polar North.*

An account of the Eskimo by one thoroughly conversant with their language.

P. Radin, editor, *Crashing Thunder; the Autobiography of an American Indian.*

A psychologically interesting account of Winnebago culture by one who was conversant both with the traditional ways of his people and the white man's civilization.

T. Whiffen, *The Northwest Amazons.*

An excellent first-hand account of a number of South American tribes.

W. Mariner, *Account of the Natives of the Tonga Islands.*

This book gives a remarkable picture of Polynesian culture, before it suffered from the inroads of white civilization.

Elsdon Best, *The Maori as He Was.* (New Zealand Board of Science and Art, Manual No. 4, 1924.)

A systematic account of another Polynesian people by one of the foremost authorities.

Langloh Parker, *The Euahlayi Tribe.*

A sympathetic description of an Australian tribe, likely to give a far better insight into native thought than more technical and intensive monographs.

Waldemar Bogoras, *The Chukchee.*

One of the masterpieces of modern ethnography. It deals with the aborigines of northeasternmost Siberia.

W. Jochelson, *The Koryak.*

W. Jochelson, *The Yukaghir and the Yukaghirized Tungus.*

These are likewise excellent monographs on Siberian peoples.

H. Junod, *The Life of a South African Tribe.*

A sympathetic and detailed treatise on the Thonga of Portuguese East Africa.

J. Roscoe, *The Northern Bantu.*

Probably the best English account of conditions developing from the contact of a primitive peasant people with a more warlike pastoral tribe.

INDEX